'Retold compellingly and fluidly, bringing to life
the cast of characters with verve'

—

'Wonderfully readable . . . John Preston is the ideal author,
having researched for years many minor characters and
talked to dozens of well-known political and literary
friends and enemies of Thorpe'

STANDPOINT

—

'Nothing comes close to the eye-popping outrageousness
of the gay murder shenanigans that engulfed and almost
destroyed a Liberal leader. Reads like a comic thriller'

RACHEL JOHNSON

—

'A gripping account. Sensational'

DAILY TELEGRAPH

—

'Devastating, scintillating'

DAILY MAIL

—

'Preston is a natural storyteller'

THE TIMES

ABOUT THE AUTHOR

John Preston is a former Arts Editor of the *Evening Standard* and the *Sunday Telegraph*. For ten years he was the *Sunday Telegraph*'s television critic and one of its chief feature writers. He is the author of a travel book and four novels. His most recent novel, *The Dig*, was published to great acclaim in 2007.

A Very English Scandal

Sex, Lies and a Murder Plot at the Heart
of the Establishment

JOHN PRESTON

PENGUIN BOOKS

PENGUIN BOOKS

UK | USA | Canada | Ireland | Australia
India | New Zealand | South Africa

Penguin Books is part of the Penguin Random House group of companies
whose addresses can be found at global.penguinrandomhouse.com.

First published by Viking 2016
Published in Penguin Books 2017
001

Copyright © John Preston, 2016

The moral right of the author has been asserted

Grateful acknowledgement is made for permission to reprint extracts from
Peter Bessell's *Cover-Up: The Jeremy Thorpe Affair* (1980),
by kind permission of Paul Bessell

Set in 10.68/13.10 pt Dante MT Std
Typeset by Jouve (UK), Milton Keynes
Printed in Great Britain by Clays Ltd, St Ives plc

A CIP catalogue record for this book is available from the British Library

ISBN: 978-0-241-97374-5

www.greenpenguin.co.uk

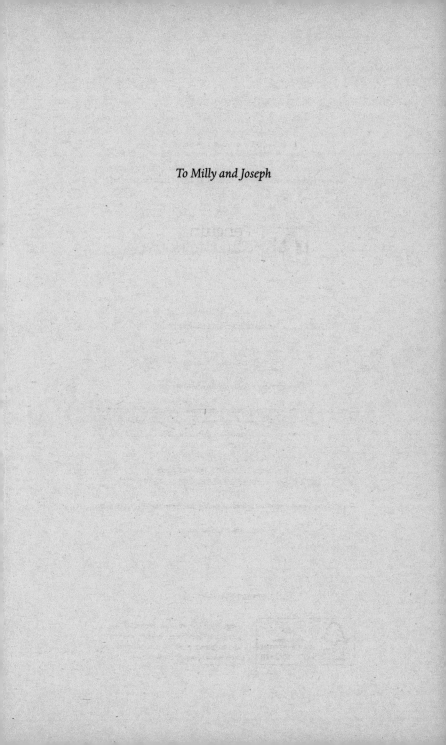

To Milly and Joseph

'Mr Holmes, they were the footprints of a gigantic hound!'

– Arthur Conan Doyle, *The Hound of the Baskervilles*

Contents

Contents

Illustrations

PART ONE

A Dinner at the House of Commons

One evening in February 1965, a man with a fondness for mohair suits, an unusually wrinkled face and a faint resemblance to Humphrey Bogart walked into the Members' Dining Room at the House of Commons. His name was Peter Bessell and he was the Liberal MP for Bodmin in Cornwall. Bessell had been an MP for only six months and he was still a little awestruck by the place. As he had few friends there, he had become used to eating on his own. On this evening, however, he heard a voice behind him asking if he would like to have dinner.

The voice belonged to another Liberal MP, Jeremy Thorpe. Although he was almost eight years younger than Bessell, Thorpe had been in Parliament since 1959. At thirty-six, he was the rising star of the party, widely tipped to become the next Leader. While some of the older members found him brash and hot-headed, no one could doubt his appeal to voters. As well as being ebullient and good-looking in a cadaverous sort of way, Thorpe had apparently bottomless reserves of charm. These had been deployed to great effect in his constituency of North Devon.

With its rolling moorland and deep valleys, North Devon may have been famously picturesque, but the people who lived there tended to have poorly paid jobs, either on the land or in the fishing industry. Thorpe was about as far from being one of them as possible: a smooth Old Etonian with a distinctive taste in clothes – he favoured a cashmere overcoat with a velvet collar and, rather more eccentrically, a brown bowler hat. However, it didn't take long for him to win them over.

Thorpe was charismatic and sympathetic. He also had an

extraordinary knack for remembering people's names and for making them feel that their problems were especially close to his heart. With his arms thrown wide and an enormous grin on his face, he would bear down on his would-be constituents as though seeing them had just fulfilled his wildest dreams. Few were able to resist. They even loved it when Thorpe – a brilliant mimic since boyhood – made fun of their broad West Country accents.

In the 1959 election, he scraped in with a majority of just 362. By 1964, this had gone up to 5,136. As a reward for his success, Thorpe had recently been made the party's official Spokesman on Commonwealth Affairs. He and Bessell had first met ten years earlier at a by-election in Torquay in which Bessell had stood – and lost. Although they didn't know one another well, Bessell had been convinced from the start that the two of them shared an unusual bond. Physically, they were roughly the same height, with dark hair and narrow, brooding features. Politically too their views tended to coincide. But it was the similarities in their characters that Bessell was most struck by: 'We were both wilful, quick to take offence, capable of arrogance and incurably sentimental.'

And there was something else they had in common, something that would soon become apparent – each in his own distinctive way was a colossal chancer. Bessell had left school at sixteen, then become a Congregationalist lay preacher. Setting up a small tailoring business in the Devon town of Paignton, he had drifted into Liberal Party politics, prompted in part by ideology and – possibly in larger part – by a desire to spice up his already hectic love-life.

Bessell did not look like a conventional Lothario. He once likened his face to 'a badly tessellated pavement' and the mohair suits he wore caused him to shimmer slightly whenever he stood near an electric light. The effect was capped by his extraordinarily gravelly voice, which made him sound like a lounge-lizard in an Edwardian melodrama. None the less, he enjoyed considerable success with women. Soon after the death of his first wife – from tuberculosis – Bessell married again. He and his second wife, Pauline, went on to have two children, a boy and a girl, but marriage and fatherhood did nothing to curb his appetite for philandering. However rackety Bessell's love-life was, it was nothing compared with his business dealings. Over the years, he had been involved in a number of schemes that he was convinced were going to make his fortune, including one to market hot-drink vending machines and another to open a chain of motels across Britain. Yet Bessell's fortune stubbornly failed to materialize. Instead, most of his schemes came hopelessly unstuck, leaving a trail of debts in their wake.

According to Bessell's account of what happened next, the two men sat at the long table reserved for Liberal MPs. That evening, the place was almost deserted and there was no one nearby to overhear what they were saying. The Members' Dining Room was not a place that naturally lent itself to gossip. Everything about it – the coffered wooden ceiling, the royal coat of arms hanging above the door, the stern Victorian portraits on the walls – seemed designed to foster an air of solemnity. In keeping with their surroundings, their conversation began conventionally enough. They spoke about the party, and about their Leader, Jo Grimond, in particular. Leader of the Liberals for the last eight years, Grimond had largely been responsible for the revival of the party's fortunes – in 1964 the Liberals had polled more than three million votes, a swing of more than 5 per cent since the last General Election.

The 1964 election had been won by the Labour Party, led by Harold Wilson. With his pasty face and his flat Yorkshire accent, Wilson neither looked nor sounded like a man gripped by visionary fervour. But Britain, he declared, stood on the brink of a New Age, one that would see the end of economic privilege and the abolition of poverty. Not only that, 'the British [will] again become the go-ahead people with a sense of national purpose.'

But this snazzy Utopia still seemed a long way off. Having won a majority of only four seats and with the economy floundering, Labour faced a constant struggle to cling on to power. Luckily for them, the Conservatives had just elected a new Leader – the defiantly charmless and far-from-magnetic Edward Heath. As the third main party, the Liberals were ideally placed to pick up disenchanted voters from both sides. There were even those who believed that, for the first time in more than fifty years, power was within their grasp.

Jo Grimond was only fifty-one, but ever since the election the House of Commons had been swept by rumours that he was about to retire. While Bessell felt that Thorpe would be an ideal replacement as Leader, he was surprised, even a little shocked, by rumours that he had heard about his private life. As the party's only other West Country MP, Bessell thought that he might be quizzed about Thorpe in the event of a leadership contest. Under the circumstances, it might be prudent to furnish himself with as much information as possible. That at least was how he rationalized it to himself. But, as always, Bessell had other, rather less lofty motives. An inveterate collector of tittle-tattle, he was curious to find out if these rumours had any substance to them.

Hoping to draw Thorpe out on the subject of sex, he started talking about his secretary, Diana Stainton. Clearly not much interested by this turn in the conversation, Thorpe asked idly if she was any good.

'Oh, yes,' Bessell replied. 'Particularly in bed.'

Thorpe stared at him for several seconds, then burst out laughing. He told Bessell that he had him marked down as a happily married man. Bessell insisted that his marriage was perfectly happy – this was different.

'I suppose you might call it a hobby,' he said. 'Some people collect stamps, play golf or breed horses. I like screwing.'

By now Bessell had Thorpe's full attention. But he also knew that Thorpe was easily bored. If he wanted to lure him into any indiscretions, he had to make his next move count.

'Of course,' Bessell said, 'when I was a young man it was more difficult. Years ago, nice girls didn't get into bed with you until you married them.'

'So what did you do?' Thorpe asked.

'Ah well,' said Bessell wistfully. 'In those days I still had homosexual tendencies.'

In fact, this was nonsense. Bessell had never been anything other than unflaggingly heterosexual: he was just fishing to see what the response would be. It could hardly have been more dramatic. Thorpe was galvanized. Leaning forward, he said, 'Did you? Tell me about that.'

Slightly taken aback, Bessell babbled something about once having had a homosexual fling in a Vienna nightclub. When he had finished, Thorpe didn't say anything at first. Instead, he signalled for the waiter.

'Peter, this calls for a drink. What will you have?'

Bessell said that he would have a port.

'Couldn't be better,' said Thorpe. 'I'll have the same.'

While they waited for their drinks, Bessell decided to press home his advantage.

'What about you?' he asked. 'Surely you don't live like a Trappist monk?'

Thorpe seemed to tense up, and for a moment Bessell wondered if he had overplayed his hand.

'When I was at Oxford I had homosexual tendencies,' Thorpe admitted cautiously. 'Of course, that was a long time ago now.'

They were interrupted by the waiter bringing the drinks. After they had raised their glasses to one another, Bessell said, 'I suppose people like us never quite lose it, do they?'

There was another pause, and then Thorpe's face broke into a grin. 'Peter,' he said in a half-whisper, 'we're nothing but a pair of old queens . . . Tell me,' he went on as they sipped at their ports, 'what would you say you were – 50/50?'

'No,' said Bessell hurriedly. 'I would say more like 80/20.'

'Do you mean 80 or 20 per cent gay?' Thorpe asked.

Bessell had never heard the expression 'gay' before and it took him a moment or two to work out what Thorpe meant.

'I mean 80 per cent for girls,' he said.

'Really? It's the other way with me,' said Thorpe. 'I'm 80 per cent gay.'

By now Bessell felt that he and Thorpe had more in common than he had ever imagined. As he was to recall later in characteristically grandiose fashion, 'Like Jeremy, my extraordinary physical and mental energy was coupled to a desire for conquest in many things.' Or, to put it another way, when faced with the faintest glimmer of sexual temptation both of them were powerless to resist.

Thorpe went on to talk about how disastrous it would be if his constituents ever found out about his homosexuality. As well as signalling the immediate end of his political career, the revelation might also land him in prison – homosexuality still being a criminal offence in 1965.

'But we've done pretty well so far,' he said. 'Nobody in the House knows about me.'

'Would anyone care?' Bessell asked.

'Oh, yes,' said Thorpe glumly. 'Neither of us could ever be Leader of the Party if they found out.'

By now the dining room was closing and Thorpe called for the bill.

'Very well,' said Bessell. 'Then we shall have to see to it that no one ever finds out.'

'You're right,' said Thorpe with a sudden burst of passion. 'And by Christ, Peter, we'll see that they never do.'

Four weeks later, Bessell was in his office on Clarges Street one morning when the phone rang. It was Thorpe. Could they meet for lunch, he asked. Bessell noticed that Thorpe sounded much more tense and less ebullient than usual. Something was clearly wrong.

At Thorpe's suggestion, they went to the Ritz. This also struck Bessell as odd, as both were members of the National Liberal Club, which was much nearer the House of Commons, but he didn't say anything. By the time Bessell arrived, Thorpe was pacing impatiently around the lobby. After giving him a cursory greeting, they went through to the dining room, where they were given a table overlooking Green Park.

The spring flowers were just coming into bloom, and Bessell, who prided himself on having an eye for beauty in all its forms, thought the park was looking especially pretty. However, the view was plainly the last thing on Thorpe's mind. Glancing briefly at the menu, he ordered the steak tartare. As soon as the waiter had gone, Thorpe took a letter from the inside pocket of his jacket and handed it to Bessell.

'Read it,' he said.

Bessell saw that the envelope was addressed to Thorpe's mother, Ursula, at her house in Oxted, Surrey. The letter inside was written on blue notepaper. Although it was very long – seventeen pages – and the handwriting hard to decipher, Bessell soon got the gist of it. The writer began by apologizing for bothering Mrs Thorpe but reminded her that he had once been a guest in her house. He went on to claim that he and Jeremy Thorpe had been lovers.

'For the last five years as you probably know, Jeremy and I have had a "homosexual" relationship. To go into it too deeply will not help either of us. When I came down to Stonewalls [Ursula Thorpe's house] that was when I first met him. Though he told you something about the TV programme and Malta. This was all not so true. What remains is the fact that through my meeting with Jeremy that day, I gave birth to this vice that lies latent in every man.'

Thorpe, the man claimed, had promised to look after him. But the affair had ended and he had reneged on his promise. All his subsequent attempts to get in touch with Thorpe had failed. The man was now living in Dublin and needed help. In particular, he wanted Thorpe to return his National Insurance card, without which, he wrote, he was unable to get a job. But to tide him over he wondered if Mrs Thorpe would be kind enough to lend him £30.

'I hate asking because I know it may cause friction and I know how close you both are. This is really why I am writing to you. Jeremy owes me nothing, possibly I owe him a lot, although I feel we balance out. Now instead of a cast-off friend I appeal to his finer feelings as a man to help me who is in real need. I promise I shall repay every penny as soon as I am on my feet – believe me I mean this.'

He ended with an apology and a plea. 'Can you understand any of this, Mrs Thorpe? I'm so sorry. Please believe me, I'm desperate for help.'

The letter was signed Norman Lianche Josiffe.

Bessell looked up to see Thorpe staring intently at him.

'Is it true?' Bessell asked.

Slowly Thorpe nodded.

'What did your mother think?'

'She didn't believe it,' he said.

Then Thorpe took out another letter. This one was much shorter, just two pages long. He explained it was the draft of a letter he was going to ask his solicitor to send to Josiffe. In the letter, Thorpe vehemently denied that any sexual relationship had ever taken place and threatened a libel action if Josiffe ever repeated his allegation: 'Our client utterly rejects the damaging and groundless allegations which you have made against him and desires us to give notice that he will not hesitate to issue a writ, whether in the English or Irish Courts, claiming damages for defamation upon receiving the slightest scintilla of evidence that you have repeated this wholly obnoxious and untrue allegation.'

There was more, all in a similar vein. Bessell read the letter, and strongly advised him not to send it.

'Why not?' Thorpe wanted to know.

'Have you forgotten Oscar Wilde?' Bessell asked.

To Bessell's surprise, Thorpe seemed to have no idea what he was talking about. Bessell had to remind him that Wilde had been destroyed by a libel action he had brought against the Marquess of Queensberry in 1895 alleging that he was a 'somdomite' (*sic*).

'Then what the hell am I to do?' Thorpe muttered.

Bessell told him that he couldn't really give him any more advice until he knew all the facts of the case. Thorpe looked thoughtful, then warned him that it was a long story. That was fine, said Bessell; he had no particular plans for the afternoon.

He couldn't possibly have known it, of course, but it was a decision that would ruin his life.

2

The Postcard

It had all begun with another letter, Thorpe told him – or rather a postcard. On the afternoon of Friday, 26 February 1960, Buckingham Palace issued a statement saying that the Queen had given her consent to the engagement of her younger sister, Princess Margaret, to Antony Armstrong-Jones.

This news prompted tremendous excitement. Like Thorpe, Armstrong-Jones had been educated at Eton – he was a year younger. But, while his background may have been conventional enough, in other respects Armstrong-Jones was quite unlike any other royal consort. Raffish, bohemian and boundlessly self-assured, he had become a highly successful photographer – despite failing his final exams in architecture at Cambridge.

The Princess's unhappy romantic history gave the story extra piquancy. Four years earlier, she had been forced to break off her romance with a highly decorated RAF officer, Group Captain Peter Townsend, because he was a divorcee. But now it seemed that she had finally found happiness. As well as coverage of the engagement itself, there were lots of articles about its social implications. A number of commentators confidently predicted that it heralded the dawning of a new era – one that would be far more egalitarian and less hidebound by stuffiness and tradition.

When Thorpe heard the news, he was in the House of Commons. Immediately, he dashed off a postcard to a friend of his, the Honourable Brecht Van de Vater.

'What a pity,' Thorpe wrote. 'I rather hoped to marry one and seduce the other.'

The next day the postcard arrived at 'Squirrels', the thatched cottage where Van de Vater lived in the Cotswold village of Kingham. With his tweed suits, his club ties, his Land Rover, his horses and his five springer spaniels, Van de Vater gave every impression of being a well-heeled English gentleman. In fact, everything about him was a carefully constructed charade. It wasn't only his title that was made up; even his name was. He had actually been born plain Norman Vater, the son of a Welsh miner. Nor was he well-heeled – far from it. Unbeknownst to his neighbours, he was an undischarged bankrupt.

Van de Vater was not living alone in Squirrels. Two months earlier, he had taken on an assistant, a young man called Norman Josiffe. Although Josiffe didn't receive any wages – he was classified as a 'working student' – he was given free accommodation. Van de Vater was also responsible for paying his weekly National Insurance contributions. Like Van de Vater, Josiffe had his secrets. He had never known who his father was. After the death of her first husband, his mother, Ena, had gone on a world cruise, paid for by his former employers as a token of their respect. By the time she returned, she was pregnant. Two years after she gave birth to Norman, she married Albert Josiffe, an accountant who had been her late husband's best friend. To make everything above board, her son was given her new husband's surname.

With little in the way of parental guidance, Norman Josiffe grew up with a very fragile sense of his own identity. Starved of affection at home, he found it in the company of animals – and horses in particular. It was this that had first got him into trouble. Soon after he turned fifteen, Josiffe asked his mother to buy him a pony. She refused, but he managed to get one for free from the animal welfare charity the Blue Cross. When his mother also refused to give him any money to feed it, Josiffe stole some food and a saddle.

On 23 April 1956, aged sixteen, he appeared at Bromley Juvenile Court in Kent and was put on probation. Keen to foster Josiffe's interest in horses, his probation officer encouraged him to become a pupil at the Westerham Riding School near Oxted in Surrey.

There, he became a qualified riding instructor, and, shortly after leaving, was offered a job by Brecht Van de Vater.

By now Josiffe was nineteen. With his thick black hair, dark eyes and full lips, he had become a remarkably good-looking young man – a striking mix of the cherubic and the saturnine. Sexually, he had had a couple of heterosexual fumbles at the riding school, but was still a virgin. Josiffe's duties at Van de Vater's consisted mainly of mucking out the stables and exercising the four horses that were kept there. But it wasn't long before he found out that he was expected to perform other, rather more unusual, duties.

When the postcard arrived, Van de Vater proudly showed it to Josiffe and explained that it was from a very important friend of his. He also showed him several letters from the same friend, claiming mysteriously that they were his 'insurance policy'. Although Josiffe was not allowed to read any of the letters, he noticed that the writing paper had a House of Commons letterhead.

A few days later, Van de Vater told him that his friend was coming to stay. Before he arrived, Van de Vater wanted to have a bath and asked Josiffe to accompany him into the bathroom. Josiffe was surprised to see that the room was lit only by candles. Van de Vater then took off his dressing gown and got into the bath. Josiffe was even more surprised when he handed him a can of shaving foam and a razor and told him to shave his back. Feeling this was a little out of the ordinary, but not liking to say anything, Josiffe duly lathered him up and set to.

That evening he went to bed before Van de Vater's visitor arrived. The next morning Josiffe got up, had breakfast and – as he always did – went out to the stables to muck out the horses. Parked outside the cottage, he saw the visitor's car – a Sunbeam Rapier. At around nine o'clock a tall man in a black overcoat with an Astrakhan collar came out and introduced himself. His name, he said, was Jeremy Thorpe.

Josiffe was vaguely aware that Thorpe was a Liberal MP, but otherwise knew nothing about him. The two men began to chat. What struck Josiffe most of all was how charming and attentive

Thorpe was. 'I just thought what a super chap.' Although it was obvious that Thorpe knew absolutely nothing about horses, he insisted that he had always adored them.

Thorpe, for his part, was even more taken with Josiffe. As he would later tell Peter Bessell, 'He was leaning over a stable door; he was simply heaven.'

The two of them talked, somewhat stiltedly, about horses for several minutes, and then Thorpe paused. 'You'll find this a bizarre thing that I'm about to say to you,' he said, 'but if you ever have problems with Van, I want you to get in touch with me.'

Then he gave Josiffe one of his cards. This too had a House of Commons emblem on it, Josiffe saw, along with Thorpe's private telephone number. After he put the card in his wallet, the two of them said goodbye. Greatly impressed, if somewhat puzzled, Josiffe watched as Thorpe walked back to the house.

That evening, before he went to sleep, Josiffe took Thorpe's card out of his wallet. As he gazed at it, he thought once again about how charming Thorpe had been, and he wondered what on earth he could have meant by 'problems with Van'. He didn't have to wait long to find out.

A couple of months later Josiffe and Van de Vater went to the Tidworth Horse Trials in Wiltshire. While they were there, Josiffe was brushing down a horse called Harbour Light when it was startled by a sudden noise and bolted. Van de Vater promptly lost his temper. In front of several friends, he started berating Josiffe for his incompetence, loudly telling him to fuck off. No one had ever spoken like this to Josiffe before and he was extremely upset – so much so that he decided to leave straight away.

He got a lift into Salisbury and then caught a train to Oxfordshire. Josiffe had been away for only two days, but when he arrived back at Squirrels he was surprised to find that a great many letters had been delivered in his absence – so many that he had difficulty opening the front door. But there was another, much bigger, shock in store. To his astonishment, he saw that most of the letters were addressed to him. Opening them, Josiffe found that they were all receipts – for things that Van de Vater had bought in his name on hire purchase. These included a new Land Rover and a horse box.

Unsure what to do, Josiffe ran across the village green to a house owned by a woman he had befriended called Mrs Barton. Breathless and distraught, he explained what had happened. A sympathetic Mrs Barton told Josiffe to go back to Squirrels and collect all his possessions and the bills. He should write a note for Van de Vater, telling him where he had gone, she said, and come back to her house. Josiffe duly ran back to Squirrels and packed up his possessions. Having done so, he collected all the bills that had arrived addressed to him and left a note for Van de Vater explaining what he had done.

Then, just before he left the house, he paused. On the spur of the moment, he decided to take something else with him – the letters that Jeremy Thorpe had sent Van de Vater. Ever since he had met Thorpe, Josiffe had had an odd sense that he might prove to be his saviour. There was nothing rational about this – it was simply that Thorpe had been one of the few people who had ever been kind to him. In his wilder moments he had even fantasized that he, rather than Van de Vater, was the 'Dear Norman' to whom the letters were written.

Remembering how Van de Vater had bragged about the letters being his insurance policy, Josiffe thought he would repay Thorpe for his kindness by sending them back, just in case there was anything in them that might embarrass him. Josiffe knew where the letters were kept – in a drawer in the living room. There were about thirty of them in all, including the postcard Thorpe had sent Van de Vater about wanting to marry Princess Margaret and seduce Antony Armstrong-Jones. Josiffe put the whole lot in his suitcase along with his clothes. Then he shut the door behind him and went back to Mrs Barton's.

Two days later, Van de Vater returned from Tidworth. As soon as he found Josiffe's note, he stormed over to Mrs Barton's house. There, an unpleasant scene ensued. Mrs Barton accused Van de Vater of having behaved appallingly, while Van de Vater, blustery as ever, again accused Josiffe of incompetence. Clearly Josiffe couldn't carry on living at Squirrels. He moved into Mrs Barton's for a while, but over the next few weeks Josiffe's mental state, never robust, began to disintegrate. Shortly after moving on again, he had a nervous breakdown – brought on, he believed, by the shock of finding that Van de Vater had made purchases in his name.

Josiffe began telling people that he'd been having a relationship with Jeremy Thorpe – although at this point they had only ever met once. On one occasion the police were called to a house where he was living in the village of Church Enstone. There, they found Josiffe in desperate straits. As one of the policemen, PC Frederick Appleton, recalled years later, 'In the house I found this pathetic creature sitting at the bottom of the stairs crying and mumbling all sorts of queer and wonderful things. I gathered from what he was saying that he had been let down by a male occupant of the house whom he had found with a female. I gathered that he had had a homosexual relationship with the male . . . Josiffe seemed to be talking for most of the time we were there and he kept blubbing pathetically. He kept talking about Jeremy, saying he would tell Jeremy about this and tell Jeremy about that. Eventually one of us asked, "Jeremy who?" and he said, "Jeremy Thorpe." '

Josiffe was taken off in an ambulance to a new clinic for psychiatric patients outside Oxford called the Ashurst Clinic – part of the Littlemore Hospital – where he was put on a regime of sedatives and anti-depressants. After a few weeks, he discharged himself and went to live in a flat in Oxford with two other patients. But soon afterwards Josiffe was readmitted to the Ashurst Clinic. In October 1961 the doctor in charge of the place, Dr Anthony Willems, called him into his office and told him that he didn't think there was anything more they could do for him.

Dr Willems asked if there was anywhere that he could go. To begin with, Josiffe was stumped. He didn't feel he could impose on Mrs Barton any more and he didn't really have any close friends. Then, all at once, he thought of Jeremy Thorpe. He explained that Thorpe had offered to help him if he was ever in trouble. Dr

Willems said he thought this was an excellent idea and promptly discharged him – but not before prescribing yet more drugs and telling him it was imperative he should keep taking them.

From Oxford, Josiffe went back to the Cotswolds to pick up his suitcase – containing the letters he had taken from Van de Vater's – and his dog, a Jack Russell called Mrs Tish. Then, on 8 November 1961, with all his worldly possessions in one hand and his dog in the other, an extremely befuddled Norman Josiffe caught a train to London.

3

The Eye of Urse

Shortly after two o'clock in the afternoon, Josiffe and Mrs Tish arrived at the House of Commons. Josiffe told the Serjeant at Arms that he had come to see Jeremy Thorpe and, like all visitors to the Commons, he was asked to fill out a green form stating who he was. But then came an unforeseen snag. The Serjeant at Arms explained that dogs were not allowed in the House of Commons.

Josiffe wondered what he was going to do with Mrs Tish. On his way to the Commons he had walked down Whitehall, and he remembered passing the headquarters of the British Union for the Abolition of Vivisection. Thinking that Mrs Tish was unlikely to come to any harm there, he went back and asked if he could leave her with them for a couple of hours. The anti-vivisectionists could not have been more helpful. When Josiffe returned, he was shown into St Stephen's Hall and asked to wait. This was the first time he had been to the Palace of Westminster and he watched fascinated as various familiar faces passed by. Ten minutes later, Thorpe came striding splay-footed across the tiled floor.

Any fears Josiffe might have had that Thorpe wouldn't remember him were instantly dispelled.

'Norman!' he exclaimed delightedly, with his arms flung wide.

Thorpe sat down beside him and asked how he was. Josiffe started to explain about all the misfortunes that had befallen him, but he hadn't gone far when Thorpe decided it might be better if they adjourned to a private office. Josiffe followed him up and down staircases and along various corridors, until Thorpe eventually showed him into an interview room – as a junior MP, he didn't have his own office.

There he fetched Josiffe some tea and listened attentively to what he said. At the mention of Van de Vater, Thorpe muttered 'silly bastard', but otherwise stayed silent. When Josiffe had finished, he asked where he was staying.

Josiffe admitted that he didn't have anywhere to live.

Was there anywhere he could go?

Josiffe shook his head.

Thorpe explained that he had to go off to Malta the next day to interview the former Prime Minister, Dom Mintoff. But why didn't Josiffe come and stay the night with him at his mother's house in Surrey? Apart from anything else, they would be able to have another conversation about his predicament on the drive down. As far as Josiffe was concerned, all his prayers had been answered. Then he remembered Mrs Tish. He told Thorpe about his dog, and not being able to bring her into the Palace of Westminster. Thorpe told him not to worry; he would sort everything out. Turning the full force of his charm on the Serjeant at Arms, Thorpe asked if he might be prepared to make an exception.

The Serjeant at Arms swiftly melted. Having collected Mrs Tish from the anti-vivisectionists, Josiffe went back to the Commons, where Thorpe was waiting by his new car – by now he had swapped his Sunbeam Rapier for a black Rover. On the way to Surrey, they stopped off at a house in South London where two friends of Thorpe – both men – lived. There, Thorpe asked one of the men to look after Josiffe if he ever needed help. More than ever, Josiffe felt that he had landed among friends. After the traumas of the last few months he had finally found people who would care for him. He was so relieved that his plan to give Thorpe back the letters he had sent Van de Vater temporarily slipped his mind.

Soon after seven o'clock they arrived in Oxted. But before they reached his mother's house, Thorpe pulled over to the side of the road and stopped the car. On reflection, he said, it might be better if Josiffe pretended to be a cameraman who was going to be accompanying him to Malta. What's more, he shouldn't give his real name. Instead, he should call himself – Thorpe pulled a name out of the air – 'Peter Freeman'. By now the combination of the drugs and the stress of the day had taken its toll. Assuming that Thorpe had good reasons for this subterfuge, but not much caring what they were, Josiffe agreed. They then drove the few hundred yards to his mother's. Stonewalls was an austere, stone-built late-Victorian house set on a rise just outside the centre of the village.

If the house was intimidating enough, Thorpe's mother was even more so. Ursula Thorpe had a reputation for being formidable. A stalwart of the local Conservative Party, she wore a monocle, smoked cigars and came from a long line of redoubtable women. Her mother, Lady Norton-Griffiths, had once ridden a mule across the Andes. Thorpe's father – a former Conservative MP – had died when he was fifteen. Even though Ursula Thorpe also had two daughters, she had always lavished a disproportionate amount of attention on her son. While she may not have shared his political views, she was determined to do everything she could to further his career.

Immediately after Josiffe was introduced, Mrs Thorpe asked him to sign the visitors' book. Gazing in horror at the open book lying on the table in the hall, Josiffe desperately tried to remember what name Thorpe had said he should use. After some discreet prompting, he signed himself 'Peter Freeman'. Then, in a whisper, he asked Thorpe what address he should give.

'Just put Colchester,' Thorpe whispered back.

The house was as gloomy on the inside as it was on the outside. Shortly afterwards the three of them sat down to supper. Although this consisted only of boiled eggs, it was served with great ceremony – on a table in the drawing room that had been laid with a tablecloth and napkins.

Throughout the meal, Joliffe was so frightened that he might be asked some technical question about being a television cameraman that he could hardly eat. But he needn't have worried: Mrs Thorpe was only interested in talking to her son. Toying with his boiled egg, Josiffe noticed that Thorpe was much less outgoing when he was in his mother's company. It even crossed his mind that he might be frightened of her.

As soon as he finished, Josiffe asked if it would be all right if he went to his room. Of course, said Mrs Thorpe, and went to turn down his bed. By now it was shortly after nine o'clock. Josiffe changed into his pyjamas, brushed his teeth – there was a basin in the room – and took some more of the pills he had been given by Dr Willems. He then got into bed with Mrs Tish.

He hadn't been there long when there was a knock on the door. It was Thorpe. He said that just in case Josiffe wanted something to read, he had brought him a book – a novel called *Giovanni's Room* by the American writer James Baldwin. After wishing him goodnight, Thorpe shut the door. Josiffe was far too sleepy to read. He did, however, glance at the book and was surprised to see that it was about a love-affair between two men. As he lay in bed, he could hear Thorpe and his mother talking to one another downstairs. He was particularly struck by the fact that Thorpe always called her by her Christian name – 'Urse' – and never 'Mum' or 'Mummy'.

He heard Thorpe wish her goodnight – 'Goodnight, Urse' – and then the sound of her footsteps as she went upstairs to her bedroom, which was next door to Josiffe's. Turning out the light, he settled down to go to sleep. But, just as he was dropping off, there was another knock on the door – softer this time.

Once again Thorpe came in. By now he was in his pyjamas and dressing gown. At first he sat on the end of the bed. 'You look just like a frightened rabbit,' he told Josiffe. Leaning forward, he embraced him and called him 'Poor Bunny'.

To his embarrassment, Josiffe began to cry.

Thorpe then went out and came back with a towel and a tube of Vaseline. Laying the towel on the sheet, he got into bed with Josiffe, then put some Vaseline on his penis. Having done so, he told Josiffe to roll over and proceeded to bugger him. Josiffe was in agony – 'It was like being cut in half; I thought he was going to kill me.' But he knew he couldn't scream because Mrs Thorpe was lying in bed next door. Just to make sure he was aware of this, Thorpe pointed at the wall and hissed in his ear, 'Mother's room!' For Thorpe, who both basked in his mother's approval and resented her dominance, the knowledge that she was only a few inches away must have lent the occasion an extra frisson of danger.

To stop himself from crying out, Josiffe bit the pillow. After what seemed like an age, Thorpe withdrew and wiped himself clean. Then he patted Josiffe on the thigh and left. The next morning, when he woke up, Josiffe found that his pyjama bottoms had blood on them. So did his thighs. After he washed himself as best as he could in the basin, he got dressed and took Mrs Tish out into the garden. Behind the house was a series of terraces, and Josiffe wandered back and forth along them as the sun came up. 'For some reason it was more painful when I was still, so I just kept walking. All the time I was thinking, what am I going to do?'

In the end he went back to his room, sat on the bed and waited. At eight o'clock Thorpe banged on the door and asked him how he wanted his eggs done. Downstairs, Josiffe found Thorpe and his mother in the kitchen. Thorpe was reading a newspaper while his mother sat impassive behind her monocle. As he sat and stared at yet another boiled egg, Josiffe kept thinking that he was about to burst into tears again. Seeing that something was clearly wrong, Thorpe bolted his breakfast and told his mother they had to leave right away.

'Peter,' he added, 'has a number of things to do before we fly to Malta.'

For a moment Josiffe had no idea who Thorpe was talking about, before remembering that he was meant to be 'Peter'. On the doorstep, Mrs Thorpe gave Josiffe a lingering look and said, 'My dear, I hope we see you again.' She then extended her hand. As he shook it, Josiffe had the disconcerting sense that, while she may not have known what had gone on, she wouldn't have been particularly surprised to find out.

For much of the journey, neither of them spoke. Nearing London, Thorpe told Josiffe he had to pick up his secretary, Jennifer King, and give her a lift to the House of Commons. He said that Josiffe shouldn't say anything about what had happened to anyone. They would talk about it later, and decide what to do. After they dropped Jennifer King off at the Commons, the two men went to a Lyons' Corner House on the south side of Westminster Bridge.

Over coffee, Thorpe took out his wallet, handed Josiffe a £10 note, and said that he should find somewhere to live. He gave him directions on how to get to Sloane Square on the Tube and told him about a newsagent's opposite the department store Peter Jones. In the newsagent's window was a noticeboard offering rooms to let. Josiffe should choose somewhere, put down a deposit on the rent, then call Thorpe and let him know the address. Although he was going to Malta that evening, Thorpe said he would be along to see him later.

Josiffe duly found a room in a lodging house in Draycott Place, Chelsea, owned by a woman called Mrs Flood. As he had promised, Thorpe turned up soon after lunch. Once again the two of them had sex – not penetrative this time – and then Thorpe went off to catch his plane, saying that he would be back in two weeks' time. He left Josiffe feeling more confused than ever. Although Thorpe had been his saviour, salvation had come at a much heavier cost than he had anticipated.

But, however confused he was, there was one thing he was quite sure about. He no longer had any intention of giving Thorpe back the letters that he had written to Brecht Van de Vater. Once, they had been Van de Vater's insurance policy. In future, they would be his.

4

Bunnies

A fortnight later, when Thorpe returned from Malta, he went straight round to Draycott Place. Over the next few weeks, his life with Josiffe settled into a pattern of sorts. Sometimes Thorpe would drop by for sex. Sometimes Josiffe would go to watch him give a speech at the House of Commons and then they would have dinner at the Reform Club. Sometimes Josiffe would go round and spend the night in Thorpe's flat in Marsham Court, Westminster – although he never cared for this, as he was expected to sleep on a camp bed.

And sometimes Thorpe would ring the bell at Draycott Place and tell Josiffe to come straight down. They would then drive to a secluded spot near Battersea Bridge. Afterwards Thorpe would rush back to the Commons, while Josiffe walked home. By now something had become clear to Josiffe, something he had very mixed feelings about – he was a kept man. Thorpe had insisted that Josiffe should throw away all his clothes and buy himself a new wardrobe. He sent him to Gieves outfitters on Old Bond Street to buy himself a suit, and to his shirt-maker on Jermyn Street. Part of Josiffe loved being made a fuss of. He was also relieved to have a measure of security in his life. But another part resented being at Thorpe's beck and call.

And then there was the sex. Brought up as a Roman Catholic, Josiffe was keenly aware that the Church regarded homosexuality as a sin. At one stage he even went to confession at Westminster Cathedral and told the priest he was sleeping with a man – but without saying who. Josiffe's sense of shame became even deeper when the priest refused him absolution unless he promised never to do it again.

As time went on, Josiffe began to feel that Thorpe had infected him with what he called the virus of homosexuality – and that if he had never met him, he would have been leading the sort of conventional heterosexual life the Church approved of. But still he couldn't tear himself away. He liked the glamour, he liked the money, and, apart from anything else, he couldn't think of where else to go. On several occasions, Josiffe accompanied Thorpe down to his constituency in North Devon. Over Christmas 1961, Thorpe arranged for him to spend the holiday with some friends of his, Jimmy and Mary Collier – Jimmy Collier was the prospective Liberal candidate for Tiverton. To allay any concerns the Colliers might have had about his emotional state, Thorpe told them that Josiffe's father had recently died in a plane crash.

While Josiffe was there, he and the Colliers met up with Thorpe and his mother for lunch at the Broomhill Hotel in Barnstaple. After lunch, Ursula and the Colliers suggested they all go for a walk. Thorpe, however, said he wanted Norman to try on some new shirts – and took him upstairs to his room. If anyone thought this was odd, no one said so.

Then, in January 1962, a former patient at the Ashurst Clinic called 'Jane R' turned up in London. While they were both in hospital, she and Josiffe had become friends. At her suggestion, they had discharged themselves and rented a house in Polstead Road, North Oxford, together with another Littlemore patient called Ian B. It was a disastrous arrangement from the very start. On their first night there Ian had tried to seduce Josiffe. Running downstairs to the kitchen to tell Jane what had happened, Josiffe found her on her knees with her head in the oven. Pulling her out by her feet, he had to smash the window with a chair to get rid of the gas.

Coming out of his room in Draycott Place one morning, Josiffe was astonished to see Jane R walking towards him, wearing only a dressing gown. He was sure he hadn't given her his address, but she'd clearly tracked him down and seemed hell-bent on seducing him. After his experience in Polstead Road, Josiffe thought this might not be a good idea and spurned her advances. Two days later Jane went to the police and complained that he had stolen her sheepskin coat. When the police told Josiffe that they wanted to question him about the alleged theft, Thorpe insisted that as Josiffe's 'guardian', he had a right to be present.

The interview was scheduled for 4.15 p.m., on 8 February 1962, at Thorpe's office in Westminster. Arriving early after a sleepless night spent worrying about his future, Josiffe told Thorpe that he thought it would be better for both of them if they stopped seeing one another. Confronted by news that he didn't want to hear, Thorpe did what he always did – he ignored it. Instead, he tried to kiss Josiffe and stick his hand down his trousers.

When the police arrived, the two men hurriedly sprang apart. One of the detectives, Detective Constable Raymond Whitmore-Smith, noted in his account of the interview that 'It was patently obvious that Josiffe was a rather weak personality, apparently labouring under considerable mental strain and completely dominated by Mr Thorpe who was acting in an advisory capacity to Josiffe. During the period when Josiffe was writing a statement, Mr Thorpe left his office to attend a Division in the House of Commons, and during his absence, Josiffe was noticeably relaxed and more talkative.'

As soon as the police learned that Josiffe and Jane R both had histories of mental illness, they decided not to pursue the case. Afterwards Thorpe decided that it might be prudent if Josiffe made himself scarce for a while and sent him off to stay with the Colliers again. From there, Josiffe wrote to Thorpe enclosing a reply he'd had to an advertisement he'd placed in *Country Life* magazine a few weeks earlier. The advertisement read: 'Ex public-schoolboy, 21, wishes to live with family and work on farm. Skilled horses. Former Badminton competitor. Willing to undertake any work. Pocket money only expected.'

Josiffe also wrote about how he hoped to go to France to study dressage. Unusually, he expressed a degree of optimism about his future. Things, he felt, were finally looking up.

On 13 February 1962, five days after the police interview, Thorpe wrote back on House of Commons-headed notepaper:

My dear Norman,

Since my letters normally go to the House, yours arrived all by itself at my breakfast table at the Reform, and gave me tremendous pleasure.

I cannot tell you just how happy I am to feel that you are really settling down, and feeling that life has something to offer.

This is really wonderful and you can always feel that whatever happens Jimmy and Mary and I are right behind you. The next thing is to solve your financial problems . . . The really important point is that you are now a member of a 'family' doing a useful job of work – with Tish – which you enjoy. Hooray!! Faced with all that no more bloody clinics . . .

In haste.

Bunnies can (and will) go to France.

Yours affectionately,
Jeremy.
I miss you.

This was a letter that would come back to haunt Thorpe. Although it didn't prove that he and Josiffe were lovers, it was couched in unmistakably affectionate terms. Thorpe had also wrongly dated the letter February 1961 instead of 1962 – a potentially catastrophic mistake. In early February 1961, Josiffe was still twenty years old. While buggery remained illegal between people of any age, anyone under the age of twenty-one was classified as a minor. Thorpe therefore could have been prosecuted not only for homosexuality but also for something far more serious – homosexual rape.

In the meantime, there was a more immediate problem. Josiffe had left his National Insurance card with Brecht Van de Vater. Given the circumstances of his departure, he could hardly ask for it back. Without it, though, he couldn't get work. Once more, Thorpe stepped into the breach. In March 1962, he telephoned the Ministry of Pensions and National Insurance to ask if they could provide a replacement. The following month, a new card – number ZT711516O – arrived.

But what Thorpe had failed to anticipate was that this new card came with some tiresome strings attached. As far as the Ministry was concerned, he was now Josiffe's employer – and, as such, was legally obliged to pay his weekly National Insurance contributions. By now Josiffe's brief flare of optimism about his prospects had burned out. Over the next few months he drifted about in a purposeless haze, working as a Liberal Party canvasser in North Devon and at a couple of riding stables. All the time his mental health continued to deteriorate.

Then came another disaster – his dog, Mrs Tish, had to be put down after savaging some chickens belonging to Josiffe's doctor. In a state of deep gloom, Josiffe wrote to Thorpe telling him what had happened and asking if he could send him a photo of Mrs Tish that Thorpe had taken.

On 30 September 1962, Thorpe wrote back:

My dear Norman,

This is indeed terribly sad news about poor little Mrs Tish, and I know what a blow this must have been to you. You have all my sympathy.

I am afraid I shall not be home for a little while and cannot therefore send you the photo (at the moment I'm in N Devon). I have a horrible feeling I may have pasted it into an album which will make it difficult for me to dislodge. However . . .

I hope otherwise things go well.

Yours
Jeremy

A few days later Josiffe tried to commit suicide, cutting his wrists after taking an overdose of sleeping pills. In his depressed mental state, Josiffe was rapidly turning Thorpe into the author of all his misfortunes – a combination of heartless lover and absentee father. None the less they continued to see one another, although there were increasingly frequent rows. After a particularly bad one, on the night of 18 December 1962, Josiffe stormed out of Thorpe's flat. Having wandered the streets for several hours, he went, on a whim, into the Easton Hotel in Victoria. By a remarkable coincidence, Mary Collier (wife of the Devon Liberal candidate who had taken in Norman the previous year) was working on the reception desk – helping out her sister-in-law, who owned the place. Josiffe told her about his troubles, and then about his sexual relationship with Jeremy Thorpe.

Mary Collier was stunned by this information – so stunned she wasn't sure what to do. Josiffe also telephoned a woman he had met while he was staying at the Colliers', Caroline Barrington-Ward. By now in a state of full-blown hysteria, he said that he was going to shoot Thorpe and then kill himself. Understandably alarmed, Barrington-Ward telephoned the police. Shortly afterwards, at just before eleven o'clock, two policemen arrived at the Easton Hotel.

One of them, Detective Sergeant Edward Smith, asked Josiffe if he actually knew Thorpe. Josiffe said that indeed he did, and opened his suitcase. Inside were the letters that he'd taken from Brecht Van de Vater's cottage, along with three other letters he had been sent by Thorpe. Smith quickly flicked through them. But what concerned him far more was Josiffe's threat to kill Thorpe. Although Josiffe had a bullet – which he produced with a suitably theatrical flourish – what he lacked was a gun. Deciding there was no imminent risk of bloodshed, Smith told Josiffe he should report to the police station in Lucan Place, Chelsea, the next day.

When he turned up the following morning, Josiffe did not waste time with pleasantries. 'I have come to tell you about my homosexual relations with Jeremy Thorpe, MP,' he announced to a startled Detective Inspector Robert Huntley and his colleague Detective Sergeant Edward Smith. He was doing so, he said, 'Because these relations have caused me so much purgatory and I am afraid it might happen to someone else.' Josiffe went on to give graphic accounts of various sexual encounters with Thorpe at Marsham Court: 'Then he put his penis into my anus and worked it in and out until he ejaculated into me. After that he wiped himself with a Kleenex. I want to say now that I didn't like doing this, not merely to clear myself, but I honestly did hate doing it. I was attached to Jeremy because he had helped me, and of course, I didn't like to say no.'

He described other incidents too, including one that had taken place at the Broomhill Hotel in Barnstaple. Although Thorpe had booked them separate rooms, Josiffe had woken up to find Thorpe in bed with him: 'He didn't use Vaseline this time, but some other lubricant which was in a tube. I didn't see the colour of the substance. He put this on his penis and put his penis in my anus. Then he asked me to put my penis into his anus. I didn't use the lubricant, but I put my penis into his anus, but I didn't ejaculate. I just felt sick. He was very angry with me. He then left the room.'

After signing a statement – it ran to six pages – Josiffe showed Huntley and Smith some of the letters from his suitcase. These included the misdated 'Bunnies can (and will) go to France' and the postcard. He also handed over another letter, which began 'My angel, all I want is to share a Devon farm with you', and then went on to describe, in some detail, how much Thorpe enjoyed having sex with him. Before he left, Josiffe was examined by a police surgeon. Humiliatingly, he had to bend over while the surgeon stuck a probe up his anus. The surgeon confirmed that Josiffe had recently had penetrative sex. Josiffe then left and, after once again wandering the streets for several hours, went back to – of all places – Jeremy Thorpe's flat.

All this presented Huntley and Smith with a dilemma. Should they delve deeper, and risk infuriating an influential public figure? Or should they wash their hands of the whole business as quickly as possible? Predictably enough, self-preservation won the day. To cover himself, Huntley asked Barnstaple Police in Devon to investigate Josiffe's story. They made a few cursory inquiries and reported back that they'd been unable to substantiate it. Huntley then sent a file containing everything – including Josiffe's letters – to Scotland Yard. From there it was passed on to Special Branch, with a copy sent to MI5, which kept files on all Members of Parliament. Having examined all the material, Special Branch decided that they too would take the path of least resistance. Josiffe's original statement – and the correspondence – was locked in a safe in the office of the Assistant Commissioner (Crime) and promptly forgotten about.

And there the matter might have rested – except that it didn't. In January 1963, Josiffe was offered a job at the Castle Riding School in Comber, Northern Ireland. He packed a suitcase and caught the ferry from Cairnryan to Belfast. There was only one problem. In order to work, he needed his National Insurance card. Although Thorpe promised to send him the card, it never arrived. As a result, Josiffe was told to leave after a couple of months. He then found unpaid work with a family who offered him free accommodation in return for helping to look after their horses. Again, he wrote to Thorpe asking him to send him his National Insurance card, but still he heard nothing. Possibly Thorpe had decided that he didn't want anything more to do with him, or possibly he just had something else on his mind.

In June 1963 the country was plunged into the biggest political scandal for forty years. John Profumo, Secretary of State for War in Harold Macmillan's Conservative government, was forced to resign after swearing in the House of Commons that he had never had a relationship with a young prostitute called Christine Keeler, who had also been sleeping with a Soviet naval attaché, Eugene Ivanov. In the face of mounting pressure, Profumo changed his story and admitted that he had lied.

The story caused a sensation. There was widespread disbelief that a government minister – and an Old Harrovian – should have been sleeping with a prostitute. That he should then have lied about it in Parliament deepened the sense of outrage still further.

Although Thorpe played no part in any of this, he did make a characteristically imprudent intervention. In the Commons, he claimed to have inside knowledge that two other ministers would soon be forced to resign for 'personal reasons'. His speech prompted a bout of feverish speculation as newspapers frantically tried to identify the ministers in question.

But three months later, when the Master of the Rolls, Lord Denning, published his report into the affair, he found no evidence to support these claims and Thorpe was forced to apologize. 'I accept Lord Denning's findings and I would wish to apologize for any pain which this publicity might have caused,' he declared in the Commons. Then, in a characteristic display of humbug, he sought to turn the situation to his advantage. 'This in itself indicates that standards of our public life stand higher than many at times thought possible.'

Denning also recommended that Members of Parliament should compile secret dossiers on one another to ensure that this sort of thing never happened again. Thorpe must have realized how vulnerable he would be in this new era of paranoia and media scrutiny. Given that Profumo had been vilified for sleeping with a glamorous young woman, Thorpe would be torn apart if news of his affair with Josiffe ever got out. But if this gave him pause for thought, it didn't last long.

The government limped on for another year before Macmillan resigned in the mistaken belief that he had terminal cancer. In the October 1964 General Election, Thorpe's majority increased almost fifteen-fold and he looked more unstoppable than ever. But, while his star continued to rise, Josiffe's had gone into freefall. In the summer of 1963 he had been competing in the Royal Dublin Show when his horse fell while taking a jump. It landed on top of him, crushing six vertebrae.

He went back to England to recuperate and found a job at a stables in Wolverhampton. It didn't last. Another suicide attempt followed, then another. But throughout it all he continued to see Thorpe, spending occasional nights on the camp bed in Marsham Court. They had continued to write to one another too, with one letter of Thorpe's containing the sentence, 'I wasn't going to write anything compromising but can't stop myself saying I love you and can't wait to see you.' At this stage, Thorpe had no inkling that Josiffe had already told the police about their relationship.

One evening, in December 1964, when the two men were together, Josiffe showed him an advertisement he had seen in *Horse and Hound* magazine. A vet in a small town near Berne in Switzerland was looking for a groom. As always, whenever there was any prospect of Josiffe finding employment, Thorpe sprang eagerly into action. He sent several telegrams to the vet, a Dr Choquard, telling him how wonderful Josiffe was with horses. A week later Dr Choquard wrote back telling Josiffe the job was his. As Josiffe had never had a passport before, Thorpe also took him to the Passport Office in Petty France to help him get one.

In January 1965, clutching his suitcase and dressed in a thin suit and a pair of Oxford brogues, Josiffe set off from Victoria Station. Inside the suitcase were Thorpe's letters. But, once again, disaster struck. First of all, Josiffe left the suitcase on the train. Then, when he arrived in Switzerland, he was shocked to find that no one had come to meet him. Hopelessly underdressed, he tramped two miles through the snow to Dr Choquard's house.

There was another shock when he got there. The horses, he found, had been badly neglected and his accommodation was a loft above the stables. Not only was it freezing cold, but a strong smell of manure rose through the floorboards. To cap it all, the loft was full of rats. Josiffe lasted for one night before deciding that he couldn't stand it any more. Dr Choquard, who doesn't seem to have been greatly disappointed to see him go, lent him 300 francs to buy a train ticket back to England. By way of collateral, Choquard told him he would keep the suitcase – when it turned up – until the loan was repaid.

By the time he got back to London, Josiffe had only 50 centimes in his pocket and the clothes he stood up in. He went straight round to Marsham Court and rang the bell. Thorpe, who had clearly allowed himself to hope that this time Josiffe might finally stick at something, was not best pleased to see him. But this was nothing compared to his alarm when he learned that the missing suitcase contained some of his letters. It was vital that Thorpe got the suitcase back as quickly as possible. He phoned the British Consulate in Berne, and then, a few days later, wrote to the Foreign Office demanding action.

In the meantime Josiffe, sensing that he was no longer welcome at Marsham Court, was soon on his travels again. He went back to Ireland, where he lasted a week as a riding instructor at a hotel outside Dublin before being sacked for allowing a friend to sleep in his room. Almost immediately he found another job with a couple called Quirke who owned a stud in County Wicklow.

On 6 March, after Josiffe had been there three weeks, Mrs Quirke wrote a heartfelt letter to Thorpe:

Dear Mr Thorpe,

Three weeks ago Norman Josiffe came here to learn Stud work. I met him in Dublin and drove him down. The first morning, within half an hour, he came in and told me he was going and would I take him back to Dublin. A friend staying with us drove him into Wicklow where he could catch a bus. Even though he insisted he could take a taxi – Dublin is thirty-eight miles from us! That afternoon he telephoned from Dublin to apologise and said he would like to come back. A friend drove him down the next day but wouldn't come in.

My husband offered him pocket money whilst he was learning the job £3 a week and he would live with us as one of the family. Norman said he would not dream of accepting anything and it was very good of us to have him. We just put it down to foolish pride.

We did everything we could to make him feel at home, especially as he then told us he was an orphan. He then went on to say that his mother was French and his father a well-known English Peer. He travelled on a French passport and his name Josiffe was his mother's name also, his mother was dead.

Three times in as many weeks he said he was going and the last time, two evenings ago when he was talking about a certain horse with my husband and they disagreed as to ownership, I told him to look it up in Horses in Training. He did so and was proved wrong. He turned on my husband and said 'I'm not spending all night arguing with you. I will be leaving here tomorrow morning.'

Frankly we were shocked. The next morning (yesterday) we drove him into Dublin parting on good terms . . .

I am writing to you as he told us you were his Guardian and we feel there is something wrong with the boy. We have made all the efforts, especially as he was widowed [sic] at such an early age and his past history seemed to play on his mind . . . He will certainly have to pull his socks up if he intends to settle down to anything, and as his Guardian I feel you have a right to know what happened here . . . It's such a pity as he can be such a charming boy and just as quickly he can turn very nasty . . .

Yours sincerely
Mrs M. Quirke

However predictable this was, it must have come as very unwelcome news to Thorpe – all the more so as he was still trying to track down Josiffe's missing suitcase. On 11 March, he replied on House of Commons-headed notepaper:

Dear Mrs Quirke,

Thank you so much for your letter of 6 March. I am very sorry you had so many unfortunate experiences with Norman Josiffe.

In fact, I am not his Guardian, but merely tried to help him on occasions which have proved at times rather hair-raising. I think honestly that he has a split personality and does seem incapable of standing on his own feet for long.

I fear that I have no responsibility for his actions. I believe that his mother is alive and living in Kent.

Yours sincerely
Jeremy Thorpe

Thorpe, clearly, was trying to put as much distance between himself and Josiffe as possible. But if he thought that would be the end of it, he was hopelessly mistaken.

Meanwhile, Josiffe had done something that no one could have predicted: he had gone into a Trappist monastery. Mount Melleray was a Cistercian abbey on the slopes of the Knockmealdown Mountains in County Waterford that offered free accommodation to people who wished to spend some time in retreat. Although Josiffe didn't know it, he can't have been far away from Brecht Van de Vater. Having moved to Ireland, Van de Vater changed his name back to Norman and become the Master of the United Hunt in County Cork; he went on to become a member of the Irish equestrian team at the 1976 Montreal Olympic Games.

All the other guests at Mount Melleray – an unusually diverse bunch, including the Chairman of the Irish Potato Board – were battling demons of one sort or another. After the upsets of the last few months Josiffe immediately felt that he was among friends. For several weeks he was blissfully happy. Then he started an affair with one of the other residents, the brother of one of the monks. Together the two of them went back to Dublin, but the relationship soon fizzled out and Josiffe sank back into depression.

One evening he went to confession in a church near St Stephen's Green and told the Jesuit priest that he wanted to kill himself. The priest – Father Michael Sweetman – arranged for him to stay in lodgings in Ballsbridge on the south side of the city. There, Josiffe sat and brooded on his misfortunes and decided that the time had come to take direct action. He wrote to Ursula Thorpe – the letter which Thorpe showed Bessell when they had lunch at the Ritz – telling her about his relationship with Jeremy and asking her to lend him £30. He needed the money, he explained, to pay for his suitcase to be sent back from France.

As Josiffe had already suspected, Thorpe and his mother had a very complex relationship. 'She was a woman of strong character, fearless in her convictions, outspoken and often tactless,' Thorpe later wrote of her. She was also a colossal snob with an unassailable belief in her own importance. When Thorpe was about five years old, he remembered his mother ringing the bell in the first-floor living room of their Knightsbridge house and summoning the maid to put some coal on the fire. This entailed the maid climbing two flights of stairs from the basement. When he asked his mother why she hadn't done it herself, she told him that she didn't want to get her hands dirty.

From the start, the two of them were unusually close. While Ursula paid little attention to her two daughters, Lavinia and Camilla, she doted on her son, seldom squandering an opportunity to laud his accomplishments. Thorpe's relationship with his father, a barrister and a former Conservative MP, was more straightforward – 'I adored my father,' he recalled simply. But at home it was the monocled Ursula who held sway. A proficient pianist, she encouraged Thorpe to learn the violin because it gave them an opportunity to spend more time together. At a concert at his nursery school, the headmaster told the audience, 'Thorpe will play – and Mrs Thorpe will accompany.'

In a sense, Mrs Thorpe carried on accompanying her son for the rest of her life. Never a physically robust child, Thorpe developed tuberculosis just before his sixth birthday and had to spend six months immobilized in a spinal carriage. Once he recovered, he had to learn to walk again – in adulthood, he suffered a good deal from back pain. During the Second World War, Thorpe's father stopped practising as a barrister to concentrate on much less well-paid war work. As the family's fortunes declined, Ursula grew even more possessive, and determined to ensure that her son was a success.

While Thorpe may have been sickly, he didn't languish in the shadows. Imbued with his mother's self-belief, he eagerly sought out any glimmer of limelight he could find – so much so that he soon gained a reputation for being a dreadful show-off. But, for all his prancing exhibitionism, he was not an unkind child. At Eton, he took boys more vulnerable than himself under his wing. In a way, of course, this was what he had done with Josiffe – the more dam-aged someone was, the more they aroused his protective instincts.

The death of his father when Thorpe was fifteen shattered him – 'our relationship was almost that of two brothers and I was intensely proud of him.' However upset Thorpe was, his outward assurance remained fixed in place. By now something else had become apparent about Jeremy Thorpe, something that would stand him in great stead in later life: he had a magnetic personality. To be in his company was to be with someone who crackled with energy, yet at the same time exuded an air of unhurried ease. It was a beguiling combination. Above all, Thorpe was terrific fun. Even when he was trying to be serious a gleam of amusement was never far from his eye.

Not everyone was smitten – there were those who found him slippery and arrogant. But, whatever you thought of Thorpe, he was difficult to ignore. At Oxford, he deliberately dressed in a way that would attract as much attention as possible, wearing brocaded waistcoats and carrying a silver-topped cane. Yet, beneath his pop-injay trappings, Thorpe didn't lack political principle. He could easily have opted to follow his parents' example and joined the Con-servative Party. Instead, he plumped for the Liberals – motivated partly by ideology, partly by a wildly romantic notion that he was destined to lead the party back to power and partly by a desire to move out from under his mother's shadow.

Thorpe, one suspects, could have joined an anarchist collective and Ursula would still have done whatever she could to advance his career. The older he became, the more he grew to resent his moth-er's interference. But the nearest he ever came to thumbing his nose at her was having sex with Norman Josiffe while she was lying in bed next door. For the next thirty years the two of them remained locked together – each in thrall to the other.

Josiffe's letter was delivered to Ursula Thorpe's house on the morning of Friday, 26 March. It arrived as she was eating her cus-tomary boiled egg. As soon as she had finished reading it, she picked up the telephone and called her son.

5

Mr Bessell Goes to Dublin

When Thorpe finished telling Peter Bessell about his relationship with Josiffe, he again asked him what he should do. He wasn't particularly concerned about his mother's reaction – however fearful he was of her, he knew he'd always be able to win her round. But he had finally realized just how dangerous Josiffe could be. Flattered that Thorpe had confided in him, keen to curry favour with a man who was looking more and more like the next Leader of the Liberal Party, and unable to resist the idea of being in the thick of the action, Bessell immediately offered to go to Dublin and talk directly to Josiffe.

Thorpe leaped on this suggestion. How soon would he be able to go? Bessell said that he would have to check his diary, but he couldn't see why he shouldn't go later that week. Before, Thorpe hadn't touched his steak tartare; now, he was suddenly ravenous. Mixing some oil and vinegar together, he poured it over his salad, mashed a raw egg into his chopped steak and wolfed down the lot. As he was doing so, he began giving Bessell instructions about what he should say to Josiffe when he got to Dublin. He should tell him that his letter to his mother was a blatant attempt at blackmail, and that if he repeated his allegations he would be charged with a serious criminal offence. Bessell, who instinctively favoured a more softly-softly approach, decided to keep his feelings to himself.

Two days later he flew to Dublin. Before he left, he telephoned Thorpe to discuss the best way of approaching Josiffe. Should he invite him to his hotel room, he wondered.

'You should,' Thorpe said. 'You'd find him marvellous in bed.'

As always, Bessell was both fascinated and appalled by Thorpe's recklessness. He liked to think he was reckless himself, but he had never come across anything like this. It was all the more remarkable to find it in the House of Commons, a place where people were normally obsessed with protecting their own backs. Thorpe's air of not giving a damn, his confidence that he would be able to get away with anything he wanted, was one of the things that made him so attractive, of course. Bessell, who was more of an acolyte than he liked to admit, was captivated. On several occasions he'd asked himself what could have made Thorpe so rash. His conclusion was that it had a lot to do with his sexuality.

Bessell was not the first to have noticed that there appeared to be two distinct sides to Thorpe's character. The public Thorpe was all ebullience, all charm, confident that he could break down anyone's inhibitions. But the private Thorpe was a much darker and more solitary figure, seemingly addicted to subterfuge. Bessell felt sure this was a result of his having had to keep a large part of his nature under wraps. On some level, Thorpe seemed to relish this double-life. Time and again, he would flirt with danger, with coming as close to being found out as he dared. The Conservative MP Norman St John-Stevas once told the political journalist Paul Johnson that he had never met anyone so addicted to risk. 'Norman said that he was bound to get into trouble sooner or later. That he did the most desperate things that Norman had ever come across before or since.'

In one respect the two sides of Thorpe matched up. Despite being in his mid thirties, he was still apt to behave like a spoiled child, rushing headlong into all sorts of scrapes on the assumption that someone else would step in and sort everything out. In the past this had been Thorpe's mother's role. Now it was to be Bessell's. However eager he was to take it on, there was a part of him that wondered what he had let himself in for.

When he arrived in Dublin, Bessell checked into the Intercontinental Hotel, and then went to see Father Sweetman at his home in Milltown Park. From his limited experience of Roman Catholic priests, Bessell had assumed that Father Sweetman would be elderly and unworldly – and hence an easy pushover. He was greatly taken aback when the door was opened by an urbane man in his forties. Sweetman invited him into his sitting room, where Bessell showed him the letter that Josiffe had sent to Ursula Thorpe. Bessell insisted that there was no truth to Josiffe's claims that he and Thorpe had had a sexual relationship, but clearly an allegation of this sort against an MP – especially an MP who happened to be unmarried – could be very damaging.

Throughout all this Sweetman sat in silence. He continued to sit in silence for some time after Bessell had finished. Then he asked quietly, 'Why do you think Norman wrote this letter if there is no truth in this story?' Bessell had to admit this was a very good question. It was also one he was quite unprepared for. The only explanation he could come up with was that Josiffe must be deranged.

'No,' said Sweetman in the same calm voice, 'he's not deranged.'

Sweetman went on to tell Bessell that Josiffe had come to see him in a distressed state and shown him several letters apparently written by Thorpe. Whatever the truth of his story, Sweetman could see that Josiffe needed help. As well as finding him lodgings, he had provided him with a little money and arranged for him to do some odd jobs. Since then, Josiffe's mental health had improved a good deal, although what Sweetman called 'the healing process' would inevitably take some time. The meeting ended with his giving Josiffe's address to Bessell and the two men agreeing to stay in touch.

That afternoon, Bessell went round to Josiffe's lodgings in Ballsbridge. As there was no one in, he wrote a note on the back of one of his cards, asking Josiffe to call him at any time of the day or night at the Intercontinental Hotel. Bessell dined at the hotel, and then sat waiting in his room. The hours ticked by. By midnight, he decided that Josiffe wasn't going to call and went to bed.

What Bessell didn't know was that Josiffe – despite possessing an extensive array of sedatives – found it almost impossible to sleep.

Every night he would walk the streets of Dublin, often covering more than ten miles. At 3 a.m. Josiffe returned to his lodgings to find a letter on the doormat. The name on the bottom meant nothing to him, but he had been so confused and depressed over the last few months that he could no longer be sure who he had and hadn't met. Despite the hour, Josiffe decided that he'd better call.

Bessell was roused from his sleep by the phone ringing. Groggily, he asked if the two of them could have breakfast at eight o'clock in the morning. Josiffe agreed and rang off. But the next morning there was no sign of him. Convinced now that the whole trip had been a waste of time, Bessell went upstairs to pack his bag.

Then the phone rang again. It was the reception desk saying that a Mr Josiffe was waiting downstairs. Just as Father Sweetman had not been at all what Bessell had been expecting, neither was Norman Josiffe. He was tall and thin and had a wild shock of black hair. He also looked much older than twenty-five, partly because there were dark shadows under his eyes. Josiffe was clearly very nervous. When they shook hands, Bessell noticed that his palm was damp. As for Josiffe, his first immediate impression of Bessell was that there was something untrustworthy about him: 'He looked so smooth and had this loud, rather slippery voice.'

Bessell explained he had been sent by Jeremy Thorpe, but he also said that he had to catch a flight back to London that morning and asked if they could talk in a taxi to the airport. Although the weather was quite mild, Josiffe sat huddled in the back throughout the journey, shivering. Just in case the driver was eavesdropping, Bessell asked Josiffe to refer to Thorpe by his initials. He told him that his letter to 'JT's mother' constituted a blackmail attempt and that Josiffe could be sent back to Britain to stand trial. What's more, he claimed to have an extradition order signed by the Home Secretary, Sir Frank Soskice, in his pocket.

Like so much of what Bessell said, this was nonsense. Josiffe's letter to Mrs Thorpe may have been grossly insensitive, but it could hardly be interpreted as a blackmail attempt – he simply wanted her to lend him £30. What's more, Bessell didn't have an extradition order signed by the Home Secretary, or by anyone else, for the simple reason that at this point in 1965 there was no extradition treaty between Britain and Ireland.

Nor did his threats have the desired effect. Far from being intimidated, Josiffe asked to see the extradition order. Bessell, not surprisingly, refused to show it to him. Josiffe then said that he wanted nothing more than to go back to England. 'I told him, "That's marvellous. I have never blackmailed anyone. I would be very pleased to come back to England. At least I would be able to tell the court my story. And at last I might be able to sort out the National Insurance card situation." '

This was not at all what Bessell wanted to hear. But he was even more alarmed when Josiffe told him about his missing suitcase – which Thorpe had omitted to mention – containing several letters that Thorpe had written him. Mention of the letters caused Bessell to look particularly shaken, Josiffe noted. But Bessell could at least take heart from the fact that Josiffe sounded genuinely contrite about having written the letter to Mrs Thorpe, particularly at the thought that he might have upset her. All he wanted, he reiterated, was a new National Insurance card and the return of his suitcase. Bessell promised to do his best to help. Executing a rapid about-turn, he told Josiffe to stay in Ireland for the time being – on the grounds that it would be safer to keep him and Thorpe as far apart as possible.

When the taxi reached the airport, Bessell gave Josiffe £5 as well as the taxi fare back to Dublin. He also gave him his address in London and told him to get in touch if he had any 'pressing problems'. Then he caught his flight back to London. All in all, Bessell felt, it had gone pretty well. True, there had been some unforeseen glitches, but, as he told Thorpe later that day, he was confident that Josiffe had finally learned his lesson and wouldn't cause any more trouble.

Thorpe was delighted. Another awkward mess had been sorted out. A few weeks later, he presented Bessell with an engraved gold cigarette lighter as a token of his appreciation. Given how mean

Thorpe could be, often showing an almost pathological reluctance to put his hand in his pocket, Bessell felt deeply touched.

By then Thorpe had had another piece of good news. Josiffe's suitcase had at last been found and sent to the British Consulate in Zurich. Bessell, helpful as ever, arranged for it to be shipped back to the UK. But his own affairs were looking increasingly rocky. He was now in debt to the tune of almost half a million pounds. In order to keep himself afloat, he had to fly to New York to try to arrange yet another loan. Bessell was away for two weeks. Towards the end of his trip, he met two friends for dinner. They had brought along a woman friend of theirs – 'a girl of Lithuanian parentage'. However, it was not the girl's antecedents that captivated Bessell so much as 'her astonishing beauty'. Two days later they dined together. 'As I was returning to London the following morning, we spent the night together at the International Hotel at Kennedy Airport.'

Bessell returned to London feeling a little sheepish and wondering if Diana Stainton, his mistress/secretary, might suspect that he'd been on one of his 'amorous adventures'. But, as it turned out, Stainton had a much more dramatic story of her own to tell. Knowing that he was likely to be away when Josiffe's missing suitcase turned up, Bessell had asked her to call Thorpe as soon as it arrived at Victoria Station. One evening in June 1965, Stainton left a message with Thorpe's office, saying that the suitcase was now in the Victoria Left Luggage office.

Later that night Thorpe called back. 'Diana, darling,' he began, 'are you in a gorgeous negligee?'

He went on to ask if he could go with her to Victoria the next morning. Then the two of them could take the suitcase to the Aer Lingus office in Piccadilly and have it sent on to Dublin. If Stainton thought it odd that Thorpe was taking such a close interest in Josiffe's suitcase, she decided to keep her feelings to herself.

The next morning Thorpe picked her up in his car as arranged, and they drove to Victoria. There, Stainton signed for the suitcase while a porter put it in the boot of the car. Afterwards they started driving towards Piccadilly. But they hadn't gone far when Thorpe said that he wanted to stop off at his flat in Marsham Court. When they arrived, Thorpe took Josiffe's suitcase out of the boot, then ran upstairs, with Stainton following. Inside the flat, she watched in disbelief as he flung the case down on the hall floor and began forcing open the locks. Rummaging through the contents, Thorpe found two bundles of letters, both of them neatly tied up with string. Without explaining what he was doing, he took the two bundles into the bathroom, along with Josiffe's shirts. When he came out, Thorpe was empty-handed. After he had managed to jam the locks closed, he took the suitcase back down to the car.

He and Stainton carried on to the Aer Lingus offices, where she made out the luggage labels to Norman Josiffe at his Ballsbridge address and arranged for the suitcase to be air-freighted to Dublin. The cost of the air freight came to £3.17s.8d. – which Thorpe reluctantly paid. However irksome this was, he could at least console himself that it was money well spent. As far as Thorpe was concerned, he was finally in the clear. There was no longer any evidence to link him with Norman Josiffe, and therefore – he believed – nothing to worry about. For his part, Bessell was less pleased. He was shocked to hear about Thorpe having removed Josiffe's letters from the suitcase and annoyed that Stainton had been involved in a possible felony.

He also wondered how Josiffe would react when he found out that his letters were missing. Given everything that had gone before, it seemed unlikely he would do nothing. In all likelihood, Bessell thought, Josiffe would talk to Father Sweetman, who would then contact him again. If that happened, he would have to lie, he decided. Although he had done quite a bit of it in his life, Bessell did not like lying. He was still enough of a Christian to be troubled by the idea of committing a sin. Besides, there was always the possibility that he might be found out.

6

The Creature

As Bessell had anticipated, Norman Josiffe was not at all happy when he picked up his suitcase from Dublin Airport. First, he saw that the handle was broken. Then, when he opened the case, he found that his letters were missing, along with half his clothes. For a while he was baffled by the question of why Thorpe had taken his shirts. Then he remembered they had been laundered at Thorpe's flat and had the Marsham Court laundry stamp on them.

When Father Sweetman wrote to Bessell asking if the suitcase could possibly have been interfered with between Switzerland and Dublin, Bessell replied in tones of high indignation. 'I can hardly imagine my secretary rifling the contents of his suitcase and I am sure he received it in exactly the same state as when it left Switzerland.' He finished off by saying, 'I only hope that he will manage to keep a job of some sort, and that he will not leave too great a trail of victims in his wake.'

Clearly Bessell didn't hold out much hope of either of these things ever happening. Yet, despite his fears, Josiffe continued to improve. He met a woman who owned a boutique in Dublin and embarked on an affair with her – by no means his first heterosexual relationship, but still against the usual run of play. Although he had no formal training, Josiffe had always been interested in fashion and began designing men's clothes for her. As he was still plagued with guilt about his sexuality, she offered to pay for him to see an Irish doctor called Peter Fahy, who claimed to be able to cure homosexuals of their 'disease'. This involved patients being put to sleep for a week and then – so the theory went – awakening to find they had turned into fully fledged heterosexuals.

Josiffe duly turned up at the Portobello Nursing Home in Fitz-william Square on 2 November 1967. There he signed a consent form, was told to undress and given an injection which promptly sent him to sleep. His only memory of what happened next is of being given more injections and helped to the lavatory every so often by two nurses. After a week he was woken up, offered a cup of tea and discharged. That evening Josiffe went to a pub. He hadn't been there long when he struck up a conversation with another man who was also drinking at the bar. They then went back to Josiffe's place and had sex. The so-called cure, he concluded glumly, had been a dead loss.

But if his sex life remained as complicated as ever, his social life had also improved. Through the boutique, he became friendly with Tara Browne, the son of the fourth Baron Oranmore and Browne, and an heir to the Guinness brewing fortune. Soon Josiffe was being invited to spend weekends at the Guinness family home at Leixlip Castle in County Kildare. He was acutely aware that all the other guests came from very different backgrounds to his, and he felt sometimes as if he was there only as an unofficial court jester. None the less, he was fascinated by the milieu and flattered by the attention.

At dinner one weekend, he found himself sitting next to Nancy Mitford. A few weeks later, in March 1966, he was invited to Browne's twenty-first birthday party at Leixlip, where he mixed with members of the Rolling Stones. It was to be Browne's last birthday. Nine months later he was killed when his Lotus Elan went through a red light in Earls Court and collided with a lorry – an incident reputed to have inspired another friend of Browne, John Lennon, to write the lines: 'He blew his mind out in a car/he didn't notice that the lights had changed' in his song 'A Day in the Life'.

At Browne's twenty-first, Josiffe met a woman who told him she had just started a modelling agency in Dublin. She complained that there was a terrible shortage of handsome men and asked if he was interested in doing some modelling. Josiffe was greatly taken by her proposal. Soon his brooding features were appearing on television and staring out of fashion magazines advertising all kinds of exotic outfits. But, while Dublin had its own lively fashion scene, it was nothing compared with London. That, people kept telling Josiffe, was the real hub of the action. He listened to what they said and, as he pondered on his changed circumstances, began to think that the time might have come for him to return.

Thorpe's optimism that he might be shot of Josiffe didn't last long. Shortly after rifling through his suitcase, he had some unwelcome news. Through a member of the Liberal Party in North Devon, he heard that the Barnstaple Police were investigating his relationship with Norman Josiffe. In fact, Thorpe's informant was hopelessly out of date: it had been more than two years since the Barnstaple Police had set up an inquiry. What's more, they'd swiftly concluded there was no substance to the story. Thorpe, though, didn't know this. As far as he was concerned, the Barnstaple Police had only just started snooping around. By now Thorpe knew that the police in London had interviewed Josiffe in December 1962 – and kept hold of some letters. Appalled by the thought that the Barnstaple Police might somehow get to see them, Thorpe did something that was fast becoming second nature to him: he turned to Peter Bessell.

The two men met in Thorpe's office in No. 1 Bridge Street, just across the road from Big Ben.

'Christ Almighty!' said Bessell when Thorpe told him about the inquiry.

Leaning across his desk, Thorpe said, 'Peter, can you think of any way to prevent the Devon Police from getting hold of those letters?'

The wheels of Bessell's brain obligingly sprang into motion. Within a few seconds, he had a thought.

'George Thomas,' he said.

George Thomas was the Labour MP for West Cardiff and the only member of the government that Bessell knew well. He was a devout Methodist who had once been national President of an interdenominational organization called the Brotherhood

Movement – an office that Bessell, incredibly, had also been nominated for. But, far more importantly, Thomas was Joint Parliamentary Under-Secretary of State at the Home Office, a job that allowed him access to police files. Bessell suggested that he should go to see Thomas and discreetly sound him out about getting hold of Josiffe's letters. Thorpe thought this was an excellent idea and asked how quickly he could set up a meeting.

That afternoon Bessell wrote a note to Thomas explaining that he had a problem – he didn't go into details – and asking if they could have a chat. A day or two later, they bumped into one another in the Tea Room at the House of Commons. In one hand Thomas was carrying a cup of tea. With the other he patted Bessell on the shoulder. 'Well, my boy,' he said. 'What can I do to help you?'

Bessell ushered him to a secluded corner. 'The problem I wanted to talk to you about isn't mine,' he explained. 'It's Jeremy's.'

He saw Thomas's eyebrows lift slightly.

'What's the bad lad been up to now?' he asked.

Bessell told him that a few years earlier Thorpe had taken pity on a destitute young man who had turned up at the House of Commons.

'I see,' said Thomas. 'Go on . . .'

At this point Bessell's nerve failed him. He had little or no idea how much to tell Thomas about Thorpe's homosexuality. For all his affability, the unmarried Thomas had a disconcertingly puritanical air. 'He gave the impression of being like a Roman Catholic priest – concerned with matters higher than sex.' As he had done before with Thorpe, Bessell tiptoed cautiously forward. 'Jeremy became quite fond of this boy,' he went on. 'In fact, they became good friends . . .'

'Did they now?' said Thomas.

'After a bit he made certain allegations against Jeremy . . . He said there had been a homosexual relationship between them.'

Thomas nodded, almost as if he had been expecting this.

What's more, said Bessell, the young man had gone to the police and given them a statement, as well as some letters. To make matters worse, the Barnstaple Police were also conducting their own inquiry. All at once, Thomas became markedly less friendly. He drained his cup of tea, pushed back his chair and seemed on the verge of walking off. Immediately, Bessell abandoned the idea of asking him to get hold of the letters. 'I thought to myself, it's no good asking him to do that because I damn well know he will shit himself on the spot.'

A rapid change of plan was called for. Wildly, and with no thought to the consequences, Bessell asked if Thomas could arrange for him to see the Home Secretary, Frank Soskice. As Bessell conceded later, this was 'a preposterous request' – so preposterous he suspected that Thomas would dismiss it out of hand. Instead, to Bessell's surprise, he settled back in his chair, gave another nod and said that he'd do his best to fix up a meeting. Thomas, Bessell realized, was happy to be helpful, just as long as the problem didn't end up in his lap. What Bessell didn't know was that Thomas had very good reasons of his own for not wishing to become involved. It wasn't until after Thomas's death, in 1997, that his own homosexuality became public knowledge; he was also being blackmailed over his private life at the time.

Several days went by. Then Bessell received a summons to go to Soskice's private office. When he walked into the oak-panelled room, Bessell saw to his surprise, and relief, that Soskice was alone – it was unusual for a minister to see an MP without an aide being present. A distinguished barrister who had become a Labour MP in the 1945 General Election, Soskice was in poor health and partly crippled. But, however infirm he was, there was nothing frail about his manner.

'How may I help you?' he asked.

Initially nervous, Bessell soon relaxed. 'I was surprised by how easy it was to talk to him.' He told Soskice about the letter Josiffe had sent Thorpe's mother, about the letters the two men had exchanged and about his own trip to Dublin. After he had finished, Soskice asked if Bessell believed Josiffe's allegations.

Bessell admitted that he did.

On the face of it, Soskice had no reason to help Thorpe – they weren't even members of the same party. But, as Bessell knew only too well, there was an unwritten code that MPs closed ranks if there was any risk of their sexual indiscretions becoming public knowledge. When he next spoke Soskice tapped his index finger on his desk to emphasize what he was saying. 'It is very important to keep them apart. You must try not to let Jeremy get into a position where this creature can blackmail him.'

Bessell then raised the subject of the police inquiry in Barnstaple. Soskice told him not to worry about this – almost certainly it was nothing more than a routine investigation prompted by scurrilous tittle-tattle.

'But what if the Barnstaple Police ever extend their inquiry to London?' Bessell asked.

As he spoke, Bessell noticed something that he had not seen before: there was a brown file on Soskice's desk. Almost as a reflex action, Soskice moved his left arm sideways a few inches until it was resting on the top edge of the file. 'It's a pity about the letters,' Soskice said, almost to himself. Now he began to pluck at the edge of the file with his fingers. All at once Bessell felt as though an electric spark had just jumped through his head. 'In that instant I felt sure the slim brown folder under his arm contained the letters to which he had referred.'

Soskice went on to say that anyone who was homosexual was always at risk. Legislation to reform the law was long overdue, he believed – personally he was in favour of legalizing homosexuality between consenting adults. Bessell made appropriate noises of agreement. Soskice then returned to the subject of Thorpe. 'It is important,' he said even more deliberately now, 'to keep Jeremy away from the creature. Treat him rough. If he makes any demands on Jeremy, get rid of him – tell him to go to hell! He must be kept out of Jeremy's life.'

Bessell sensed that the meeting was at an end. He got up and Soskice limped around to the other side of the desk. There, he put his hand on Bessell's arm. At the same time he gazed into his eyes.

'They must be kept apart,' he repeated.

When Bessell told Thorpe about their meeting, he mentioned the file that he'd seen on Frank Soskice's desk – the file he felt certain contained the letters that Thorpe and Josiffe had exchanged. Far from allaying Thorpe's fears, this only exacerbated them.

'Do you think he'd read them?' he asked.

Bessell replied that it would have been very odd if he hadn't. At this, Thorpe grew even more agitated. Whenever he was embarrassed or annoyed, Thorpe had a habit of slapping his head with his right hand, then smoothing his hair to the side. He did it now as he admitted that one of the letters was particularly damaging. Gently, Bessell probed for details.

'I said how it felt to screw him,' said Thorpe. 'And that I cared a lot about him.'

Bessell did his best to reassure him that Soskice did not strike him as a gossip, and eventually Thorpe calmed down. The next time Bessell ran into George Thomas – again in the Tea Room – he thanked him for fixing up the meeting with Soskice.

How had the meeting gone, Thomas wondered.

Bessell said that it had gone well.

'Good,' Thomas told him. 'I'm sure there's nothing to worry about. Tell Jeremy to forget about it, my boy.'

A few minutes after leaving the Tea Room, Bessell saw Thorpe coming towards him along the library corridor.

'I've seen George, and I've got good news,' he told him.

Together they walked towards the Speaker's House. 'You'll hear no more of that file,' Bessell continued. 'George has told me that there's nothing more to worry about.'

'But does that mean it's been destroyed?' Thorpe wanted to know.

It was at this point that Bessell made a characteristically impulsive – and imprudent – decision. While he had no hard evidence that Soskice had the file, let alone had destroyed it, Bessell knew that Thorpe would never stop fretting until he believed it was gone. It was therefore his duty, he reasoned, to set his friend's mind at rest.

'Yes,' said Bessell. 'It has. It's been destroyed.'

Thorpe stopped in his tracks. As he turned to him, his face split into an even wider grin than usual.

'Marvellous!' he said.

Over the next few months, Bessell occasionally thought about the brown file, and where it might be. Every time he did, 'there would be a faint question mark in my mind.' But, as time went on, the question mark grew fainter and fainter, and after a while it disappeared altogether.

7

This Filthy Subject

In the summer of 1965, shortly after Norman Scott had received his missing suitcase, Leo Abse, the Labour MP for Pontypool, went to see a Conservative peer, the Earl of Arran. The two of them had important business to discuss. Abse was a flamboyant dresser with a fondness for billowing silk scarves and brightly patterned shirts. He also liked to drop references to Freudian psychotherapy into his Commons speeches, undeterred by the fact that these tended to be greeted with hoots of derision, or looks of utter bafflement, from his fellow MPs.

Although Abse was not homosexual himself, he had long taken a keen interest in homosexual law reform, believing the law as it stood to be absurdly outmoded. In 1957 the Wolfenden Report had recommended decriminalizing male homosexuality, but the government, horrified by the prospect, had done nothing. In March 1962 Abse began a campaign to make some of Wolfenden's recommendations law. He didn't go as far as proposing that homosexuality should be made legal – he knew there was no chance of that for the time being. Instead, he came up with three compromise measures. He suggested that all prosecutions for offences between consenting adults in private should be authorized by the Director of Public Prosecutions before being launched. This was intended to curb the excesses of the police.

Abse's second proposal was that all prosecutions for homosexual offences should commence within twelve months of their having allegedly been committed – in order to decrease the chances of people being blackmailed. And lastly he wanted to make it obligatory for the courts to obtain a psychiatrist's report before sentencing anyone, hoping this might 'let a little of the light of understanding into the darkness of the judicial mind'.

But Abse soon met an immovable object in the shape of the Lord Chancellor, Lord Kilmuir, who refused to sit in any Cabinet meeting where what he referred to as 'this filthy subject' would be discussed. In 1964 Abse tried again, but in the face of continued hostility from the government his bill was easily talked out. While the tide may have been slowly turning, the effort of trying to hurry it along had left Abse feeling tired and frustrated. In future, he decided, he would need an ally, someone who felt as passionately about homosexual law reform as he did. Ideally, this ally would be a peer who could propose a Private Members' Bill in the Lords, where – all being well – it would win enough support to enable it to be sent on to the Commons.

He could hardly have chosen a more unexpected figure than the eighth Earl of Arran – or Sir Arthur Strange Kattendyke David Archibald Gore, as he had been before succeeding to his title seven years earlier. Known as 'Boofy' to his friends, the Earl had seldom spoken in the House of Lords. The few speeches he had made had been devoted exclusively to protecting the rights of badgers. A small, excitable man with a brick-red complexion and snowy-white hair, Arran was prone to ending his remarks with the words 'What, what?' rather in the manner of George III. He too was a married man. His wife, the Countess of Arran, was a champion powerboat racer who shared his love of badgers.

At their home near Hemel Hempstead they allowed badgers to have the run of the place and always wore gumboots indoors to stop their ankles from being bitten. This was not the only hazard involved in keeping badgers. On several occasions Arran and his wife – as they proudly demonstrated to visitors – had caught ringworm.

To widespread astonishment – including Abse's – Lord Arran had taken up the cause of homosexual law reform. 'I could not unravel why this heterosexual man, lacking formed philosophy, should so relentlessly pursue this path.' It was only later that Abse learned that Arran's elder brother had been gay. After receiving psychiatric help for many years, he had committed suicide a few days after succeeding to the title. By championing the cause of reform, the Earl hoped to create a fitting memorial to his late brother.

Together the two men decided to introduce a Private Members' Bill into the Lords – one that this time would abandon all thoughts of compromise. Instead, it would grasp the key Wolfenden recommendation and seek to make homosexuality legal between consenting adults over the age of twenty-one.

On the afternoon of 12 May 1965, Lord Arran stood up and asked the House of Lords: 'What is homosexuality? What causes it? Answer: no one knows. Some call it a disease, others call it a diversion from the biological norm. Others call it a weakness, others quite simply a vice. What is the cure? No one knows. Some even doubt whether a cure exists, at least in extreme cases.' It was quite possible, Arran conceded, that 'normal people' might regard homosexuals as 'unpleasant. We do not want to think about them; we try to regard them as evil; our instinct is to want to stamp them out.'

No one was more determined to stamp them out than his fellow peer Lord Montgomery of Alamein. Montgomery was one of Britain's greatest heroes, the man who had masterminded the defeat of Field Marshal Erwin Rommel at El Alamein in northern Egypt in 1942, thereby changing the course of the war. When Montgomery had taken over command of the Eighth Army just two months before the battle, he had told his men that some of them might think he was mad. 'I assure you I am quite sane,' he declared. '[But] I understand there are people who often think I am slightly mad; so often that I now regard it as rather a compliment.'

Back then, with the country desperate for a military saviour, people had been happy to take Montgomery at his word. Twenty years on, these protestations had a less convincing ring. In his distinctive, yapping lisp, the 78-year-old Field Marshal told a packed House of Lords that he regarded 'the act of homosexuality in any form as the most abominable bestiality that any human being can take part in, and which reduces him almost to the status of an animal. The time will come when we have to choose a title for this Bill, and I think that instead of "Sexual Offences Bill" the proper title should be "A Charter for Buggery".'

When someone pointed out that France and some other European countries took a more relaxed attitude towards homosexuality, Montgomery retorted, 'We are not French; we are not other nationals. We are British, thank God.' He went on to propose one of the most bizarre amendments in British parliamentary history: if there was to be a change in the law, he said, let the age of homosexual consent be set at eighty. That way 'at least one has the old-age pension to pay for any blackmail which may come along.'

Even the normally unshockable Abse was left speechless. What demons lurked in Montgomery's psyche, he wondered – a question echoed thirty years later by Montgomery's biographer Nigel Hamilton, who suggested that Montgomery spent his life furiously trying to repress his sexual attraction to young boys.

But Montgomery was not alone. Another peer, the former Lord Chief Justice Lord Goddard, had heard of what he called 'coteries' where 'the most horrible things go on. As a judge one has to listen to these stories which really make one feel physically sick.' Others, though, couldn't understand what all the fuss was about. Lord Stonham, Parliamentary Under-Secretary at the Home Office, said that during a fairly active life among men, 'including twenty-five years' participation in team games', he had never encountered homosexuality and seriously doubted if it even existed.

Meanwhile Abse had introduced a Private Members' Bill into the Commons. In his opening speech, he declared, 'For any person to suffer the misfortune of homosexuality there are clearly grievous burdens. Certainly for most of them it means they are permanently denied the blessings of family life, the rearing of children and the gift of a mature love with a woman.' Typically, Abse could not resist invoking Freud – telling startled MPs that anyone who voted against his bill was only doing so because they were repressing their homosexual desires.

Predictably enough, this did not go down well – especially with the Conservative MP for Louth, Sir Cyril Osborne. 'The vast majority of our people consider, rightly or wrongly, that sodomy is wrong, unnatural, degrading and disgusting,' Osborne said, 'and I agree with them.' Once again Abse picked up a strong whiff of repression. Osborne, he suspected, had been so affected by 'curbs placed on his infantile masturbatory activities' that he was hell-bent on removing any whiff of homosexual temptation from society.

Although Abse's bill was defeated by nineteen votes, Lord Arran had more success in the Lords, where the Sexual Offences Bill had another two readings. At the Third Reading, Arran confessed that there had been several occasions when he wished he could be shot of the whole thing and go back to his badgers. 'There is no fun in it, and sometimes one feels desperate at some of the letters one receives.'

What he particularly disliked was the aggressive tone of the letters. A great many of them quoted the Bible at him – usually Deuteronomy or Leviticus. Why didn't anyone ever mention something more open-minded like the Sermon on the Mount, Arran wondered. In fact, he did receive one letter that mentioned the Sermon on the Mount. His heart lifted as he read this, and then plummeted as his correspondent referred to it as 'That masterpiece of appeasement'. On another occasion a parcel containing human excrement arrived at his office. Apparently, under the impression it was pâté, his secretary told him, 'I threw it away, Lord Arran. It wouldn't keep.'

But by now the momentum was building. In early 1966, Arran's bill was passed in the Lords by 116 votes to 46. It then moved to the House of Commons, where it was taken up by a Conservative MP called Humphry Berkeley. Although Berkeley was openly gay, he was another unlikely ally for Abse – 'not the sort of man whom I would choose to accompany for a skate on thin ice'. Sent down from Oxford for writing hoax letters to a number of public figures – he pretended to be a crazed public school headmaster called H. Rochester Sneath – Berkeley had a reputation for being as mercurial as he was unreliable.

Yet Abse could not fault the way in which he steered the bill through the house. Passed by 179 votes to 99, it went through for a Second Reading. While another hard struggle lay ahead, for the first time Abse and Arran allowed themselves to believe that reform might finally be in sight.

Like Thorpe, Peter Bessell was in favour of homosexual law reform, but it was a long way from being uppermost in his thoughts. He had other, more pressing concerns. After a rare period of solvency his finances had plunged back into the red. Bessell was now so deeply in debt that there was a strong likelihood of his going bankrupt. This had all kinds of alarming implications. Apart from anything else, MPs who are declared bankrupt immediately have to resign their seats.

Now it was Bessell's turn to confide in Thorpe. The prospect of his having to resign appalled Thorpe. Not only would it do the Liberals' image considerable damage, it would also trigger a by-election which they were far from certain of winning. Thorpe agreed to try to find Bessell some money. In June 1965 he approached the Liberal Party's main benefactor, an Anglican priest of independent means called the Reverend Timothy Beaumont. The Reverend Beaumont agreed to lend Bessell £5,000. Helplessly optimistic as ever, Bessell was confident this would be enough to tide him over until the end of the year.

Just two months later it had all gone – yet more grand plans having come to nothing. Again Bessell went to see Thorpe, and again Thorpe agreed to help. How much did he need this time? Badly burned by his previous experience, Bessell decided to set his sights a little higher and asked for £15,000. Beaumont agreed to lend another £5,000 on the condition that someone else stumped up the remaining £10,000. Thorpe then approached a former President of the Liberals, a wealthy businessman called Sir Felix Brunner. It turned out that the Brunners were cruising in the Mediterranean, but their yacht was due to put in to Corfu in a few days' time. About to go on holiday to Greece, Thorpe suggested that he and Bessell should fly to Corfu together. When they turned up at the Brunners' hotel, Thorpe went to talk to Sir Felix while Bessell sat making small talk with his wife, Elizabeth. Bessell prided himself on being able to talk on almost any subject, but on this occasion he rapidly ran out of things to say. Lady Brunner had founded the Keep Britain Tidy group in the 1950s and retained a keen, almost obsessive interest in litter.

The moment Thorpe and Brunner joined them it was clear from Thorpe's manner that he had been successful. He did, however, tell Bessell later on that a shocked Brunner had exclaimed, 'That's not peanuts, Jeremy!' when he made his approach. After saying goodbye to the Brunners, Thorpe and Bessell boarded a Douglas DC-3 plane and flew to Athens. That evening they celebrated in a restaurant at the foot of the Acropolis.

Thorpe was holidaying with an old friend of his from Oxford – a tall, slim, bespectacled merchant banker called David Holmes. Bessell was struck by the fact that Holmes and Thorpe 'shared an intimate relationship which they made no effort to hide'. Although he was not quite as relaxed about homosexuality as he liked to pretend, Bessell decided that he approved of Holmes. He liked his sense of humour and found that all three of them shared an interest in classical music. 'He was the kind of man I had expected Jeremy would find attractive.' And there was another, and far more important, consideration. 'Unlike Norman Josiffe, he would not endanger his career.'

Six months later, on 28 February 1966, the Prime Minister, Harold Wilson, announced that Parliament would be dissolved on 10 March and a General Election held on 31 March. Wilson had been in power for less than eighteen months, but he had a majority of only four and was finding it increasingly hard to govern. Labour ran its campaign under the slogan 'You Know Labour Government Works'. In fact, there was little evidence that people knew any such thing. A disastrous series of by-elections the year before had seen Labour's majority cut to just two. But Wilson was confident that, faced with a choice between the party in power and the Conservatives led by Edward Heath, the electorate would opt for familiarity.

As for the Liberals, they hoped to build on what they saw as mounting dissatisfaction with the two main parties and increase their number of seats from a modest tally of nine. The portents, though, were gloomy: judging by post-war election results, Liberals tended to do badly whenever Labour was in power.

Peter Bessell was feeling particularly sorry for himself when he sat down for lunch with Thorpe in the Members' Dining Room shortly before Parliament was dissolved. Repeated financial disasters had inflamed his tendency towards self-laceration. Despite all the evidence to the contrary, Bessell continued to regard himself as a man of high ideals. The trouble was he kept falling a long way short of them.

Thorpe did his best to cheer him up, invoking the spirit of a man he revered above all others, David Lloyd George, the last Liberal Prime Minister. Lloyd George too had encountered great disappointments. 'But,' Thorpe said, 'he never thought of giving up. Liberalism was the most important thing in his life, as it is in ours. That's why we're here.'

Also in the Members' Dining Room that day was Leo Abse. He too was feeling gloomy. Wilson's announcement had come as a heavy blow to his hopes of introducing homosexual law reform. Whenever a General Election was called, any bills that were still making their way through Parliament were automatically abandoned. As a result, Abse and Arran faced the prospect of having to start all over again.

8

Bessell Pulls Another Rabbit Out of His Hat

'Good God, is that all?' muttered Thorpe when the election results were announced in North Devon. His majority, which had risen to 5,136 in 1964, had dropped to 1,166. The situation was even worse for Bessell, who had fought what he described as a 'half-hearted campaign' in Bodmin and saw his majority cut to just over 2,000. Overall, the Liberals enjoyed mixed fortunes in the March 1966 election. Their share of the vote went down – from 3,099,283 to 2,327,533 – but they gained three seats, taking their total to twelve. There was no doubting the winner, though – Labour romped home with a majority of ninety-six. As Harold Wilson had anticipated, it was going to take a lot to make the British electorate vote for Ted Heath.

Why had Thorpe done so badly? In part, this was because of a recurrent incident during his election campaign. On a trip to Tangier the year before, Thorpe had tried to seduce a young man. After angrily rebuffing his advances, the man had gone and told both the local Liberal and Conservative associations in North Devon about it. Whenever Thorpe gave a speech, he'd had to contend with groups of raucous young Conservatives shouting anti-homosexual abuse. The North Devonians liked Thorpe; they warmed to his bluster, relished his eccentricities and laughed at his jokes. But the idea that he might be homosexual was too much for some of them to contend with.

A month later, Bessell was in his favourite place in the Palace of Westminster – the Tea Room – when a fellow Liberal MP called Alasdair Mackenzie approached him. Mackenzie was a 62-year-old Scottish Highland farmer who was the party's spokesman on agriculture. A nervous, diffident man, he had led a cloistered life before becoming an MP – so cloistered that he had never been to London until he won his seat. Arriving at the House of Commons, Mackenzie was refused admission as he spoke only Gaelic. Thorpe had had to arrange for him to have a crash course in English so that he could take the Oath of Allegiance. Since then he had gained a reputation for making unusually short but – due to his accent – often largely incomprehensible speeches.

Mackenzie asked if he could have a word.

'Of course,' said Bessell.

Mackenzie then lowered his voice. 'It's about Jeremy.'

Bessell noticed that Mackenzie appeared to be having difficulty speaking. Also that he was blushing.

'Aye,' said Mackenzie. 'I feel I must tell you about it.'

He went on to tell Bessell that he had heard rumours – rumours about a man, currently living in Dublin, who was claiming to have had a homosexual relationship with Thorpe. Mackenzie was known to have very definite views about homosexuals. He thought they should be locked up – preferably for ever.

'Oh, I know about him, Alasdair,' said Bessell, trying to sound as relaxed as possible. 'His name is Norman Josiffe.'

'You know?' said Mackenzie. 'Oh, that's terrible, terrible. So it's true, then?'

'Certainly not,' said Bessell. This man Josiffe had a history of mental illness, he explained. Thorpe had met him and endeavoured to help, but after a while had decided there was nothing more he could do – whereupon Josiffe had turned nasty and started claiming they had been lovers.

Mackenzie was greatly relieved. But it turned out he hadn't quite finished yet. 'Of course,' he went on, more reflectively now, 'Jeremy's never been married . . . Aye, never married.'

Bessell sensed danger. He realized that he had to defuse Mackenzie's suspicions. But how could he do this without inviting further questions? It was at this moment that he had a flash of something like genius. He remembered that his heroically long-suffering wife Pauline had once joked that if Bessell were to meet an untimely end, she would have to consider marrying Thorpe for the good of the party.

'Between ourselves, Alasdair, it's very sad,' he told Mackenzie. 'Jeremy fell in love – years ago – with a married woman.'

Bessell saw that Mackenzie's eyes had opened very wide. It occurred to him that, as a devout Presbyterian, Mackenzie was likely to take almost as dim a view of adultery as he did of homosexuality. Bessell quickly reassured Mackenzie that nothing improper had happened. As a matter of honour, Thorpe had refused to break up a marriage. Mackenzie then did something Bessell had been half expecting, even hoping for. He asked if he knew the woman in question. Bessell said that he did know her. In fact, he knew her well – very well indeed.

After a significant pause he added, 'Perhaps now you'll understand why Jeremy and I are such good friends.'

By now Mackenzie's eyes were bulging out of their sockets.

'You mean . . .'

Bessell said nothing; he simply nodded. But there was no mistaking the implication – he and Thorpe were bonded by their love for the same woman. When Mackenzie got up to go a few minutes later, Bessell noticed that he was still looking dazed.

However much Bessell liked being the custodian of Jeremy Thorpe's big secret, it also made him uncomfortable. Should the secret ever get out, his part in the cover-up might also become known – in which case his fellow MPs would blame him for having failed to alert them. It might be prudent if he took another MP into his confidence, Bessell decided. The man he chose was Richard Wainwright, a Methodist lay preacher like himself, albeit with a much less rackety private life.

Wainwright listened in silence as Bessell told him about Thorpe and his affair with Norman Josiffe. Afterwards he thanked Bessell for his frankness and told him that should he ever feel the need to unburden himself again he was welcome to do so. As Bessell went away, he had one of those fierce blasts of moral certainty that came over him from time to time, and which were invariably accompanied by twinges of pride. He had, he felt sure, done the right thing.

*

Ever since the election, there had been rumours that Jo Grimond might be about to stand down as Liberal Leader. His son had committed suicide during the election campaign and, stricken with grief, Grimond's appetite for stopping the Liberals from squabbling among themselves – always an uphill struggle – was clearly waning. In any succession battle, Thorpe was reckoned to be the front-runner. But he did himself no favours at the Liberal Assembly in Brighton in September 1966 when he made what was widely seen as a call for Britain to declare war on Rhodesia.

Thorpe was a passionate opponent of the Rhodesian Prime Minister Ian Smith, whose policy of racial segregation had resulted in the white settlers owning all the property in the country and black Rhodesians being reduced to a pitifully paid servant class. The Rhodesian economy was dependent on oil, most of which was brought into the country by rail. Thorpe felt that if only Rhodesia could be denied oil, there was a good chance that Smith might be toppled. He therefore proposed what he called 'selective bombing of supply lines'.

This wasn't such a mad idea – the only rail line went through virtually uninhabited territory so the risk of civilian casualties was small. None the less, Rhodesia was still a member of the Commonwealth, and many Britons had friends and relatives living there. Conservative right-wingers had long been itching to have a go at Thorpe, seeing him as a traitor to his class as well as a bumptious gadfly. Their dislike had been compounded when, in a typically deft jibe, Thorpe referred to Ted Heath as 'The plum pudding around which no one has succeeded in lighting the brandy'.

Now they seized the opportunity to ridicule him, shouting out 'Bomber! Bomber!' whenever he stood up to speak in the Commons. The furore badly tarnished Thorpe's image. Along with the rumours that continued to swirl around Westminster about his sexuality, it left some Liberals wondering if he really was such an attractive prospect as Leader.

That winter an incident occurred which Peter Bessell didn't think that much about at the time. Later on, though, it came to assume an ever greater significance in his mind. As relations between Britain and Rhodesia continued to deteriorate, Harold Wilson proposed that Britain should impose mandatory sanctions.

Bessell was one of three MPs – one from each of the main parties – who proposed asking Ian Smith if he would agree to a Royal Commission visiting Rhodesia. This, they hoped, would preclude the need for sanctions. He showed the proposed telegram to Thorpe, who – after tinkering with the wording – agreed that it should be sent. The telegram, sent on 7 December, asked for a reply before 8 p.m. GMT the next evening.

The following afternoon Harold Wilson spoke for two hours, laying into the opposition for being racist or lily-livered, or both, and arguing there was no viable alternative to sanctions. Wilson knew about the telegram, but thought the idea of a Royal Commission was a waste of time. He also didn't think much of Bessell personally, having marked him down as unusually shifty even by Westminster standards. Towards the end of the debate an attendant handed Bessell a small brown envelope. Inside was a telegram from Government House in Salisbury, the Rhodesian capital. In response to Bessell and his colleagues' three proposals, the telegram said simply, '1, Yes. 2, Yes. 3, Yes.'

Having read it, Bessell stood up as the Prime Minister was speaking and asked if the Right Honourable Gentleman would give way. Wilson ignored him. A few minutes later he tried again. This time Wilson stopped and glared across the Chamber before saying, 'If there is one honourable gentleman to whom I will not give way it is that honourable gentleman who has played his unworthy part!'

Bessell was astonished by what he regarded as a wholly undeserved attack. Immediately, he looked to Thorpe to protest. But Thorpe, he saw, was staring at the floor. He did not look up. After the debate was over, Bessell, as usual, headed for the Tea Room. There he tried to work out why his friend, whose secrets he had shared and for whom he had done so much, had made no effort to defend him.

9

The Blessings of Family Life

The General Election was not the disaster that Leo Abse and the Earl of Arran had feared. It did, however, spell the end of Humphry Berkeley, who lost his Lancaster seat – midway through the campaign his Labour opponent very publicly and pointedly got married. Undeterred, Lord Arran once again set about trying to pilot a bill through the Lords. Even though it was passed on three occasions, it still faced strong – at times apoplectic – opposition. 'I cannot stand homosexuals,' declared the Earl of Dudley at the bill's Third Reading. 'They are the most disgusting people in the world, and they are, unfortunately, on the increase. Prison is much too good a place for them; in fact, that is a place where many of them like to go, for obvious reasons.'

Abse and Arran soon found a new ally in the Labour Home Secretary, Roy Jenkins, who shared their reforming zeal. In the hope that they might finally 'dismantle our barbaric homosexual laws', Abse gave notice of his intention to introduce another Private Members' Bill in the Commons. A few days later, Jenkins asked Abse to come and see him. As far as Abse was aware, Jenkins was a staunch heterosexual. In fact, Jenkins had had a passionate homosexual affair with a fellow undergraduate, Tony Crosland, while the two were at Oxford. Crosland had also gone on to become a Labour Cabinet Minister – he was now the Secretary of State for Education and Science.

Like Abse, Jenkins was Welsh – his father, Arthur, had been the MP for Abse's constituency, Pontypool, in the 1940s. But that was about all they had in common. While there were not many people in politics that Jenkins actively disliked, Abse was one of them. On several occasions Abse had criticized Jenkins for betraying his roots by seeking to anglicize himself. He had also accused Jenkins's mother – not without foundation – of being a social-climbing snob. As Jenkins later admitted, he wished that someone else could have led the fight for reform, preferably someone who was less besotted with the sound of his own voice. But, realizing that he was stuck with Abse, Jenkins told him that if his Private Members' Bill gained a decisive majority, he would persuade his Cabinet colleagues to grant a full debate.

This time Abse decided it might be prudent to give Freud a miss – not that his views had changed. However, to have banged on about sublimated desires might, he felt, 'have alarmed too many in the House, insufficiently secure in their own heterosexuality'. At the same time, Abse decided to steer a careful middle way. He sought to disarm his opponents who were concerned about the corruption of minors by introducing heavy penalties – up to five years in prison – for any homosexuals caught having sex with someone under the age of twenty-one, irrespective of whether that person had consented. This in turn infuriated the Homosexual Law Reform Society, which wanted the age of consent set at eighteen.

The majority in favour of Abse's bill at its First Reading – 244 to 100 – was even higher than he had expected. After receiving an unopposed Second Reading on 19 December 1966, it was scheduled for a Third – and final – Reading the following summer. But, as the time for the debate grew nearer, Abse became increasingly uneasy. What worried him most of all was what he regarded as the disproportionately high number of mummy's boys in the House who might back down at the last moment. 'There is a type of homosexuality that finds its psychical genesis in an intense attachment to a female person, mother or nanny, in the first period of childhood; and those who, while not practising homosexuals, remain, unconsciously, excessively fixated to the mnemic image of a mother or mother substitute, can react over-determinedly to a plea for a toleration to homosexuality, for they are ever fearful that they might yield to its attractions.'

Those MPs not fixated with the mnemic images of their mothers might simply be too apathetic to vote, he felt. There was a danger that success could be taken for granted – giving his opponents, who until now had been so vitriolic they were practically incoherent, a chance to muster their resources. What Abse hoped for above all was a single issue that would unite the opposition. This would allow him to call on his supporters, whom he suspected of growing over-confident, to mount a counter-attack.

Help came from an unexpected quarter. Alarmed by the effect that a change in the law might have on discipline in the Merchant Navy, the National Maritime Board went to see Abse. He explained that it was not within his, or anyone else's, power to prevent buggery in the Merchant Navy. The Board, however, was not convinced. Did he not realize that the whole future of the Merchant Navy was at risk?

Getting wind of this, the press began to speculate that the bill might be defeated. Abse was delighted. As he had anticipated, the thought of failure galvanized his supporters. But still the National Maritime Board was implacable. Eventually Abse suggested a compromise every bit as bizarre as anything Lord Montgomery had proposed: to allow Merchant Navy seamen to have sex with passengers and foreign seamen while they were at sea, but not with each other. Much to his amazement, the Board bought it.

At the start of the Third Reading, the opposition's tactics soon became plain: they were going to try to filibuster the bill – to keep on talking until the allocated time had expired. One MP after another voiced their objections in as long-drawn-out a fashion as possible. As the hours dragged by and the speakers droned on, the prospect of an all-night debate became evermore likely. Tired, disheartened or just in need of a drink, MPs began to drift out of the Chamber. This put Abse in a very tricky position. In order for the bill to be passed, more than 100 MPs had to be in the Commons at any one time.

Anxiously, he scanned the benches and did his sums. On nine occasions he realized the numbers were getting desperately tight.

Each time, Abse left his seat and went through the lobbies half cajoling, half pushing his supporters back into the Chamber. By the time the final vote was taken, on 4 July 1967, it was after 5 a.m. Counting the votes, the tellers found that 99 MPs had voted in favour of the bill and only 14 against.

An exhausted Roy Jenkins stood up to congratulate an equally exhausted Leo Abse on having put through an important and civilizing measure. As Abse walked out of the Commons, the gas lamps were still burning in Westminster Palace Yard. Getting into his car, he drove along the Mall just as the sun was rising behind Admiralty Arch – a pleasingly symbolic touch, he thought. At home in St John's Wood, Abse's wife was in bed, 'still awake anxiously awaiting me and my news'. When he told her what had happened, she didn't say anything – 'She just took me into her arms.' Ever alert to his own emotional paradoxes, Abse found his earlier euphoria had swiftly been succeeded by a strange sense of melancholy. 'I needed her comfort,' he recalled, 'for nothing fails like success.'

Ten days later, the bill was ratified by the House of Lords. Afterwards Lord Arran was asked why his homosexual law reforms had succeeded, while his efforts to protect the rights of badgers had not. Arran paused, and then said ruminatively, 'There are not many badgers in the House of Lords.'

10

Two Pledges

Shortly after 9.30, on the morning of 17 January 1967, Peter Bessell was in his office in Pall Mall when the phone rang. He heard Thorpe's voice on the other end of the line.

'Peter, it's Jeremy. Jo's made up his mind at last.'

'About what?' asked Bessell, his mind still fogged with constituency business.

'He's announcing his resignation this morning.'

The fog instantly lifted.

'Good God!' Bessell exclaimed.

They agreed to meet at Thorpe's office in Bridge Street before lunch. All that morning Bessell paced up and down, trying to work out who to vote for as Leader. There were three serious contenders – Thorpe, Emlyn Hooson and Eric Lubbock. Bessell's first loyalty was to Thorpe, of course. But he was still smarting from Thorpe's refusal to support him during the Rhodesia debate, and he was also worried about what would happen if news of the Josiffe affair ever got out.

Hooson, another Welshman, was not exactly a friend of Bessell, but their political views had often coincided. His one drawback in Bessell's eyes was that he had an unusually high-pitched voice, making him a far from impressive public speaker. None the less, as Bessell paced about, he began to lean increasingly towards Hooson. Then came a characteristic rush of blood to the head. On impulse, he phoned Hooson's office to ask if he intended to stand. Hooson said that he hadn't made up his mind, but wanted to know if Bessell would support him if he did. Again, Bessell didn't stop to think. Yes, he said. If Hooson stood, then he would support him.

It was only after he had put down the receiver that the implications of what he'd just done hit home. How was he ever going to tell Thorpe that he wouldn't be voting for him? Walking over to Bridge Street, Bessell kept running through possible scenarios in his mind. None of them ended happily. He grew even more anxious when he made a mental list of the likely candidates and their supporters. In the event of a run-off between Thorpe and Hooson, Thorpe looked set to get six votes and Hooson five. If Bessell voted for Hooson – as he had promised to do – then the result would be a tie.

When he arrived Thorpe too was pacing about. As soon as he saw Bessell, he grabbed him by the shoulders. 'We'll shake this old party up!' he cried. 'I'll lead it as ruthlessly as Lloyd George. Harold and Ted won't know what's hit them. No more farting about. Now it's a crusade!'

These words had a dramatic effect on Bessell. Once, long ago, Thorpe had told him that he would be Prime Minister. Suddenly, it didn't seem like such an absurd idea. All Bessell's doubts disappeared – and so too did his promise to Hooson. 'From that moment I was his man. That was what Jeremy would do: lead a crusade . . . The fact that I was breaking my pledge to Hooson did not enter my head.'

After they had lunched together, Bessell went to the House of Commons Library, hoping to close his eyes and gather his thoughts. But he had only been there a few minutes when he felt a hand on his arm.

Opening his eyes, Bessell saw Emlyn Hooson standing before him.

'Peter,' said Hooson, 'I've decided to ask you to be my proposer.'

'Emlyn, I can't . . .' Bessell mumbled.

Hooson looked confused. 'What do you mean?' he asked.

'I – I must support Jeremy.'

To begin with Hooson didn't say anything; he just stared at him. When at last he did speak, his voice wasn't in the least high-pitched.

'If you hadn't said you'd support me,' he said, 'I wouldn't have stood.'

Then he turned and walked away. Reflecting on his own behaviour, Bessell felt an all-too-familiar sensation: remorse. 'I had treated him abominably.' But, as always, this didn't last long. Soon the clouds lifted and he brightened up again. After all, he reasoned, 'there was still ample time for Hooson to withdraw his name.'

But Hooson didn't withdraw. Both he and Eric Lubbock decided to stand against Thorpe. The following afternoon the ballot took place in the Whips' Office. With an air of great ceremony, the twelve Liberal MPs placed folded-up pieces of paper in a champagne bucket. The count didn't take long. Thorpe had won six votes and Hooson and Lubbock three apiece. Thorpe then went off to the office of the Minister of Technology, Tony Benn – Benn had lent it to him for the afternoon – while the other Liberal MPs decided what to do next.

At this point Richard Wainwright asked Bessell if they could have a quiet chat. They went downstairs to the Committee Corridor, directly below the Commons Chamber, and into a private room – a room that Wainwright appeared to have booked specially. Closing the door, he turned to face Bessell. Was there any risk of these rumours about Jeremy becoming public, he wanted to know.

Bessell did not hesitate.

'If I thought there was, I wouldn't have supported Jeremy.'

Wainwright nodded. 'That's good enough. I trust your word.'

Quite possibly, this was something that Bessell had not heard for a long time. At any rate he was very moved – so moved that he had a stab of conscience. When they left the private room, Wainwright headed back upstairs, while Bessell stayed where he was. 'As Wainwright rounded a corner to disappear from sight, I wavered. I started to call his name, then stopped. A few more seconds and it was too late.'

Shortly afterwards Thorpe was summoned to the Whips' Office. There he was told that Hooson and Lubbock had decided to withdraw, leaving only one man standing. At the age of thirty-seven, Jeremy Thorpe was now the Leader of the Liberals – the youngest man to lead a British political party in more than a century.

An hour later, Thorpe and Bessell were sitting alone in Tony Benn's office. Thorpe was so excited he could hardly sit still; the job he had dreamed of ever since he was a boy was now his. Perhaps hoping to take a little of the gloss off Thorpe's delight, Bessell mentioned what Richard Wainwright had asked.

At once the smile disappeared from Thorpe's face. 'Christ Almighty! What did you tell him?'

Bessell said that he had reassured Wainwright there was nothing to worry about.

'I hope you did more than that,' said Thorpe sharply. 'Surely you said you knew I wasn't gay?'

Remembering his earlier conversation with Alasdair Mackenzie, Bessell said – quite falsely – that he had also told Wainwright about Thorpe's doomed love-affair with a married woman.

Thorpe started to relax. 'Couldn't be better. Who did you invent to play the part of the woman who broke my heart?'

Bessell admitted that he had chosen his own wife, Pauline.

Thorpe roared with laughter.

'Superb, Besselli, you're a genius.'

But Bessell hadn't finished yet. This time, he didn't want Thorpe to go away without realizing just how much he owed him. He pointed out that if he had not lied to Richard Wainwright, Thorpe would almost certainly have lost the election. As he had hoped, this brought Thorpe swiftly down to earth. However unlikely a lay preacher Bessell may have been, he'd had plenty of experience delivering sermons. Assuming his sternest manner, he told Thorpe it was imperative that he must not be so reckless in future.

'If you do anything that puts the party at risk, you'll have betrayed everything we've fought for. If anything in the past ever became public, you'd have to resign immediately.'

Seeing how serious Bessell was, Thorpe nodded solemnly. 'I give you my word,' he said.

There could be no more casual pick-ups, Bessell told him. No more flirting with danger, no more imprudent letters. However hard he might find it, he must learn to control his sexual desires. Thorpe did not speak for some time after Bessell had finished.

'All right,' he said eventually.

But Bessell wanted his word on this too. Several more seconds went by with the two men staring stonily at one another. Then Thorpe pushed his chair back and stood up. Walking over to where Bessell was sitting, he looked down at him.

'Peter,' he said, 'I give you my word that if anything should become public, I will blow my brains out.'

11

Unexpected Developments

At first Bessell assumed the letter was from one of his constituents. After he had read a few lines, he turned it over and looked at the signature. As he did, his spirits plummeted. The letter was signed Norman Josiffe. In it Josiffe explained that he had recently returned to England – not on the back of his newfound success as a male model, but in the depths of another, particularly severe, depression.

'I have no money left,' he wrote. 'I cannot model because my nerves are so shot to shreds that I soak everything I put on. I can't showjump because I have no riding kit, it's all sold. I have no real qualifications, I am still on a vast amount of drugs which means I'm not too strong . . . I cannot come up to London for I have no money. So I beg you Mr Bessell to help somehow.'

In retrospect, Bessell might have seen this coming. Three months earlier, in April 1967, he had received a letter from Josiffe. But any disquiet he felt on opening it quickly evaporated. Writing from Dublin, Josiffe said that he was planning to go to America to make a fresh start. The only problem was that he had burned his passport. Could Bessell help him to obtain a new one? To mark this new beginning, he had also decided to change his name – to Norman Scott. He wondered if Bessell might also help in making this official.

Far from being downcast, Bessell had been delighted. Judging by the tone of his letter, Josiffe/Scott was both happy and relatively optimistic about his prospects. The next afternoon Bessell told Thorpe about it. After he had read the letter, Thorpe tipped his chair back and took a deep breath.

'Marvellous!' he said.

If Scott was going to America, the risk of his making any more trouble was smaller than ever. Bessell promised Thorpe that he would help him to obtain a new passport and to change his name. And that, they had assured one another confidently, would finally be that.

'Christ,' said Thorpe. 'What a relief.'

But Scott hadn't gone to America. Instead, he had come back to England, travelling on a visitor's passport. He was now staying at his stepbrother's home in Kent and seeing a doctor called Brian O'Connell at the psychiatric unit of St George's Hospital in Knightsbridge. Once again Bessell was faced with being the bearer of ominous tidings. This time Thorpe, fired up by his election victory, decided the time had come to take action. He arranged an appointment with his solicitor for the following afternoon and asked Bessell to come with him.

Arnold Goodman – Baron Goodman of Westminster – was the most famous, and feared, lawyer in Britain. As well as having a raft of wealthy and well-known clients, Goodman was the official solicitor to the Labour Party and a close confidant of the Prime Minister, Harold Wilson. With his mop of curly black hair, colossal girth and array of chins cascading down his shirtfront like swagged curtains, he cut an unforgettable figure.

Bessell, who knew Goodman only by reputation, was prepared to be impressed. In the event, he found him 'a trifle oily' and was disappointed by how small his office was. First of all Thorpe explained – in general terms – the nature of the problem. He then showed him the seventeen-page letter which Norman Scott had written to his mother. Goodman read it and took a copy for his files. Afterwards they discussed how to proceed. Thorpe told Goodman that he was keen on the idea of writing Scott a letter threatening him with something, although he wasn't quite sure what.

Goodman advised against this, saying it was best not to put anything on paper. He did, however, suggest that Bessell should see Scott and persuade him to go to America at the earliest possible opportunity. Bessell duly wrote to Scott in Kent asking him to come to see him and enclosing the rail fare. When Scott turned up at his office two days later, Bessell was shocked by his appearance. 'Taut, sweating and nervous, he sat on the edge of the chair and stammered badly.' For his part Scott was 'full of trepidation' and far more intimidated by Bessell's suave self-assurance than he had been in Dublin. 'He was courteous, but not at all friendly,' Scott recalled. 'I got the strong impression he thought I was a complete and utter nuisance.'

All Scott wanted, he repeated once again, was a new National Insurance card. Then, when his health improved, he might at least have a chance of finding a decent job. For the first time Bessell grasped just how tricky this was going to be. Shortly after Scott had been issued with a replacement card, in April 1962, Thorpe had lost it.

That wasn't so serious – people lost their National Insurance cards all the time and simply asked for new ones. The trouble was that Scott was in no position to make the backlog of payments his 'employer' – Thorpe – owed. But if Thorpe offered to pay the money, that would be tantamount to admitting he was legally responsible for Scott. There was even the possibility he might be prosecuted for failing to stamp his card.

But there was even more to it than that. Bessell had begun to realize how much the National Insurance card meant to Scott in other ways. In his eyes, it had turned into a kind of identity card, an official confirmation of who he was. Without it, he felt more adrift than ever.

Once again, Bessell promised to try to help. In the meantime Scott was penniless. To tide him over until his circumstances improved, Bessell suggested paying him a weekly retainer. However desperate Scott was, he didn't much like the sound of this – he had unhappy memories of being a kept man. Nor did he like any implication that he was a sponger. But in the end he agreed to accept £5 a week – the same sum he would have received in unemployment benefit if he'd had a fully stamped National Insurance card. Bessell gave him two weeks' money – £10 – on the spot and promised to send a weekly cheque thereafter. He also promised that he would try to find Scott a job in one of a chain of hamburger restaurants he intended to open in the States – yet another business venture he was certain would make his fortune.

Scott went back down to Kent far from convinced that his promised retainer would ever materialize. But exactly a fortnight later a cheque for £5 arrived. Along with it was a note – a note which Bessell, without thinking, had written on House of Commons notepaper.

When Bessell went to New York to see for himself how fast-food restaurants operated, he realized straight away that Scott would never be able to cope with the pressures of a professional kitchen. There was also a strong likelihood that he wouldn't even be allowed into the country. Under US Immigration Law, Scott was likely to be classified as 'undesirable' if the authorities ever learned about his homosexuality. On his way home Bessell stopped off in Nassau in the Bahamas and asked the Governor if there was any chance of Scott finding work there. The Governor was not optimistic. Bessell even went to see the owner of riding stables to ask about employment opportunities. That too proved fruitless.

By now Bessell's attitude towards Thorpe had gone through a subtle change. Although he liked him as much as ever, his admiration had slipped a little. In the six months since Thorpe had become Leader, there had been no great leap forward. There had also been a distinct shortage of eye-catching new policies. Instead, things were much the same as they had been before, with voters still confused, baffled even, about what the Liberals stood for. On several occasions Bessell had implored Thorpe to issue more clear-cut policy statements, but each time the response had been the same. To begin with, he would respond with characteristic enthusiasm, but then he would lose interest, his attention snagged by something else.

Bessell had begun to suspect that Thorpe, for all his nonconformist talk, was a much more conservative figure than he liked to pretend. His suspicions were confirmed when Thorpe turned up for his first Armistice Day Parade as Liberal Party Leader wearing a silk top hat and Edwardian morning dress – in contrast to the other two party Leaders, Harold Wilson and Edward Heath, who wore suits. Bessell had noticed too that Thorpe showed little taste for dirtying his hands with the less glamorous aspects of political life.

For all his philandering, this was not an accusation that could ever have been levelled at Bessell. Partly as a reaction to Thorpe's inactivity, he became deeply involved in one of his more unexpected passions: transport reform. Bessell played a key role in the 1968 Transport Act, an enormously ambitious plan to coordinate road, rail and waterway services. The passage of the bill soon attained Wagnerian proportions. In its committee stage, it broke every record in parliamentary history, the record of its debates taking up more than 4,000 pages in Hansard. For the first time in a standing committee, over a million words were spoken, of which 200,000 were credited to Bessell.

Yet still he found time to lead a hectic love-life, cook up yet more money-making schemes and send Scott's weekly retainers to his stepbrother's house in Kent. Every three months Bessell would give Thorpe a note saying how much he had sent Scott. Thorpe would then cash a cheque at the Members' Post Office at the House of Commons and, invariably with some reluctance, hand over the cash to Bessell. There was never any mention of Scott on these occasions – Bessell assumed that Thorpe was pursuing his usual strategy of ignoring a problem in the hope that it would go away.

As it turned out, Thorpe had other things on his mind. One evening he asked Bessell to come to the Liberal Leader's office in the Commons. This was a small, rather austere room with a large lead-paned window overlooking the Speaker's Court, oak-panelled walls and an unusually high ceiling. The only furniture was a desk facing the window, an easy chair and a green leather sofa. Since becoming Leader, Thorpe had tried to brighten it up by hanging new curtains and pictures on the walls – including several framed cartoons of himself – and putting in a drinks cabinet. There had been other changes too. Thorpe had become more concerned about his public image than ever, so much so that he'd had a tiny wart on the side of his nose removed because it apparently showed up on television.

Now he sat behind his desk while Bessell lay on the green sofa with his feet up. 'Pedro,' Thorpe announced without any preamble, 'I've decided to get married.'

At first Bessell assumed he was joking. 'Really?' he said. 'Who do you have in mind, the Queen Mother?'

Thorpe's laugh had a peculiarly hollow ring to it, Bessell noticed. As he looked at him more closely, he saw that Thorpe was serious. Bessell pointed out there was a problem here – after all, hadn't he once told him he was 80 per cent gay? Thorpe admitted there were difficulties, but said that it wasn't a matter of personal preference; he had his reputation to consider. If he remained a bachelor, that was bound to become a talking point. It could easily cost the Liberals votes at the next election.

'But what about the sex?' Bessell wanted to know.

'If I close my eyes and grit my teeth, I'll manage it somehow,' Thorpe replied. 'Then after a few months I can say I've become old and impotent.'

Drawing on his considerable stock of experience, Bessell said he thought that any woman of reasonable intelligence might suspect that something was amiss.

'It's true I need a girl who's led a rather sheltered life,' agreed Thorpe. 'But I've someone in mind.'

Bessell didn't like the sound of this. As he often did when his sense of outrage was stirred, he clambered on to his high horse. It was a ludicrous idea, he told Thorpe. Not only was it ludicrous, it would also be an unforgivable deception. With that, he stood up and walked towards the door.

Curtly, Thorpe told him to come back.

Bessell hesitated, and then retraced his steps. Often, he'd noticed, Thorpe's mouth seemed to creep up at the edges, as if he were trying, none too successfully, to keep his amusement in check. But when he was displeased, he would put on what Bessell called 'His Mandarin Mask', making his face eerily expressionless. The Mandarin Mask was in place, Bessell saw. This time when he sat down, he kept his feet on the floor. As he sat there, something else occurred to him, something he hadn't really thought about before. The fact that Thorpe was now party Leader had had a fundamental effect on their friendship. Once it had been a marriage of equals – or so Bessell had believed. Now, there was no doubting who was in charge.

Abruptly, Thorpe started laughing.

A moment or two later, Bessell joined in.

'Tell me, Besselli, what's it like making love to a woman?' Thorpe asked.

When Bessell tried to explain that it was one of the things that made life worthwhile, Thorpe just looked puzzled. But he was not wholly inexperienced with girls. At Oxford Thorpe had gone out briefly with a fellow student, Marigold Johnson. They had even kissed, although, as she recalled later, 'It was the most chaste kiss I've ever had in my life.'

Once, Thorpe told Bessell, he had tried sleeping with a girl, but he'd been put off by the way she smelled. Bessell advised that the feminine aroma was an acquired taste like – he groped for an analogy – whisky. Thorpe was not convinced. None the less, he repeated that he intended to take a woman to bed to see what happened. A week went by. Then Thorpe and Bessell were both invited to the same official lunch. Afterwards they shared a taxi back to the Commons. Leaning over, Thorpe closed the glass partition so that the driver couldn't hear.

He had another important question to ask.

'Pedro, how the hell do you fuck girls?'

Bessell found himself in the rare position of being lost for words. He was still trying to think of a suitable response when Thorpe launched into a description of what had happened when he had taken his female companion on a date. After having dinner in a restaurant, they had gone back to his flat. There he had proceeded to undress her. That part had gone smoothly enough, but then disaster had struck. 'When I saw her on the bed, legs open, all I wanted to do was roar and roar with laughter.'

This did not bode well, Bessell felt – certainly not for any prospect of marriage. Arriving back at the Commons, they went to Thorpe's office. Again Bessell lay on the sofa while Thorpe sat behind his desk.

'What is it that sets your blood coursing, Besselli?' Thorpe asked.

With his thoughts still scrambled, Bessell began to blather about the sensual power of great music. How in Beethoven's Pastoral Symphony, for instance, the composer had conveyed the impression of water tumbling over rocks by the use of muted violins. It seems safe to say that this was what Thorpe neither wanted, nor expected, to hear.

'Oh, God, why is it all so complicated?' he moaned.

Bessell went away with the impression that Thorpe had given up on the idea of heterosexual sex. However, he had underestimated his Leader's persistence. Another week went by, then Thorpe summoned him again. His second attempt had proved more successful than his first, he told him – even though he'd had a bad stomach. 'I was in and out of the bathroom all night. But in between I managed to screw her. So, you see, I can do it!'

Bessell did what he thought was appropriate under the circumstances: he offered his congratulations.

Thorpe, though, was in no mood for triumphalism.

'It's a bloody bore,' he said. 'But if it's the price I've got to pay to lead this old party, I'll pay it.'

In August 1967, Thorpe and his friend David Holmes went on holiday to Greece. Their trip did not get off to a promising start. At Heathrow the passport officer looked at Thorpe's passport and asked him who had inserted the words 'Rt Hon' in ink in front of his name. Thorpe claimed that his secretary had done so without consulting him – she later denied it. The passport officer was not impressed, telling Thorpe that only the Passport Office could make amendments like this.

'Yes,' said Thorpe airily. 'But they are not always competent.'

In Greece, they met up with two young women. One, Charlotte Prest, was a childhood friend of Thorpe. The other was Caroline Allpass. Educated at Roedean, then at a finishing school in Gstaad, Caroline Allpass was the daughter of a wealthy businessman who owned a chain of furniture stores. Tall – several inches taller than Thorpe – with a wide, expressively mobile mouth, Caroline was now twenty-nine and working as a PA to the head of the Impressionist Paintings Department at Sotheby's.

Although she and Thorpe had met before, their relationship hadn't progressed beyond polite chit-chat. But, as they swam and sunbathed on the beaches of Kos and Rhodes, the two of them got on increasingly well. In his account of what happened next, Thorpe claimed that he and Holmes had both wanted to marry Caroline and, like true gentlemen, agreed that whoever was unsuccessful would be the other's best man.

This seems fanciful to put it mildly – given that Holmes never pretended to be anything other than homosexual. But then Thorpe's account of his and Caroline's courtship had a number of significant holes in it. Not surprisingly, he made no reference to another incident that happened on holiday, when he and Holmes picked up a male prostitute. The three of them had gone to the beach, where Thorpe and Holmes both had sex with him.

By the time they came back to England, Thorpe had contracted gonorrhoea. As usual, he turned to Bessell to sort it out. Bessell sent him off to a doctor in Hampstead who gave him some antibiotics and told him to lay off sex until his symptoms had disappeared. Soon afterwards he returned, Thorpe asked his press officer, Mike Steele, how the Liberal poll ratings might be affected if he were to marry. Taken aback, Steele said that he thought they might rise by 2 per cent.

Thorpe did not try to hide his disappointment. 'Come on,' he said. 'Surely not less than 5 per cent?'

Bessell's chain of hamburger restaurants had still failed to take off, and that autumn he went back to New York to try to raise yet more money. While he was there, Thorpe arrived for a meeting with President Kaunda of Zambia. Beforehand, he and Bessell had a drink at Thorpe's hotel – the Waldorf Astoria. Thorpe said that he expected his meeting with Kaunda to finish early and wanted to know where he might find some company for the night. It was clear to Bessell that his earlier lecture about the importance of being discreet had had no effect. For a moment he thought of delivering another warning, then he decided it was pointless. Instead, he steered Thorpe, none too enthusiastically, towards Greenwich Village.

'What do I do when I get there?' Thorpe asked.

'Just walk around,' Bessell told him. 'I don't think it will be difficult for you to spot the right place.'

The next morning, when Bessell phoned up Thorpe's hotel, there was no reply from his room. He began to grow concerned. Asking to be put through to the Assistant Manager, Bessell learned that Thorpe had already checked out and gone to the airport. Back in London, Thorpe told him what had happened. The trip to Greenwich Village had been a waste of time, he said. 'But it turned out all right. I found someone on Times Square and took him back to the hotel.' What seemed to please Thorpe more than anything else was how cheap it had been. 'The whole thing only cost twenty-five dollars!'

It was not long afterwards that Thorpe told him about his plans to marry Caroline Allpass. He had taken her on a date to the revolving restaurant at the top of the Post Office Tower, he said, where he had made his intentions clear – albeit in starkly unromantic terms. 'I said I was too old to talk about falling in love. I think she liked me for being honest about it.'

Typically, Bessell was more concerned with more practical considerations. 'Have you slept with her?' he asked.

'Certainly not,' Thorpe replied.

He should do so without delay, Bessell advised. Then, if that went without mishap, he should live with her for six months before even considering marriage.

Thorpe brushed this aside. 'It wouldn't be possible for me to live with a woman unless I was married to her,' he said loftily.

Bessell was no stranger to humbug – far from it – but once again he found himself lost for words.

Early one January morning in 1968, a brand-new blue Ford Corsair travelling at high speed drove straight into a roundabout near Altrincham in Greater Manchester. Thrown clear, the driver escaped with a few cuts and bruises. If he had been wearing a seatbelt, he would have been killed instantly, the police told him. The car was crumpled to half its original size, the steering wheel pushed into the driver's seat with such force that it punctured the upholstery.

Although it would be more than ten years before breathalysers were widely introduced, people suspected of drink-driving were routinely given blood and urine tests. But in this case the police decided that no tests were necessary – despite the fact there was ample evidence to suggest the driver had been drinking heavily. Instead, they let him off with a caution, and a very mild caution at that. The driver was already familiar to them. His exploits – usually involving gambling and always drink – had earned him a reputation for wild, even self-destructive behaviour. His name was George Carman, and he was a 38-year-old barrister specializing in criminal law at a leading Manchester chambers.

Born in Blackpool to devoutly Roman Catholic parents, Carman had gone on to study law at Balliol College, Oxford. There he had soon been singled out as unusually bright and invited to speak at the Oxford Union by its then-President, Jeremy Thorpe. The two were never close friends, but they got on well enough; indeed, Carman is believed to have helped Thorpe write some of his essays.

In 1952 Carman left Oxford with its top degree – an unvivaed first, one of only two to be awarded to law graduates that year. Thorpe, by contrast, scraped a third. After qualifying as a barrister, Carman went to work in Manchester. However, there was a general feeling in his chambers that he wouldn't be staying around for much longer. Just where he would end up, or what sort of state he'd be in when he got there, was another matter. A few months after writing off his car, Carman lost so much playing blackjack that he had to sell his house. But, while his private life may have been a shambles, nobody who had seen him in action doubted his skill as a barrister. Nor did Carman make any secret of his ambition. Above all, he dreamed of making his mark in London – ideally in as high-profile, as sensational, a case as possible.

12

A Happy and Joyous Occasion

On Thursday, 30 May 1968, Jeremy Thorpe married Caroline Allpass in the private chapel at Lambeth Palace. The service was conducted by Wilfrid Westall, the Bishop of Crediton, and the blessing pronounced by Thorpe's old friend Michael Ramsey, the Archbishop of Canterbury. As the chapel was small, there were few guests present apart from family members. These included his constituency agent, Lilian Prowse, and David Holmes, who was the best man.

While the wedding may have been a fairly simple affair, the reception was anything but simple. More than 800 guests were invited to a lavish party at the Royal Academy in Piccadilly. A number of people in the Liberal Party complained that this show of opulence was sending out entirely wrong messages. Thorpe, they said, was behaving more like an old-fashioned Tory grandee than the Leader of the most socially progressive party in the country. They even began to talk about trying to oust him. If Thorpe was aware of this, it didn't trouble him. He was far more preoccupied with poring over the arrangements. For weeks beforehand he regaled visitors to his office in the Commons with lists of the various dignitaries who were coming.

On the day itself he and his new bride stood at the top of the staircase greeting guests – among whom were the Prime Minister, Harold Wilson, as well as the Leader of the Opposition, Ted Heath, who, unusually for him, had forgiven Thorpe for his Christmas pudding jibe. However, there was one notable absentee. Peter Bessell had decided not to go, much to his wife Pauline's annoyance. He had a good excuse – he was still in New York trying, more frantically than ever, to persuade investors to part with their money. None the less, as he later admitted, he could easily have come back if he'd wanted to. Yet something – he wasn't quite sure what – made him stay away. He could only define it as a sense of apprehension, almost of foreboding. A feeling that somewhere a fuse was smouldering away.

Even though Bessell had stayed away from the wedding, he soon found himself being sucked back into Thorpe's orbit. Not long after he returned from New York, he went round to Thorpe's flat in Marsham Court to drive him to a reception. What struck Bessell first of all was how different the place looked. In the past it had had a rather spartan air, relieved only by Thorpe's collection of chinoiserie and his Max Beerbohm cartoons. Now, thanks to Caroline, it felt much warmer and more homely.

Then he was struck by something else, something he would never have believed possible. The two of them gave every impression of being very happy together. As Thorpe told him later, he liked being married. He liked Caroline's company, he liked being in a relationship that he didn't have to lie about and – the biggest surprise of all – he even found his new wife physically attractive.

Beforehand Bessell had assumed that Caroline must be hopelessly naive, but he soon revised his opinion. However shy she may have been, she was also lively and charming. This was an opinion shared by many of Thorpe's friends, who had also suspected she was likely to be on the dim side. What's more, Bessell noted with approval, she wasn't in the least deferential to her new husband. As they were leaving, Caroline asked what time Thorpe would be back. He said he didn't know as he had no idea how long the reception would last. Smiling affectionately at him, she said, 'I don't trust you an inch.'

Did Caroline know about Thorpe's past? Bessell thought not. When he asked Thorpe about it, he insisted she didn't suspect anything. Once, he said, he had tentatively brought up the general subject of homosexuality, but Caroline 'had made it clear that she did not want to discuss it'.

Yet there are suggestions that she did know and wasn't in the least concerned. After all, she was also close to David Holmes, who never tried to hide his homosexuality. But the feeling among those who knew her well is that, for all her outward gloss, Caroline was still something of an innocent, especially when it came to sex. Far from being blasé about homosexuality, it seems more likely that she never imagined her husband was anything other than staunchly heterosexual. What she definitely didn't know was that Thorpe carried on having gay flings after their marriage – although he was more discreet than he had been before.

At first Caroline found the life of a party Leader's wife understandably daunting, but she soon settled into it, becoming more assured and mounting a stout defence of her husband, whom critics had accused of spending too much time with his smart friends. 'It's a lot of nonsense, this talk of Jeremy being a socialite,' she told the *Daily Mail*. 'From the moment I met him I was impressed by the wide variety of friends in his life. He likes people and is interested in them.' She even defended his values. 'Jeremy is a true Liberal. He believes in Liberalism. He would never lead a party which was not truly Liberal. He would rather resign.'

The only sign that Caroline might not have been quite as happy as she appeared was that within a year of their marriage, she began having persistent nightmares – so much so that she became frightened of going to sleep. Thorpe talked to Bessell about it and said that she'd been to see a doctor but he had been unable to do anything – apparently sleeping pills made little difference. Bessell advised him to take her to a psychiatrist. Although this was hardly an outlandish suggestion, Thorpe reacted badly, brusquely telling Bessell that he was being absurd. The matter was never raised again.

By the time Bessell returned from New York, he had been forced to confront an unavoidable fact: his proposed chain of hamburger restaurants was never going to get off the ground. Yet another grand scheme had come to nought, leaving him in more desperate straits than ever. He decided that there was only one possible course of action if he was to avoid bankruptcy. He must leave politics and devote all his time to trying to keep his head above water.

In very low spirits, Bessell went to see the local executive of the Liberal Party in Bodmin and told them that he would not be standing at the next election. Understandably, they wanted to know why. Reluctant to tell them about his financial difficulties in case they became alarmed, he alluded vaguely to difficulties in his private life. With regret, as well as some puzzlement, they accepted his decision. All Bessell could do was hope that he'd be able to last out until the next General Election. That, though, was still two years away.

He also told Thorpe about his decision to stand down. As he had done before, Thorpe tried to talk him out of it, but this time his efforts struck Bessell as being oddly half-hearted. At first he wondered if Thorpe was distracted by the prospect of fatherhood – Caroline had just become pregnant. Then another, more ominous explanation occurred to him – could his old friend be losing faith in him? This thought made him even more depressed.

He reacted by trying to make himself as useful to Thorpe as possible. In the summer of 1968 he gave him a written record of the retainer payments he had sent to Norman Scott. He also agreed to look after some papers that Thorpe gave him – papers that Thorpe didn't want falling into the wrong hands. Bessell put them into an old briefcase, along with some bank statements of his, and hid the briefcase in a safe place in his office. By then, Bessell and Scott had had a further meeting – at which Bessell gave him £75 to try to relaunch his modelling career. As he hadn't heard anything since then, he believed that everything was under control. Bessell therefore reassured Thorpe that there was little likelihood of Scott's talking about their relationship.

'Do you think anyone would believe him?' Thorpe asked.

Bessell said he thought it was unlikely, especially now that Thorpe was a married man.

'I mean, it's not as if he's got any proof, has he?' said Thorpe. 'No letters or anything?'

'No, no,' said Bessell.

And then he paused. 'Not exactly . . .'

'What do you mean?'

To his dismay, Bessell saw Thorpe had put on his Mandarin Mask again. Now he came to think of it, he said, he did have a faint recollection that Scott had mentioned something about having a few letters from 'JT' – this was when the two of them were in a taxi on their way to Dublin Airport.

Thorpe practically levitated. '*What?*'

Bessell told Thorpe to stay calm while he tried to remember just what Scott had said. Slowly his memories cohered. He remembered telling Scott that he didn't think Father Sweetman believed he had ever had a relationship with Thorpe. Scott had replied that Sweetman might not have believed him at first, but he certainly did after Scott had showed him some of Thorpe's love-letters.

Thorpe was furious. How could he have forgotten something as important as that?

Bessell had no answer for this, beyond that his memory was full of convenient holes. Trying to sound more in control than he felt, he said, 'All right. We've got to get hold of them.'

But how, Thorpe wanted to know.

Bessell was stumped – he could hardly just come out and ask Scott to give him the letters. Thorpe, meanwhile, had started striding about, muttering to himself. Several times he started sentences and then broke off, saying, 'No, that won't do.' Abruptly, he stopped and pointed his finger at Bessell. 'David!' he said. 'That's the answer. David's got to get them.'

Bessell agreed this might work. Whoever made an approach to Scott, it couldn't be anyone he had met before. David Holmes fitted the bill here. Then Bessell had an idea of his own. What if Holmes posed as a reporter, saying that he'd heard rumours about Scott's relationship with Thorpe and offering to buy his story? If Scott was willing, Holmes could ask if he had any proof – whereupon Scott was sure to produce the letters.

'Superb!' said Thorpe.

But then Bessell realized his plan had a fatal flaw. If Holmes claimed to represent a Fleet Street paper, it would be easy for Scott to phone up and check him out. What if Holmes said he was from *Der Spiegel*, Thorpe suggested. Scott would never go to the trouble of contacting a German magazine. Briefly it occurred to Bessell that this would involve Holmes trying to pass himself off as German – something that might well tax his powers of dissimulation. At the same time another, bigger question was troubling him. Why would Holmes be willing to become involved at all?

'Oh, he'll do anything we ask,' said Thorpe. 'He loves being around us. Tells all his friends in Manchester he's going to London to see the Liberal Leader!'

While Holmes certainly enjoyed mixing with glamorous and powerful people, there was more to it than that. From the moment they first met at Oxford, he had adored Thorpe. But Bessell's assumption that Holmes and Thorpe were lovers may have been wide of the mark. Although they clearly shared sexual partners, it's not clear if they ever had an affair. As for Thorpe's attitude towards Holmes, that was rather less dewy-eyed. However much Thorpe enjoyed Holmes's company, he found him useful to have around – he was yet another person who could be relied upon to clear up the mess Thorpe left behind.

A week later Holmes came down to London and called Thorpe, suggesting they meet. The three of them had lunch together in the Strangers' Dining Room at the Commons. Over lunch Thorpe explained that he had a problem that Holmes might be able to help him with. As Thorpe had predicted, he was keen to be of assistance. However, Holmes's enthusiasm rapidly waned when he heard what he was expected to do. He pointed out that Scott was unlikely to believe him if he simply turned up in Kent claiming to be a journalist who wanted to buy his story.

Thorpe explained patiently that he would need to be subtler than that. The first step was for Holmes to see Scott so he'd be able to recognize him later. That shouldn't be a problem, said Bessell. He could arrange for Scott to come to his office at a certain time.

All Holmes would have to do was hang about inconspicuously on the other side of the road, staring up at Bessell's office window on the second floor. When Scott was leaving, Bessell would signal to him.

'What should I do then?' Holmes wanted to know.

He should approach Scott and ask him if he had a light, Thorpe suggested. Then he had a better idea. 'Got it! Let him know you're gay and ask him to have a drink.'

Holmes, who had had a good deal of experience of picking up men on the street, said he thought he could manage this easily enough.

'You may have to screw him to get the letters,' warned Thorpe.

Foreseeing yet more complications, Bessell hurriedly said he thought this would be a very bad idea. To his surprise, Thorpe agreed. Perhaps it would be safer to keep everything on a strict financial footing. How much did he think Scott would want for the letters? Bessell reckoned that £200 should be enough – but he'd forgotten about Thorpe's tight-fistedness.

'Far too much,' Thorpe complained. 'I thought about twenty-five pounds.'

Amid further grumbling on Thorpe's part, they compromised on £100. That afternoon, Bessell's secretary wrote to Scott asking him to come to London the following week. The night before Scott was due to come, Bessell and Thorpe met briefly outside Thorpe's office in the Commons. Thorpe said that he'd had dinner with Holmes earlier that evening and they had gone over the details of what was going to happen.

'I told David that he's got to get those letters,' said Thorpe. 'It doesn't matter how he does it, but he's got to get them.'

At first Bessell assumed that Thorpe meant that Holmes might have to have sex with Scott. Once again, he started to say that he thought this would be a terrible mistake, but Thorpe shook his head impatiently. Speaking with great deliberation, he said, 'I told David to stop at nothing.'

Thorpe went into his office, leaving Bessell outside wondering what he could have meant. Surely he wasn't suggesting that

Holmes should use force to get hold of the letters? Then, just for a moment, an even more outlandish thought flashed through Bessell's mind. Immediately he dismissed it, telling himself – not without cause – that he was under a lot of strain and therefore prone to all kinds of disturbing ideas.

The next morning Bessell was waiting in his office as arranged. A quarter of an hour before Scott was due to arrive, he looked out of the window and saw David Holmes standing on the other side of the street. Far from looking inconspicuous, he was standing bolt upright and staring straight ahead as if he were a sentry at Buckingham Palace. This was not a good omen, Bessell thought.

As usual, Scott was bang on time. But it wasn't his punctuality that made the most impression on Bessell; it was his appearance. Since they had last met, Scott had undergone a dramatic transformation. He was now smartly dressed in a fashionable and clearly expensive suit. In one hand he even carried a briefcase. But it wasn't just that. His manner had changed too.

No longer stuttering or quivering with anxiety, he was relaxed and assured. His modelling career had undergone a sudden transformation, he said. He was getting plenty of work and earning good money. From his briefcase, Scott took a number of black-and-white photos showing him in a variety of outfits and poses. He also showed Bessell his portfolio listing his vital statistics: 'Height 5'11". Chest 38". Waist 30" . . .'

Bessell was very impressed, especially when Scott told him that he no longer needed his weekly retainer. But best of all was that he no longer seemed bitter about Thorpe. 'I can never forget Jeremy,' Scott told him. 'But I'm happy now and I don't want to think about him.'

Seizing the moment, Bessell reminded him of their conversation in the back of the taxi in Dublin. How Scott had told him that he had some letters from Thorpe which he had shown to Father Sweetman. If those letters fell into the wrong hands, that could have extremely awkward consequences. Wouldn't it be a good idea – Bessell dropped the suggestion as lightly as a handkerchief – if Scott let him look after them?

To begin with Scott seemed confused. Then his face cleared. He did remember their conversation, he said, and it was true that he had once had a couple of letters from Jeremy. However, he had destroyed them at the same time as he had burned his passport. Greatly relieved, Bessell told Scott that he was delighted that his new career was going well and asked him to keep him informed on its progress. With that, they shook hands and Scott left.

As soon as he had gone, Bessell rushed over to the window and began waving his arms about – much to the surprise of his secretary, Sheila Skelton. Holmes, who was still standing to attention on the pavement opposite, gave a jolt as if he'd been touched by a cattle prod and began to cross Pall Mall. Suddenly Bessell had a thought: there was no longer any point in Holmes trying to engage Scott in conversation; it would only excite Scott's suspicions if he did. He therefore changed his wave into a beckoning gesture.

Stopping in the middle of the road, Holmes gazed at him in confusion. Finally he got the message and went up to Bessell's office. There Bessell explained what had happened.

'Did you believe Scott when he said he had destroyed the letters?' Holmes asked.

Bessell thought about it. In the past, he had found Scott emotionally overwrought, even delusional, yet he'd had no reason to suppose he was a liar.

'Yes,' he said. 'Yes, I did.'

Holmes too was relieved – though not, it turned out, for quite the same reasons. 'I must say when I saw Scott I didn't think much of Jeremy's taste.'

After Holmes had gone off, Bessell felt an enormous sense of relief. Another awkward hurdle had been successfully negotiated. This time he allowed himself to hope that it really might be the last.

13

Shooting a Sick Dog

Bessell deliberately hadn't inquired too closely into Scott's new circumstances, thinking he was probably better off not knowing. As he might have guessed, they were complicated. After years of shuttling in and out of mental hospitals, Scott had thrown himself into life in Swinging London with hectic abandon. One of the perks of being a successful male model, he discovered, was that he was constantly being invited to parties and meeting new people.

Through some friends in Ireland, he was introduced to four girls who lived in a large flat in Earls Court Square. Among them was a trainee art restorer at the Tate Gallery called Sue Myers. She and Scott quickly became close – or, in her case, besotted. A few weeks after they met, he moved into the flat – and into her bedroom. But they didn't have sex. Scott didn't feel she was the sort of person to have a casual fling with. 'I respected her too much for that. She was so lovely; we had this immediate rapport.' Myers's own romantic history had also been troubled – there had been a number of unsatisfactory relationships with much older men.

One night another of the girls, Catherine Oliver, asked Scott if he would like to come to see Margot Fonteyn dance at Sadler's Wells. A friend of hers and Myers's would also be coming along, she said. The friend turned out to be a young man called Conway Wilson-Young, an extremely wealthy Old Etonian in his early twenties with a house in Belgravia. Scott and Wilson-Young took one look at each other – and found they too had an immediate rapport. After the performance, the three of them went backstage and met Margot Fonteyn in her dressing room – she was a friend of Wilson-Young's parents.

The next day Scott moved out of Earls Court and into Wilson-Young's house in Chester Square. In Scott's more level-headed moments, he could see that his new boyfriend was trouble: 'He was moody and intolerant and always used to getting his own way.' None the less, he was smitten, both with Wilson-Young himself and with his lifestyle. Discovering that Scott was keen on classical music, Wilson-Young took him off to Bayreuth to watch a Wagner opera, then to Salzburg for some Mozart. On the way he bought a brand-new chocolate-coloured Mercedes sports car. When Scott said how much he liked the car, Wilson-Young gave it to him – despite the fact that Scott had never learned to drive.

On their return, they went off to Wilson-Young's parents' house in Barham, Suffolk. The following morning Sue Myers turned up unexpectedly. Walking into Wilson-Young's bedroom, she found them in bed together and immediately burst into tears. A tense weekend ensued. Things didn't improve when they went back to London. Wilson-Young and Scott argued incessantly and in the end Scott decided to go to Ireland for a while – much to the annoyance of the modelling agency he was signed up with, Bonnie's in Kensington, which had booked him for a number of fashion shoots.

From Dublin, Scott wrote to Sue Myers asking her to come and stay. Dropping everything, she flew to his side, but still their relationship remained platonic. Fortified by his break, Scott returned to London at the end of November 1968 and went straight round to Earls Court Square. He had assumed that he'd be able to pick up his modelling career where he had left off, but he soon had a nasty shock. In his absence, work had dried up. However striking he may have looked in photographs, Scott had acquired a reputation for unreliability.

Once again he wrote a letter to Peter Bessell asking for help. By now Bessell had realized that Scott and Thorpe had more in common than they would have cared to acknowledge. Both liked to abdicate responsibility for their own behaviour, expecting someone else to pick up the pieces. The problem for Bessell was that he was stuck in the middle trying to keep both of them happy.

On 3 December, he wrote back a carefully phrased response, commiserating with this latest downturn in Scott's fortunes: 'I am sorry to hear of your unhappy experiences in Dublin. I am going to the States tomorrow and I hope that I might be able to find some means of helping you permanently. And in any case I shall be glad to see you on my return . . . I am enclosing an additional £5 to help you in your immediate difficulties and Miss Skelton will be sending £7 next week. Please do not be downhearted about the future. I am confident we shall be able to work something out for you. With my very best wishes for a Happy New Year.'

After Scott read this, he showed it to Sue Myers. As usual, she was sympathetic and keen to do whatever she could to stop him from sinking back into depression. That night they slept together for the first time.

Two days later Jeremy Thorpe asked Peter Bessell to join him in his private room in the House of Commons. As he had done before, Bessell lay on the green leather sofa, while Thorpe sat behind his desk. After a few minutes Thorpe asked if he had heard anything from Norman Scott.

Bessell said that he had. The news was not good – Scott's career as a model appeared to have hit the buffers again.

'Blast,' said Thorpe. 'I thought we'd heard the last of him.'

He went on to say that he couldn't see how he was ever going to be rid of Scott. Did Bessell have any idea what it was like living in a state of constant apprehension? Slumped in his chair, Thorpe made a despairing gesture towards the window. On several occasions recently, he admitted, he had imagined that the whole affair was going to destroy him.

Bessell had seen Thorpe depressed before, but never this low. He did what he could to buoy him up, saying that he was confident he could keep Scott under control and stop him from doing anything rash. But Thorpe just shook his head and kept staring out of the window. Bessell was still trying to think of some further reassurance he could offer when – to his relief – the Division Bell rang summoning MPs to the Chamber for a vote.

Thorpe said that they should continue their discussion afterwards. Tired as well as a little fed up with Thorpe's despondency, Bessell decided that he would make an excuse and slip away. On their way into the Chamber, they both went into the gents' lavatory. Again Thorpe's behaviour struck him as strange. First, he opened all the cubicle doors to make sure no one was inside. When he was satisfied they were alone, Thorpe joined Bessell at the urinals.

'What about getting him a job abroad?' he suggested.

Bessell, of course, had already tried this without success. In order to humour Thorpe, he said that he'd look into it again. As they walked into the Chamber, he noticed that Thorpe was still looking preoccupied. His head was down, his face set. Immediately after the vote, Thorpe took hold of Bessell's arm and propelled him back to his room, scuppering his chances of slipping away. Once again, he sat slumped behind his desk.

It was at this point, according to Bessell, that Thorpe said, 'Peter, we've got to get rid of him.' Bessell had a nasty feeling he knew what Thorpe was thinking of, but he decided to make light of it.

'What, are you thinking of killing him off?' he said.

Thorpe took a deep breath, pushed his chair back from his desk and stood up.

'Yes,' he said.

Walking over to the drinks cabinet, Thorpe poured himself a large whisky. He offered Bessell a drink, but Bessell said no.

Thorpe then drained the glass in a single gulp.

'Well?' he said.

Bessell was badly shaken. He'd always known that Thorpe was a fantasist. It was something Bessell believed was closely linked with his abilities as a mimic. Thorpe not only liked to play a lot of different parts, he also liked to live them – and in the process bury his own identity. Far from diminishing with age, this habit had become ever more engrained. The more successful Thorpe became, the more compulsively he would mimic people, taking on their mannerisms and cloaking himself in their characters. Even his public persona struck Bessell as being an exercise in mimicry. 'When addressing a TV audience or a large public meeting, his voice took on a different tonal quality, and those who knew him intimately recognized they were watching an exaggerated impersonation of himself.'

Only now Bessell had the strong suspicion that Thorpe wasn't fantasizing, or pretending to be someone he wasn't. To play for time, he too stood up and paced round the room.

'Jeremy, it's ridiculous,' he said.

'There is no other solution,' Thorpe told him.

What disturbed Bessell most of all was how controlled Thorpe sounded. Bessell started telling him that he was being absurd. Did he really understand what he was proposing?

'No sane person talks of murder – and certainly not two MPs in the House of Commons.'

Again Thorpe repeated that there was no other solution. The stakes had become too high. What if Scott was to sell his story? Clearly Thorpe would be ruined. Bessell decided to change tack. How did he intend to carry out his plan?

'He would have to be shot,' Thorpe said.

Seeing the look on Bessell's face, he said, 'Peter, it's no worse than shooting a sick dog.'

This was too much, even for Bessell. 'It's a bloody sight worse than killing a sick dog,' he told Thorpe. 'Scott may be a shit, but he's a human being.'

Thorpe said nothing; he just sat there glowering. Worried that he might have antagonized him, Bessell returned to the question of practicalities. How was he going to dispose of the body?

'In New York I believe they drop them in the river,' said Thorpe.

That might be trickier than it sounded, Bessell told him – American rivers being deeper and more tidal than British ones. Thorpe then said he'd read recently in a newspaper that someone had disposed of a body in America by covering it in fast-setting concrete during the construction of a new freeway.

Bessell pointed out that if he had read about it, that meant someone must have found the body.

'Oh . . .' said Thorpe, and fell silent.

All at once he had another idea. 'A tin-mine!' he exclaimed. Jumping up, he grasped Bessell's shoulders. 'That's the answer.' Scott could be thrown down a tin-mine. There were several abandoned tin-mines in Cornwall, all with deep shafts. No one would ever find a body there.

At this point Bessell announced that he was going home. Plainly irritated, Thorpe gruffly wished him good night. However, Bessell didn't go home, not directly. He walked out to New Palace Yard, where his car was parked. Then he drove through the gate and around Parliament Square. When he was halfway around the square, he changed his mind. Afterwards, trying to explain his behaviour, Bessell recalled glancing up and seeing the light on the top of Big Ben. In some odd way, the light seemed to be signalling to him, beckoning him back.

Driving into New Palace Yard again, he reparked his car and went to the Members' Tea Room. There he bought a cup of tea and sat down. Had Thorpe really been serious, Bessell asked himself. As he smoked a cigarette, he began to suspect that he might have been. It had been almost four years since their lunch at the Ritz. In that time Thorpe had become increasingly obsessed by Scott, and the damage he might do him. At first he had spoken of Scott with a few faint shreds of affection. But not any more. Now there was only fear. What's more, Bessell suspected that Scott knew just how vulnerable Thorpe was as party Leader, and that his re-emergence into their lives was more than just a coincidence.

Bessell finished his tea and returned to the Members' Lobby. By now he was no longer tired. Instead, his mind was racing with questions. If Thorpe was serious, how far would he – Bessell – go to help him? Was he really prepared to become an accessory to murder?

Looking up, Bessell saw a statue of David Lloyd George, the

greatest-ever Leader of the Liberal Party, standing at the entrance to the Chamber. It was a statue that Bessell had always been fond of – partly because, like Thorpe, he was a huge admirer of Lloyd George, and partly because it was splendidly dramatic, with Lloyd George standing there with his finger pointing and his lips open, as if words were spilling off his tongue. But now the pointing finger seemed to have something accusatory about it. Bessell wondered what the 'Old Man', as Lloyd George was known in the party, would have made of his conversation earlier.

Standing up, he walked back down the now-deserted corridors to Thorpe's room. He believed there was a strong possibility that Thorpe might already have left, and didn't bother knocking before he went in. But Thorpe was still sitting slumped in his chair with his chin on his chest. For a moment, Bessell thought he had fallen asleep. And then Thorpe slowly raised his head.

PART TWO

14

The Ultimate Solution

'The person to do it is David.'

Thorpe was speaking in a peculiarly flat monotone, Bessell noticed. Also his eyes seemed to have retreated into his head. Under the circumstances Bessell felt that he needed to be absolutely clear about what Thorpe was proposing. Was he seriously suggesting that David Holmes should murder Norman Scott?

'Well, I can't do it – it'd be too obvious. The same applies to you, so there's nobody but David.'

From what he had seen of David Holmes's behaviour when he was trying to make himself inconspicuous on Pall Mall, Bessell suspected he was just about the last person he could imagine committing the perfect murder.

'That's mad,' he said. 'David's too wet.'

Thorpe agreed that Holmes was a bit on the watery side, but repeated that he was the only possible candidate.

'There's no reason why David couldn't do it if he's properly briefed.'

Bessell wasn't convinced. 'He'd still manage to cock it up,' he said confidently.

But Thorpe refused to budge. He intended to call Holmes the next morning and ask him to come and see them both, he said. What was Bessell doing the following week? At this point he could easily have made an excuse – he was still spending a good deal of time in America – but he didn't. Instead, Bessell told Thorpe that he had no plans to go away. With that, they said good night for the second time. As he drove away, Bessell was no longer wondering if Thorpe was serious. As for the other question he had asked himself earlier that night – how far was he prepared to go to help him? – that was still going round and round inside his head.

Norman Scott spent Christmas 1968 as a guest of Sue Myers's parents at their large Queen Anne house in Spilsby, Lincolnshire. Arriving in a purple velvet suit, he did not make a favourable first impression. Subsequent impressions were no better. Myers's parents clearly regarded him as a wastrel and could barely bring themselves to acknowledge his presence. On Christmas morning, Scott came downstairs to find a present on the kitchen table. His first reaction was that this must be a goodwill gesture, an attempt to put their relationship on a friendlier footing. This feeling did not last long. Tearing off the wrapping paper, Scott found a mug inside. Printed on the side was a single word – 'Strychnine'.

Bessell thought there was a chance, if only a slim one, that the Christmas break might bring Thorpe to his senses. But Parliament had only just reconvened in January 1969 when Thorpe told him that David Holmes was coming to London and they should all meet up. By the time Bessell arrived in Thorpe's office, Holmes was already there. Once again he was bolt upright, Bessell saw. Thorpe told Bessell to lock the door, then waved him towards the chair. It turned out that he'd already started outlining his plan, and had plainly given it a good deal of thought. Holmes was going to re-create his role as the man from *Der Spiegel*. As before, he would strike up a conversation with Scott. Only this time he would say that his editor was on a trip to England and staying in Cornwall. Holmes would then offer to drive Scott down to Cornwall in order to meet the editor and do the deal.

As he spoke, Thorpe glanced at Holmes and Bessell. Neither of them said anything. Having reached Cornwall, Holmes was to take Scott to a pub, get him drunk, put him in the back of the car, drive him to Bodmin Moor and then kill him. The silence when Thorpe had finished was so intense that Bessell felt he had to do something to fill it.

'How?' he asked.

'It's quite easy to break someone's neck,' said Thorpe nonchalantly.

To prove his point he stood up, came round from behind his desk and put his arm around Bessell's neck. Taking hold of his elbow with his other hand, he jerked it sharply upwards. At this point Bessell wondered for the first time if Thorpe might have gone mad. He tried to emphasize that there were a number of flaws in this plan. What if Holmes only succeeded in half choking Scott? What was he going to do then?

Silence descended once more.

'I think you're right,' said Thorpe at last. 'In which case, David, you'll have to shoot him.'

After shooting Scott, Holmes should go through his pockets and remove anything that might identify him. All that remained was to drag Scott's body across the moor and tip it into a conveniently situated mine-shaft. Then Thorpe offered a word of warning. 'By the way, do you know that when someone meets a violent death, they always defecate? You'll have to remember that.'

Unpleasant though this prospect was, Bessell felt that under the circumstances it was a fairly minor consideration. He raised another objection. Dragging the body of quite a large man – he remembered Scott's vital statistics from his portfolio – across open moorland in pitch darkness was going to be a lot harder than Thorpe was making it sound. What's more, there would almost certainly be a trail of blood.

'All right,' said Thorpe abruptly, changing tack again. 'It'll have to be poison.'

Having driven Scott to the pub, Holmes should slip some poison into his drink. Now it was the turn of Holmes – who had not said anything so far – to point out another flaw. 'Wouldn't it look rather odd if he falls off his bar stool stone-dead?' Despite himself, Bessell began to laugh. Once he had started, he found it hard to stop. 'Don't worry, David,' he said between guffaws. 'You can apologize to the landlord and ask him to direct you to the nearest mine-shaft.'

Holmes too had started laughing – no doubt through nerves. Thorpe, however, did not laugh. He just stared at them both until they had composed themselves. 'It would have to be a slow-working poison,' he said. 'It's only a matter of research, David.' Thorpe then announced that he had to go off to a meeting and suggested that the two of them should carry on discussing the plan.

Sitting in the Strangers' Cafeteria, Bessell asked Holmes what he thought. Still clearly in a state of shock, Holmes could only shake his head and say 'Incredible!' in a hoarse voice. He went on to say that he didn't think Thorpe could really have meant it. Bessell tried to convince himself that Holmes must be right – after all, Holmes probably knew Thorpe better than anyone else. But just in case he suggested they should raise as many practical objections as possible in the hope that Thorpe might eventually lose interest. Holmes agreed this would be the best course of action. Before they parted, they exchanged phone numbers. That way, they said, they would be able to talk to one another behind Thorpe's back.

However dark Thorpe's private thoughts were, his public face remained as cheery as ever. Jeremy and Caroline Thorpe's son, Rupert, was born on 12 April 1969. When he was christened twelve weeks later in the crypt of the House of Commons by the Archbishop of Canterbury, Thorpe was on typically ebullient form, posing for press photographs with his young son in his arms. For the ceremony, the child was wrapped in a christening robe of Brussels lace which Thorpe's sister Lavinia, his mother and his grandmother had all worn when they were christened. As for Thorpe, he wore a morning suit which had belonged to his father, with a large carnation in his button hole. The godfathers were David Holmes and the Liberal MP Eric Lubbock. The wife of the Archbishop, Joan Ramsey, was godmother. Among the other guests were Peter and Pauline Bessell.

But nothing, not even fatherhood, could deflect Thorpe from his course. Over the next few weeks he referred on several occasions to the idea he had begun to call either 'the Scottish Matter' or 'the Ultimate Solution' – a phrase that struck Bessell as having distasteful echoes of Nazism. Thorpe told him that he had decided that it would be better if Holmes didn't try to poison Scott in the pub. Rather, he should offer him a drink from a lethally laced flask. As he and Holmes had agreed, Bessell immediately identified a problem. Wouldn't Scott think it odd if Holmes didn't also take a drink from the same flask?

Thorpe conceded that some further refinements might be necessary, although he remained convinced the plan itself would work. Why was Holmes taking so long to research slow-acting poisons? Surely it couldn't be that difficult? Bessell blustered and flannelled, but Thorpe was relentless. They needed to have a further discussion to finalize arrangements, he insisted.

The next time Thorpe saw Bessell, he told him that Holmes was coming down to London the following week. The three of them should meet up again in his office. Once again Bessell steeled himself for an awkward encounter. But then came news which astonished him. News that he was convinced would change everything. Two days before Holmes was due to arrive, Bessell's secretary told him that Scott had called up that morning. He had not asked to speak to Bessell; instead, he had just left a message. The message was very brief. It said simply that he had got married.

15

Doomed

On 13 May 1969, almost exactly a year after Jeremy Thorpe's wedding, Norman Scott married Sue Myers at Kensington Register Office. Scott's wedding was a much less glamorous affair. There were few guests. Sue's mother refused to attend, as did Sue's sister, Belinda, and her husband, the actor Terry-Thomas. As for Scott's mother, she wasn't invited. After the ceremony, the wedding breakfast was held in a restaurant called L'Artiste Affamé on the Old Brompton Road; not inappropriately, it was almost next door to London's most notorious gay pub, the Coleherne.

In keeping with tradition, the bride's father, Captain Myers, a bluff Australian, made a speech. But the speech Captain Myers gave wasn't in the least traditional. The marriage, he declared starkly, was doomed. When Sue said goodbye to her father after lunch, he hugged her and said, 'Oh, my darling, I wish you were coming home with me instead of that dreadful homosexual.'

Myers's dislike of Scott had been compounded by the fact that Sue was now two months pregnant. Quite possibly she would never have married otherwise. As soon as she learned she was pregnant, she decided to have an abortion – something she could now do legally as a result of the 1967 Abortion Act. However besotted Sue was with Scott, she knew enough about him to realize that he wasn't the steadfast type. Her mother was only too keen that she should have an abortion, even offering to pay for it herself. But Scott felt differently. While his religious faith may have waxed and wobbled over the years, he was still a devout enough Roman Catholic to believe that abortion was morally wrong. Not only did he want Sue to keep the baby, he wanted it to be born in wedlock. He therefore did the decent thing and proposed.

Awash with hormones and allowing herself to believe that Scott might change his ways, Sue accepted. Scott's first plan was that they should marry in the crypt at Westminster Cathedral, but Captain Myers wouldn't hear of it – he had enough religious faith of his own not to want his daughter's union sanctified by God. Although Sue's sister, Belinda, and Terry-Thomas didn't come to the wedding, they gave the newly-weds a generous present – the loan of their cottage in Milton Abbas in Dorset for a year. Rather than pay rent on Earls Court Square, the Scotts decided to move into the cottage and sublet the flat.

But their rural idyll proved short-lived. Within a couple of months the couple had run out of money. In no doubt how her parents felt about her marriage, Sue felt she could hardly ask them for a handout. To make matters worse, she learned that she wouldn't be able to claim maternity benefits without Scott's National Insurance card – despite having a properly stamped card of her own. As Peter Bessell had promised to look into the missing card, Scott wrote to him asking how he had got on. This was a letter Bessell dreaded receiving, since he'd done nothing about Scott's card – partly through inertia and partly because he didn't want to stir up further trouble. Now, worried how Scott might react if he continued doing nothing, he wrote to David Ennals, the Minister of State for Social Services, giving him a suitably abridged version of what had happened.

Ennals's reply was not encouraging. He could only suggest that Scott should apply for an emergency card at his local unemployment exchange. This was the last thing Bessell wanted. If Scott went along to his local unemployment office, there was every likelihood he would start talking about Thorpe.

And then came even worse news. On 27 August, Bessell's secretary told him that she had received a frantic phone call from Scott. By this stage he and Sue were so poor that they were living off vegetables that they scrounged from the fields around their cottage. Having lost faith in Bessell's ability to sort anything out, Scott had tried to telephone Thorpe at his house in the village of Cobbaton in North Devon – he had got the number from the Liberal Club in Barnstaple. The first time he tried, there was no reply, but the next time Caroline answered the phone.

In a state of near-hysteria, Scott began to pour out his problems: 'I told her, "I don't know if you know but I have to get back my Insurance card."' No doubt wondering what he was talking about, Caroline asked, 'Why should Jeremy have it?' Scott replied: 'Well, he was my employer. We were lovers. You have a baby and you know what it must be like for my wife with no money.'

There was silence. Then she said, 'I don't want to know anything about it. It's disgusting.' Finally she said, 'I'm sorry', and put the phone down.

Clearly Bessell had to do something to keep Scott in check – but what? After spending several hours on the phone, Bessell managed to arrange for him to receive emergency funds from his local Social Security office in Weymouth. That afternoon, Scott called his office. Bessell started to explain that all he had to do was get himself to Weymouth and his immediate difficulties would be over.

Assuming this was yet another attempt to fob him off, Scott grew even more angry. He said that unless Bessell arranged for him and Sue to get their benefits in full, he was going to sell his story to a national newspaper. Bessell thought it highly unlikely that any paper would touch the story for fear of being sued for libel. On the other hand, it wasn't a risk he wished to take. Before he could say anything else, Scott slammed the phone down. With a heavy heart, Bessell wrote him another letter. 'Dear Norman,' it began. 'Further to our telephone conversation this afternoon, we appeared to be cut off . . .'

He went on to insist that he was doing everything in his power to obtain an emergency card so that Scott and his wife could obtain temporary benefits. Then came something midway between a plea and a threat: 'It would be a great mistake if you jeopardized this in the way you suggested to me on the telephone and I hope for your own sake and in spite of your anxiety, you will accept my advice and guidance.'

Bessell finished up as follows: 'I have spoken to Jeremy Thorpe and put him in the picture regarding the present situation.' In fact, Bessell hadn't actually spoken to Thorpe about this latest development. He had decided to keep him as much in the dark as possible in case Thorpe's thoughts, like homing pigeons, should return once more to 'the Ultimate Solution'. Possibly Bessell was feeling overwrought himself, or possibly he was just being careless. At any rate in all the letters that he sent Scott, this was the only one that mentioned Thorpe by name.

As it turned out, Scott didn't need to go into Weymouth to collect his money. A representative from the Department of Health and Social Security came to see him. Scott told him that he had never stamped his NI card, as his former employer, Jeremy Thorpe – with whom he'd once lived – had promised to do it for him.

'In what capacity did you live with Mr Thorpe?' the man inquired. 'As his private secretary?'

'No,' Scott told him. 'As lovers.'

A week later Sue Scott received her maternity benefits cheque. That afternoon she went off to the nearby town of Blandford, telling Scott that she wanted to buy some baby clothes. But while she was there she changed her mind. Instead, she came back with a black Indian dress covered with mirrors, four Penguin books and twelve peacock feathers. This was not a good sign, felt Scott, but he put it down to her nerves about the impending birth. When he asked what had happened to the baby clothes, she told him not to worry; after all, they'd now be receiving money every week, and could always buy them later.

But the cheques did not arrive weekly. They received two – for £15 each – and then they stopped. The cheques from London had also stopped arriving, as their tenants had defaulted on the rent. By now Sue was almost eight months pregnant and feeling thoroughly fed up – not only with life in the country, but also with Norman.

Deciding that she would rather face the disapproval of her parents than remain where she was, she headed to Lincolnshire to have the baby. Scott was not invited to come with her. Instead, he and his whippet, Emma, went to the flat in Earls Court Square, where he managed to evict the tenants.

On 18 November 1969, Diggory Benjamin Scott was born. The next day Norman Scott travelled north to see his new baby. Reluctantly his in-laws offered him a bed. He ended up staying over Christmas. Although there was no Strychnine mug this time, the atmosphere was no better than it had been before. In January, Norman, Sue and Benjamin – as he was always known – returned to London and moved into the flat in Earls Court Square. There the Scotts lived an increasingly unhappy and isolated existence, their nerves frayed by the strain of looking after their new baby.

However, they did have one unexpected visitor. Mrs Josiffe – Norman's mother – was keen to see her grandchild. As she had never shown him much affection as a boy, Scott was sceptical about her motives. He therefore decided to play a trick on her, one that would demonstrate how little interest she really had in children. When she arrived, Benjamin was sleeping in their bedroom. While Mrs Josiffe talked to Sue, Scott slipped into another room, where he dressed Emma the whippet in a baby's bonnet and put her into the pram.

He then asked his mother to come in.

Mrs Josiffe peered into the pram. Far from noticing anything amiss, she began saying what an enchanting-looking baby Benjamin was. As soon as she had finished making appreciative noises, Scott called out 'Emma!' – whereupon the whippet leaped out of the pram, still wearing the bonnet. Mrs Josiffe gave a shriek of alarm and keeled over. She never came back.

It soon became clear to Scott that Sue was suffering from postnatal depression. She seldom went out, grew increasingly listless and took to spending most of the day in bed. Scott too became depressed. The only good news was that the cheques had resumed – he was now receiving £15 a week in Social Security. For a few weeks he went to see a psychotherapist, before deciding that he couldn't afford the £4 that each session cost. Instead, he turned to a cocktail of anti-depressants and sleeping pills.

Meanwhile Sue continued to deteriorate. One day Scott found a letter she had written to herself that made it plain just how wretched she felt: 'He lies by my side in this bed, not stirring. I try to wake him so many times wanting him to hold me. But he is lying full of sleeping pills. I think how easy it would be to go to the bathroom and cut my wrists and by morning I would be dead. This whole miserable existence would be over.'

Then they had another unexpected visitor. Having just returned from a world cruise, Conway Wilson-Young arrived with a belated wedding present – an electric kettle. He invited them both to dinner that evening at his house in Chester Square. Sue declined, but Scott did go, and stayed the night. The next morning he called Sue and told her what had happened. 'I tried to explain how I needed warmth and someone to wake up next to.' As excuses for infidelity go, this was clearly on the thin side, but Sue said he could come back on one condition – that he stopped seeing Wilson-Young. Scott agreed and returned to Earls Court Square.

Two days later he was looking after Benjamin when he saw that Sue was sitting up in bed crying. When he asked what was wrong, she wouldn't say. It was at this point that Scott snapped. Picking up an ashtray, he hurled it at the wall. 'I said, "You see what I've done? How I've made this place beautiful? I've got no work and no money, but I've done everything I can . . ."'

That afternoon Sue and the baby caught a train up to Lincolnshire. She and Scott continued to talk on the phone, and several days later she wrote him a long letter saying she still loved him and was coming back down to London. To celebrate her return, Scott invited some mutual friends round to an impromptu party. But Sue never arrived, and after a couple of hours the friends made their excuses and left. At around midnight Scott called her parents' house. Sue answered the phone. When he asked what had happened, there was a long silence. Then she said, 'I'm not coming back. It's finished.'

16

Back to Black

Throughout the 1960s Liberal Party finances had staggered from one crisis to another. As soon as he became Leader, Jeremy Thorpe was determined to unearth a rich donor. All that was stopping the Liberals from regaining power, he believed, was the lack of a well-stocked war chest. 'If only we could find just one millionaire who would open his purse,' he would say constantly to Peter Bessell.

But the millionaires proved elusive. The Reverend Timothy Beaumont felt that he had done everything he could to keep the party solvent, as did Sir Felix Brunner. Then, in May 1969, an unlikely saviour appeared out of nowhere. Jack Hayward was a man in possession of two fortunes. One had come from his father's engineering business; the other he had made himself from a scheme to construct a deep-water port on Grand Bahama Island in the Caribbean.

Despite living in the Bahamas, Hayward was passionately, almost manically, pro-British. Thanks to him, the inhabitants of Grand Bahama now rode around in red double-decker buses. He had also been responsible for arranging for portraits of the Queen to be hung in all government offices. As a result, he became known as 'Union Jack' Hayward – a nickname he revelled in.

In April 1969, Hayward was reading a copy of the *Daily Telegraph* at his home in Freeport when he saw a story about an appeal to save the island of Lundy in the Bristol Channel for the nation and turn it into a bird sanctuary. One of the people behind the appeal was Jeremy Thorpe. That night Hayward called Thorpe at his London home. Caroline answered the phone and explained that Jeremy was out at a dinner. Could he possibly call back later?

By the time Hayward called again, she and Jeremy were in bed. Any irritation Thorpe felt at being telephoned so late swiftly evaporated as Hayward told him that he was keen to become involved in the appeal. Caroline, however, was more suspicious, waving a scribbled warning in front of her husband which read, 'How do you know he's not an agent for the Scientologists?'

What price were the owners asking, Hayward wanted to know.

'Well, I think we'd get it for £125,000,' Thorpe told him.

'OK,' said Hayward. 'Count me in.'

'What?' asked Thorpe incredulously. 'You mean for the whole amount?'

Hayward confirmed that he did. 'I happened to have some spare cash at the time,' he recalled later. In fact, he ended up paying £150,000 for Lundy. After the sale had gone through, a service of thanksgiving was held in the little church on the island. Hayward sat in the front pew with the Thorpes in the row behind. Although he was a staunch Conservative, Hayward was hugely impressed by Thorpe. He had always had an intensely romanticized view of Britain and longed to see the country being run by someone with dash and vision. Someone who embraced the modern world but shared his reverence for its traditions. During the service he leaned back and whispered, 'Jeremy, you ought to be Prime Minister.'

'It's on the cards,' Thorpe replied.

An opportunity like this could not be allowed to go begging. Before Hayward went back to the Bahamas, Thorpe asked if by any chance he had any more spare cash lying about.

'How much did you have in mind?' Hayward asked.

Thorpe swallowed. 'Perhaps the same again?'

This time Hayward hesitated. Before he committed himself, he wanted to know what the money would be spent on. Could someone provide him with a breakdown? Of course, said Thorpe – he would put his finest financial brain on to it. He then called Bessell, who was back in New York, and told him to get out to Grand Bahama as soon as possible with a plausible-looking plan.

Naturally, Bessell did what he was told. If he hadn't already known that Hayward was a multi-millionaire, he would never have guessed it from the way he lived. True, Hayward had a Rolls-Royce, but it was at least fifteen years old. As for his house, it was modest in size and furnished with 'homely sofas' and 'good reproduction tables'. Bessell immediately liked Hayward, who struck him as a thoroughly decent sort. Hayward also seems to have taken to Bessell. The meeting went well and a few weeks later a cheque for £150,000, made out to 'Jeremy Thorpe', arrived – the largest single contribution to the Liberals since the 1920s.

Rather than putting the money in the party's general account, Thorpe decided to open a new account, one that would be controlled by a small group of senior Liberals – including him and Bessell. That way, Thorpe said, he would be able to keep a tighter control over expenditure. It also meant there was no need to pay off the party's debts, as they had all been run up on other accounts.

Bessell's trip to New York had been successful in other ways too. One evening he was having dinner with a friend in the Oak Room of the Plaza Hotel. At another table he saw someone he knew sitting with a beautiful dark-haired woman.

'I'd like to meet her,' Bessell told his companion.

His companion said that he should go over and introduce himself. Up close, Bessell saw that the dark-haired woman was 'even more lovely than from a distance'. For the rest of the evening he bombarded his friend with questions. Her name was Diane Kelly, he learned, and she was twenty-nine years old. She was also married. It wasn't all bad news, though: she and her husband were known to be having problems.

A few days later Diane joined Bessell and his friend for dinner. As well as having an impressive grasp of international affairs and a keen interest in the arts, she was, Bessell noted approvingly, 'essentially warm and feminine'. After dinner he drove her back to her apartment on Long Island. On the doorstep they shook hands and said good night. However much of a philanderer Bessell may have been, he was also a romantic and the idea of courtly love greatly appealed to him. Diane, he could tell, was not the sort of woman who was going to fall into his bed. Instead, any attempt to press his suit was going to take a great deal of patience. Driving back into Manhattan, Bessell prepared himself for the long haul.

Shortly before he left New York, he had a phone call from a man called Norman Graham with whom he'd had business dealings some years earlier. Graham explained that he had recently launched a new company. The company didn't have a very glamorous title – the Plastic Carton Corporation of America – nor did it manufacture a very glamorous product – extruded plastic foam. However, this foam could be turned into items that Graham predicted would soon be taking the world by storm: plastic egg cartons. He wondered if Bessell might be interested in running the company's British arm.

At this point Bessell would probably have sold eggs from the back of a lorry if he thought there was any chance of making money at it. Trying not to sound too eager, he did his best to imply that he had always been fascinated by extruded plastic foam. The two men met and quickly agreed terms. When Bessell returned to London, his life had changed in two key regards. Not only was he in love, he was also the proud owner of 20 per cent of the British subsidiary of the Plastic Carton Corporation of America. The path back to prosperity, he felt certain, was paved with plastic egg cartons.

Bessell went back to New York at the first opportunity, where he called Diane and asked her out to dinner. She said, rather pointedly Bessell thought, that she'd have to check with her husband first. As it happened, her husband was away on business and the two of them did meet up. However, 'there was no change in the friendly formality of the previous occasion.' Far from being put off, this only made Bessell more ardent.

For her part, Diane was intrigued, if wary of what she might be getting into. 'In college, I had majored in political science. You can imagine how interesting I found this sitting Member of Parliament. Then of course he was good-looking with a really fine quick mind. He was gentle, he cared about human rights, he used the English language as only a Brit can do – beautifully and persuasively – and he had a wonderful sense of humour.'

By the time Norman Graham flew to London eight months later to discuss building a large factory in Cornwall to produce his plastic egg cartons, Bessell's persistence had paid off: Diane and her husband had decided to get divorced and she and Bessell were on the brink of becoming lovers.

Bessell and Graham spent several days together talking to potential investors. The meetings went well. By dangling the prospect of creating 800 new jobs in an area of high unemployment, Bessell was able to persuade Liskeard Rural District Council in his constituency of Bodmin to buy ten acres of land outside the town. The Council then waved through planning permission for a new factory to be built on the site.

But, during the time they spent together, Bessell noticed something about Graham that he hadn't noticed before – in between meals Graham often slipped a little white pill under his tongue. When Bessell asked what the pills were, Graham told him they were nitroglycerine tablets, which he took for a heart condition. He had had a coronary a couple of years earlier and been prescribed them by his doctor. But there was nothing to worry about, he assured Bessell. Absolutely nothing at all.

On 18 May 1970, Prime Minister Harold Wilson, buoyed up by a surge in the opinion polls and a favourably received budget, announced that a General Election would be held on 18 June – five weeks away. For Jeremy Thorpe the stakes could not have been higher. It was his first election as Party Leader, and the first big test of his appeal to the nation. With Liberal Party finances now in better shape than they had been for half a century, he had no excuse not to do well.

After prolonged brainstorming, his campaign team came up with what they were convinced was a winner of a slogan, one which invested Thorpe with an almost Messianic aura – 'Faith, Hope and Jeremy'. Two helicopters were hired to fly senior party members around the country, while the latest telex equipment was installed in Liberal offices. Thorpe himself worked unflaggingly through the campaign, often for seventeen hours a day. Compared with his two rivals – Wilson and Heath – he cut a dashing, piratical figure in his Homburg hat and his double-breasted waistcoats, plunging into crowds to wring the hands of strangers as if they were long-lost intimates. The press loved him and so too, it seemed, did the people.

The only hitch in Thorpe's campaign took place at Cheadle in Cheshire, when a female protester carrying a banner stood too close to the still-spinning rotor blade of his helicopter. First it sliced her banner in two, then, to his horror, Thorpe saw a large, muddy hank of hair lying on the ground. Thinking she must have been scalped, and already envisioning disastrous newspaper headlines, Thorpe and Caroline climbed out of the helicopter – only to discover that the woman's wig had been blown off by the downdraught then trampled underfoot.

Because of his financial difficulties Peter Bessell was no longer standing as an MP. As a leaving gift, Thorpe presented him with two leather-bound volumes of Hansard recording his contributions to the 1968 Transport Bill; the bill had eventually been passed, but in a much watered-down version that bore little resemblance to what Bessell had envisaged.

The first of these volumes bore a handwritten inscription:

To Peter,

My very dear friend and loyal colleague. This is a small memento of the six years in which we served together in the House of Commons. Apart from your devoted service to your constituents in the Bodmin Division, these volumes commemorate your marathon on the Transport Bill in which you set up an all-time record for a single MP by moving 1,400 amendments and new clauses and making over 500 speeches and interjections . . .

Your affectionate colleague
Jeremy

17

The Price of a Peerage

As polling day grew closer, Peter Bessell felt more and more bereft. Thanks to the plastic egg cartons, his financial situation was no longer as perilous as it had once been, but he still had a sense of being marooned on the sidelines, forced to stand and watch as his former colleagues headed for the hustings. He yearned to be doing something to help. Yet those days, it seemed, had gone for ever. It didn't help that the Bodmin Liberal Association was still puzzled about his motives for standing down. And then there was the strain of leading a double life – pretending to be happily married to his wife Pauline while Bessell was in Devon, and spending much of his time with Diane in New York.

One evening, less than a week before the election, he was about to leave his house when the phone rang. Bessell picked it up and a voice on the other end said, 'This is Mr Hetherington.'

The name meant nothing.

The man said that he wanted to talk about 'Jeremy – and how you've looked after his friend, Norman Scott'.

Bessell trod carefully. He said that Scott was one of the great many people that Jeremy Thorpe had helped over the years.

Mr Hetherington gave a dry chuckle. Had he helped them all become homosexuals, he asked.

Swiftly Bessell vaulted on to his high horse. That was an outrageous suggestion, he said, as well as a slanderous one. Didn't he know that Jeremy Thorpe was a happily married man, and a father?

Hetherington gave another chuckle. 'Norman's told me you looked after him because you were disgusted by what Thorpe had done.'

Throughout all this, Bessell was racking his brains, trying to work out why there was something familiar about the man's voice. Dimly, he remembered that about a year before someone had phoned his office claiming to be the stepfather of Scott's wife, Sue – in fact, Sue Myers didn't have a stepfather. This man, who hadn't given his name, claimed that her life had been blighted by her association with Scott. As a result Thorpe bore some moral and – the man implied – financial responsibility for her.

The voice, as far as Bessell could tell, was the same. At the time he hadn't taken the caller seriously, but now he began to wonder. Bessell's doubts only increased when the man said, 'Norman's wife has given me three letters that Thorpe wrote to him years ago.'

Could this be true? If so, it would mean that Scott must have been lying when he said he'd destroyed the letters he had.

What did he want, Bessell asked.

Hetherington said that he had written a pamphlet in which he outlined what had gone on between Norman Scott and Jeremy Thorpe. His plan was to drive around North Devon on the night before the election, giving out as many copies of this pamphlet as possible. Then came a twist which Bessell couldn't have foreseen. Apparently under the impression that Bessell was sympathetic to Scott, Hetherington asked for his help in distributing the pamphlet.

Bessell did his best to appear calm. He figured that his only hope was to get hold of both the letters in Hetherington's possession, and the pamphlet. Plainly that would involve the two of them meeting. It was now Friday night – there were five days to go before the General Election.

'Why don't we have a drink together on Monday evening?' Bessell suggested. Hetherington agreed and said he would call again on Sunday to finalize arrangements.

Early the next morning, Bessell called Thorpe. 'Oh, Christ!' Thorpe exclaimed. 'What are we going to do?'

By 'we', Thorpe, of course, meant 'you'. However much Bessell had yearned to be back in the fray, this was hardly what he'd had in mind. None the less, he knew he had to come up with a plan.

Thorpe and Caroline were due to come to tea on the Sunday afternoon and he needed to have something by then.

All Saturday, Bessell sat and pondered. By the time he went to bed, he thought he had found a possible solution. When Hetherington called the next morning, Bessell asked where he was planning to have his pamphlets photocopied. To his surprise – and relief – Hetherington said that he didn't know. He was going to drive down from London and intended to find somewhere to get it done when he arrived in Cornwall. This was just what Bessell wanted to hear. Why didn't Hetherington allow him to help out? Bessell could meet him off the Saltash Ferry at midnight on the Monday, then take him to the Liberal office in Liskeard, where there was a photocopying machine.

'Won't someone be there?' Hetherington asked.

'Not at that time of night,' Bessell assured him. 'And I've got a key.'

That Sunday afternoon, when the Thorpes came to tea, the two wives stayed indoors while Jeremy and Bessell went for a walk in the garden. Bessell explained what he hoped was going to happen. After Hetherington arrived in Saltash, Bessell would take him to Liskeard and then, in a manner that he was still a bit hazy about, persuade him to part with the letters.

Thorpe was unconvinced. 'He won't give them to you. He'd be a fool to trust you.'

Bessell admitted that his plan depended on Hetherington being unusually gullible, but he still felt it might work.

'The bastard isn't going to part with his evidence,' said Thorpe as he paced around the lawn. What if it didn't work? Did Bessell have a fallback plan? All he could think of was that they could go to the police.

Thorpe stopped and stared at him. 'Are you suggesting that we go to them and say that shit Scott has evidence?'

Bessell pointed out that homosexuality was no longer illegal and so, on that score at least, Thorpe had nothing to worry about. 'I'm not talking about the law,' snapped Thorpe. 'The story would get out in no time and the gossip would emanate from the police station.' Stung by his tone, Bessell asked if he could suggest a better plan. Yes, said Thorpe, he could. 'Meet him off the ferry, get him in your car and instead of going to Liskeard, go to the moor somewhere and kill him.'

Bessell had experienced déjà vu several times before, but never quite as acutely as this. For the first time he began to wonder if Thorpe had turned into a homicidal maniac.

Seeing his reaction, Thorpe reminded him of his wider responsibilities. 'Peter, you've got to do this,' he said. 'It's not only North Devon; it's the entire party.'

With the election just a few days away, Bessell knew he had to do something to stop Thorpe from panicking. 'Jeremy,' he said, 'I give you my word that I'll find a way of removing the danger.' He was deliberately being as vague as possible. However, Thorpe wasn't buying it.

'You realize that means killing him?'

'I don't accept that,' Bessell told him. 'But if you're saying that if all else fails, well, that's another matter.'

As far as Thorpe was concerned, that moment had already arrived. 'How will you kill him?' he asked.

'I'd rather not discuss it,' said Bessell primly.

'Do you have a gun?'

In fact, Bessell did possess a gun, but it was an antique sporting rifle which he had never used. He wasn't even sure if it had a firing pin. He thought it best to keep this to himself.

'What about poison?'

'No, of course not.'

Then Bessell remembered that he also had some poison. 'I've got some trichloroethylene,' he said. It was dry-cleaning fluid, he explained, but was once used as an anaesthetic, like ether. Thorpe had no idea what trichloroethylene was, but he knew all about ether.

'Couldn't be better! You can soak a handkerchief in it, hold it over his face and it'll knock him out.'

'Jeremy,' said Bessell simply. 'It's murder.'

Thorpe gazed at him. 'Peter, it's no worse than killing a sick dog.'

These too were words that Bessell had hoped never to hear again.

'Once he's out cold, it'll be easy,' Thorpe went on. 'Hit him on the head with something heavy. You know how to get rid of the body – down a tin-mine.'

With that, they went back inside the house. After they had supper, Bessell and his wife, Pauline, drove the Thorpes to the Pencubitt Hotel in Liskeard, where they were spending the night. On the way there, Thorpe turned around in the passenger seat and, apropos of nothing, said to Pauline who was in the back with Caroline, 'How would you like to be Lady Bessell?'

Pauline was too surprised to answer.

'I think old Besselli would look good in ermine,' Thorpe went on.

Everyone laughed, but Thorpe insisted he was being serious. 'Peter shall be the next Liberal Life Peer.'

Bessell said nothing. He wasn't averse to being Lord Bessell – far from it. Apart from anything else, it might prompt investors to put money into the Plastic Carton Corporation of America. But he couldn't help wondering if this was to be his reward for killing Hetherington.

As Bessell left his house soon after eleven o'clock the next night – having told Pauline he was going to check that Liberal election posters were not being defaced – he realized that he was scared. He still had no idea how he was going to persuade Hetherington to give him the letters. Nor had he thought about what he would do if Hetherington turned violent. Driving his Triumph 2000 through the darkened Cornish lanes, he wondered if it might be possible to reason with him, to appeal to Hetherington's better nature – assuming he had one. If Hetherington went ahead with his pamphleteering plan, that could wipe the Liberals off the map, as well as ruin Thorpe's career. Was that really what he wanted? By the time Bessell reached Saltash he had decided that this was his best course of action.

It was now almost midnight and the streets were deserted. But as he drove into the car park by the ferry terminal, he saw a tall, thick-set man on the pavement. The man was walking in the opposite direction, but, as Bessell pulled over, he stopped. Then the man started walking again, only more slowly this time.

Bessell wound down the window. 'Mr Hetherington?'

Hetherington was older than Bessell had expected – in his mid fifties, with thick white hair. He wore a tweed suit, or a sports jacket, and in one hand held an old-fashioned bag like a Gladstone. When he got into the car, he rested the bag on his knees.

'How long will it take to drive to Liskeard?' Hetherington asked.

Bessell noticed that his breath smelled of alcohol. He also appeared nervous. Rather than going straight there, Bessell suggested they might stop on the way and talk. Hetherington agreed. About three miles outside Saltash, Bessell pulled into a lay-by and turned off the headlights.

'I expect you'd like to see the letters,' said Hetherington.

Opening the bag, he took out four sheets of paper. Bessell switched on the interior light. Three of the sheets of paper were handwritten while the fourth was typed. The light inside the car wasn't much brighter than a candle's, but, as he examined the first letter, Bessell saw straight away that something was wrong. Thorpe always wrote his letters on House of Commons notepaper, or on specially printed blue paper which bore his family crest. However, these letters were written on cheap white paper – and yet the handwriting appeared to be Thorpe's.

'Dearest Norman . . .' he read. The letter wasn't long and, on a quick perusal, seemed to contain nothing incriminating. It was, however, signed 'With love, Jeremy'. The second letter was longer. But once again Bessell smelled a rat. Thorpe had a habit when writing letters of abbreviating certain words – 'should' always became 'shd' and 'would' became 'wd'. But there were no abbreviations here.

Next Bessell read the typed sheet of paper. It outlined how Scott and Thorpe had been lovers, how Thorpe had apparently turned Scott into a homosexual, and how Scott had recently married Sue

Myers. All this was fairly accurate, but by now Bessell's suspicions had hardened. He was almost sure the letters were fakes.

How had he got hold of them, he asked. Hetherington replied that they had come from a friend of Scott's wife – but refused to say more.

'What do you suppose a set of documents like this is worth?' Bessell asked.

Hetherington did not hesitate. 'Five thousand pounds.'

Out of the question, Bessell told him. He began to explain that the Liberals had never had much money and had even less than usual with an election only two days away. Hetherington said nothing. He just took back the papers and placed them on top of the bag. Bessell started the car and carried on towards Liskeard. He was just coming into the town of Callington when Hetherington said suddenly, 'All right, Mr Bessell. I'll take two thousand pounds.'

Bessell was careful not to reply straight away.

'Mr Hetherington,' he said. 'You've got a deal.'

Hetherington wanted to know when he could have the money.

'Tonight!' declared Bessell impetuously. 'You can have the money tonight. I have an office in Plymouth and there happens to be a fairly large sum in the safe.'

Once again he was bluffing. There was no money in his Plymouth office; there wasn't even a safe. But Bessell reasoned that he would be less vulnerable in Devon, where the roads were better lit and the towns bigger. Swinging the car round, he headed for Plymouth, intending to stop as soon as he saw a policeman. But before that he needed to be certain that Hetherington was a fraud. He asked if he knew Norman Scott.

Hetherington gave another chuckle. 'Oh, I know him all right.'

As he had proved before, Bessell knew all about laying false trails. 'I never trust fair-headed men,' he said.

Hetherington patted his thick white hair. 'I used to be blond myself,' he said ruefully.

'As blond as Scott?' Bessell asked casually.

'Oh, no,' said Hetherington. 'Not that fair.'

That clinched it. Norman Scott may have been many things, but he had never – not even in his modelling days – had anything other than raven-black hair. By the time they reached Plymouth it was 1 a.m. Bessell stopped near the train station. Standing outside, he saw a policeman. Telling Hetherington that he needed to get something from the boot, Bessell fetched his own briefcase. Inside was an envelope containing some spare cash which he always carried in case of emergencies.

After he had got back into the car, he held up the envelope.

'Mr Hetherington, you see this?'

Hetherington nodded.

Inside it there was £200, Bessell told him. He then dropped the envelope into the gap between his seat and the driver's door where Hetherington couldn't reach it. If he handed over the letters and the typed sheet of paper, he could have the money, Bessell said. But if he refused, Bessell would go straight to the policeman and tell him he was being blackmailed.

To begin with Hetherington didn't cotton on. 'What are you up to?' he asked.

'Exactly what I said.'

And then all at once he did. 'You bastard . . . Fuck you. Oh, fuck you.'

Opening the passenger door, Hetherington heaved himself out of his seat and ran round to the driver's side. There he hurled the documents through the open window before grabbing the envelope Bessell was now holding.

'Bugger you,' he shouted. 'I'll get you all one day. Queers – that's what you all are. All of you, fucking queers!' With his Gladstone under his arm, he ran off into the night – never to be seen, or heard of, again.

Driving back to Cornwall, Bessell felt better about himself than he had done in a long time. As well as being quick-witted, he had displayed admirable coolness in a crisis. Far more importantly, he had saved his party – and his Leader – from almost certain disaster. On the way, he pulled into another lay-by. With his cigarette lighter, he set fire to all the papers that Hetherington had hurled at him. It was nearly 3 a.m. when he reached home. After setting the alarm for 7.45, Bessell went to bed.

At eight o'clock, he phoned Thorpe and told him that the problem had been dealt with. He did not elaborate.

'Marvellous!' said Thorpe.

Only two things clouded Bessell's sense of elation. One was that more and more people now seemed to know about Thorpe's affair with Scott. The other was that when danger threatened, Thorpe's immediate reaction had, once again, been to think of murder.

18

From Bad to Worse

The 1970 General Election was a disaster for Jeremy Thorpe and the Liberals. After spending more than £100,000 of the £150,000 that Jack Hayward had given them on their campaign, they won just six seats, compared with the twelve they had won in 1966. The helicopters, the telex machines, the 'Faith, Hope and Jeremy' posters had all been for nothing.

It was a disaster too for Harold Wilson, who had fatally misread the mood of the electorate. For the first time eighteen-year-olds were eligible to vote – previously voters had to be over twenty-one. Wilson had been convinced that hordes of these new voters would plump for Labour. But what they wanted more than anything else, it turned out, was change. Wilson wasn't the only one to get it wrong; so did the pollsters. A week before election day most of the polls put Labour at least ten points ahead. But on the morning of the election, the *Daily Telegraph* scented a change of mood. 'Conservative hopes of winning today's election, resting largely on the housewives' vote, are running high.'

Whether it was the housewives or the newly enfranchised teenagers that did it, Labour's majority of over 100 was wiped out. The party ended up with 288 seats, while the Conservatives had 330. At 5.05 in the afternoon, on 18 June, Harold Wilson and his wife Mary left Number 10 by the back door. An hour later Ted Heath entered Downing Street to be greeted by a chorus of 'For He's a Jolly Good Fellow' from the waiting crowd.

On election night Peter Bessell was invited to represent the Liberal Party during the BBC's coverage hosted by Robin Day. Sitting in Lime Grove Studios, he gazed in horror at the monitors as one

Liberal seat after another fell. Then came the news that the result in North Devon was too close to call – there would have to be a recount. Thorpe appeared on screen at Barnstaple Town Hall, his face drawn. When the results of the recount were announced, it turned out that he'd hung on to the seat by just 369 votes – compared to 1,166 four years earlier. Had it not been for Caroline's efforts on his behalf, a lot of people in North Devon felt that Thorpe might well have lost it.

The result in Bessell's old constituency of Bodmin was not announced until lunchtime the following day. By then he had grabbed a few hours' sleep and returned to Lime Grove Studios. It was Robin Day who informed him that the result had come in. Instead of telling him directly, Day handed him a piece of paper. Bessell thought he had prepared himself for the worst – but he too was wrong. The Conservatives, he read, had overturned his majority of 2,000 and won by almost 4,000 votes. When Day asked him for a comment on air, Bessell said simply that he was 'heartbroken'. Day waited, clearly expecting him to say something else, but Bessell couldn't. Only later did he realize that tears had been streaming down his cheeks.

Thorpe himself struggled to stay upbeat. He told his friend, the former MP – and sponsor of the Sexual Offences Act – Humphry Berkeley, 'I've still got my seat, an adorable little boy and a wife I love.' But he was more candid with Bessell, admitting that he had no explanation for what had happened. 'Pedro, why didn't the old magic work?'

It was a question Bessell was still asking himself ten days later when he and Pauline attended the annual dinner of the United Nations Association at the Guildhall in London. Thorpe was also due to attend. When the Bessells walked into the Guildhall, one of the officials stopped them.

'Have you heard about Mrs Thorpe?' he asked.

'Caroline?' said Pauline. 'What about her?'

'She was killed this afternoon in a car accident.'

*

That morning the Thorpes had been intending to drive up to London from Devon in their green Ford Anglia. However, they had so much luggage that they decided it would make more sense if Thorpe and the eleven-month-old Rupert caught the train. Caroline dropped them off at the station and then went back to their cottage to finish packing.

As she was driving along the A303 in Hampshire, her car suddenly veered from one lane into another. There it hit a thirteen-ton lorry travelling in the opposite direction, collided with another car and rose twelve feet into the air before skidding along on its roof. Mrs Elizabeth George of Basingstoke was one of the first on the scene: 'It was terrible. She had a bunch of white carnations with her and they were scattered all around. The car was on its roof and in a terrible mess.' Caroline was trapped inside the wreckage. She managed to speak briefly to the policemen who were trying to cut her loose, but by the time the ambulance arrived at Basingstoke Hospital she had died of a ruptured spleen.

That afternoon Thorpe was giving a speech in the Commons, congratulating the Speaker on his re-election. Afterwards he and two colleagues went into his office to talk about how they were going to muster an effective political presence with only six seats. They had not been there long when there was a knock on the door. The Superintendent of Police asked Thorpe if he would step outside. When he returned Thorpe didn't say anything; he just collapsed into a chair.

However cynical Thorpe's motives had been in marrying Caroline, there was no doubt that he had come to love her deeply. Her death devastated him – 'It felt as if my life had come to an end.' It also prompted him, not normally an introspective man, to question the nature of existence. Speaking on a BBC Radio religious programme, he said, 'Unless you believe in the Resurrection, I think the whole of this life is a very bad joke . . . People are not just snuffed out. There must be a further purpose.'

Caroline's funeral – organized by David Holmes – was held in the garden of their house in Cobbaton. Simultaneously, a public service was held in Barnstaple, where silent mourners lined the streets. At her memorial service, the violinist Yehudi Menuhin played Bach's Second Violin Partita. Any dissatisfaction with Thorpe's performance as Leader during the election campaign was washed away in a wave of sympathy.

But over the next few weeks his friends and colleagues began to grow alarmed. While Thorpe had always doted on his son, Rupert, he now became obsessed with his welfare, insisting on spending as much time with him as possible. When he came to Westminster, he drifted about in a haze of grief, taking meetings and attending functions, yet scarcely aware of where he was. At the inquest into Caroline's death there were suggestions that she too had been in a kind of trance when she died. The driver of the lorry she had collided with, Brian Knock, reported that she had been 'looking down at the inside of the car' as she drove towards them. However, his passenger in the lorry, Stephen Blythe, contradicted this. 'When I saw the Anglia car it was about one foot over the central white line. The driver seemed to be looking straight ahead and did not seem to know where she was going. I thought at the time that she was day-dreaming. She seemed to reach our lorry and shake her head as if she realized what was going to happen.'

Ever since there has been speculation about what might have occurred before Caroline left for London. According to one theory, Norman Scott turned up at the house just after Thorpe had caught the train and, in much greater detail than before, talked about his relationship with Thorpe. This – so the theory goes – was why she was staring straight ahead in an apparently distracted manner.

Scott has always insisted that the only time he spoke to Caroline was almost a year ago. On that occasion Thorpe had been able to convince her that there was no truth in his story. But what does seem clear is that, mired in grief and casting about for an explanation for what had happened, Thorpe came to believe that Scott bore some responsibility for his wife's death.

*

However distressed Thorpe was, there was one piece of information Bessell felt he had to share with him. When he went round to Thorpe's flat, he saw to his dismay that the place had been turned into a shrine to Caroline. Looking at the photographs of her that covered the walls, Bessell grew more concerned than ever about Thorpe's emotional state. 'At best it was unhealthy. At worst, it could be interpreted as a manifestation of Jeremy's morbid obsession with death.'

He told Thorpe that shortly before Caroline's death, Scott had telephoned his secretary and said that he was getting divorced. Predictable as this was, it was also dangerous – Scott might use the divorce proceedings to start talking about his relationship with Thorpe. The best way of neutralizing Scott, Bessell felt, was to find a tame solicitor who would impress upon him the folly of making any sort of public statement. Bessell suggested writing to Scott and inviting him to come to his office. There he would gently steer him in the direction of his own solicitor, a man called Leonard Ross.

Thorpe agreed, but said it would only be a temporary remedy. Then came the familiar refrain: 'It's got to be the ultimate solution.' As he talked about how Scott could be lured to America with the promise of a job, before being shot, poisoned or beaten to death with a shovel, then dumped in a Florida swamp, Bessell's head began to swim.

He was already overloaded with problems of his own. The Plastic Carton Corporation of America's plans to build a factory in Cornwall had hit a snag. Norman Graham believed he had patented a method of producing the extruded plastic foam from which his revolutionary new egg cartons were to be made. The trouble was that two large American pharmaceutical companies had challenged the patent and were preparing to manufacture foam of their own.

In the circumstances, Bessell thought it might be prudent to split off the British arm of the company from its American parent. Seeking to reassure investors who were alarmed about what was going on, he offered to act as a personal guarantor, making himself liable for any losses. By this point in his life, Bessell had already made a great many financial miscalculations. This, though, was to prove the most disastrous of all.

When Scott turned up at Bessell's office, it was clear that he had gone through yet another transformation. All his surface gloss, all his brittle assurance, had disappeared. Now he looked rougher than ever. In large part, this was because he was taking so many pills that he spent long periods of time in a semi-conscious stupor. Several weeks earlier, Sue Myers and her two half-brothers had driven down to London in a removal van. Letting themselves in, they removed the furniture. The first Scott knew about it was when he woke up and found that the flat was empty apart from the bed he had been sleeping in.

Scott was also more upset about divorce proceedings – started by Sue with enthusiastic support from her parents – than Bessell had anticipated. But, comatose or not, he had come up with a new plan. The owners of the flat wanted to redevelop it and had offered Scott £1,500 to move out. In a copy of *The Times*, he had seen an advertisement for a mill house to let in a village called Tal-y-bont in North Wales. Although Scott had never been to Tal-y-bont and didn't know anyone there, he thought the house looked delightful. He also felt like a change of scene. If all went well, he hoped to open a riding school.

Bessell had never been to Tal-y-bont either, but it sounded reassuringly far away from London. Before Scott went to North Wales, he advised him to see his solicitor, Leonard Ross, to discuss his divorce – having first persuaded a characteristically reluctant Thorpe to pay Ross's fees. Scott agreed. His main concern, he explained, was to try to secure custody of Benjamin. Privately, Bessell thought the chances of this happening were almost non-existent – family courts tending not to look favourably on promiscuous homosexuals with well-documented mental problems. He did, however, tell Scott that he would arrange – through

Leonard Ross – to pay the rent on his new house. He also said in passing that he might be able to help Scott set up his proposed riding school.

Then something happened that drove all other thoughts from his mind. In October 1970, Norman Graham dropped dead of a massive heart attack. His creditors panicked, the Plastic Carton Corporation of America went bust, and Bessell found himself saddled with debts of more than half a million dollars.

19

Big Swamp

On 5 February 1971, Norman Scott was driven up to Tal-y-bont by a friend of his – a diamond dealer with whom, not unpredictably, he had recently started an affair. Also in the car were his two whippets, Emma and Kate, an Afghan hound called Apple and a cat. Tal-y-bont knew all about nonconformists. In the nineteenth century it had been the home to the largest artists' colony in Wales. But it's doubtful if people there had ever seen anyone quite like Scott before.

It wasn't just his brooding, saturnine air that marked him out from everyone else; it was also the way he dressed. Scott's wardrobe still consisted of clothes he had been given when he was working on fashion shoots. In London, he was just another trendy young man about town. However, in Tal-y-bont his velvet suits and psychedelic shirts with their big, flapping collars made him look as if he'd just stepped out of a time machine.

To begin with, locals were courteous enough, but kept their distance. Not that this bothered Scott; he'd long ago become inured to disapproval. Besides, Tal-y-bont was just what he had been looking for. He liked the mill house, which proved just as pretty as the description in *The Times* had claimed. He also liked the fresh air and the rugged beauty of the landscape. Freed of the complications of metropolitan life, he even began to ease up on his pill intake.

But once again the idyll didn't last. Shortly after Scott arrived he received a cheque for £25 from Bessell – sent via Leonard Ross. That, though, was it. Weeks went by without another cheque and Scott soon fell behind with his rent. As his bank balance slid downhill, so did he – to the point where he took an overdose of Mogadon sleeping pills and went walking on the mountain behind his house, half hoping that he might die of exposure. Cold, sleepy, but very much alive, he was found by the man who owned the local garage – Keith Rose.

Rose and his wife took Scott in and listened agog as he told them about how all his troubles stemmed from his relationship with Thorpe. They then encouraged him to telephone Bessell and explain his predicament. A cagey-sounding Bessell said he didn't want to talk over the phone and asked Scott to come back down to London. The next morning an envelope arrived at the mill house containing a £10 note to cover his train fare.

As usual Bessell was full of excuses – excuses that now struck Scott as shimmeringly insincere. He explained that Thorpe was still stuck in the depths of grief, while he himself was in a spot of temporary financial difficulty. Scott was unmoved. Where was his rent money, he demanded. And the backing for his proposed riding school? Faced with the prospect of an angry Norman Scott, Bessell promptly backed down. He promised to pay the arrears on Scott's rent and to give him money to open his riding school. Just how much money was to prove a matter of dispute: Scott insisted that Bessell mentioned the sum of £5,000; Bessell claimed it was £500.

Scott returned to Tal-y-bont feeling reassured that another cheque would soon be forthcoming. Only it wasn't. All that happened was that on 7 April Bessell sent him a letter: 'Dear Norman, I am so sorry I have not been able to raise the money you required before going away on urgent business to the United States . . .'

When Keith Rose saw this, he was so incensed on Scott's behalf that he decided to write directly to Jeremy Thorpe at the House of Commons: 'Mr Scott's financial situation is now critical. He is not without friends who are willing to help him, but obviously the situation must be resolved. It must surely be in your interest to resolve it.' Normally Thorpe would have passed this straight on to Bessell. But Bessell was still away in the States and so he arranged for his personal assistant, Tom Dale, to reply. While the signature may have been Dale's, the tone of lofty dismissal was very much Thorpe's: 'As far as [Mr Thorpe] is aware, he does not know Mr Norman Scott. However, he believes that Mr Van de Brecht de Vater [*sic*] knew a Mr Norman Josiffe who may be the same person. Mr Thorpe asks me to say that he is under no obligation to this gentleman.'

For Scott, this letter was like a slap in the face. He grew even more depressed. A month later he had run out of money. Moving out of the mill house, he went to live in a disused caravan nearby. But once again his remarkable capacity to make people feel sorry for him came to the rescue. A woman called Gwen Parry-Jones, who had previously worked as the sub-postmistress in the village, befriended him and allowed him to stay – rent-free – in a cottage she owned.

Gwen Parry-Jones was in her early fifties. Her husband, a soldier in the Welsh Guards, had died two months earlier. She came from a devoutly religious family and was regarded as a woman of strict moral principles – she would never, for instance, go into the local pub. Kindly, vulnerable and possessed of what Scott called 'a very good Modigliani-type face', Parry-Jones also proved a good listener. At her instigation, so he insists, they soon began an affair: 'She rather pushed herself on to me.' Either way, Scott was hardly an unwilling participant – sexual confusion never having any discernibly inhibiting effect on his behaviour.

Soon they were walking around the village hand in hand. News of the affair between the middle-aged widow and the moody young interloper electrified Tal-y-bont. Suspicious of Scott to begin with, they were even more so now. Scott himself thought that if Parry-Jones noticed people's reactions, she was too smitten to care: 'I think she was terribly proud that this young giddy poof had turned up in her life when she thought it was the end.'

As well as being a good listener, Parry-Jones was a keen Liberal supporter. For years she had been friendly with the father of Emlyn Hooson, whose constituency, Montgomeryshire, was not far away. Convinced, like the Roses, that all Scott's problems resulted from his affair with Jeremy Thorpe, Parry-Jones decided that she too would take direct action. She wrote to Emlyn Hooson and – without naming Thorpe – said that a young man she knew had suffered dreadfully as a result of a relationship he'd had with a 'Liberal colleague'. By trying to conceal the affair, this unnamed colleague had not only ruined the young man's life, but damaged the reputation of the party.

Hooson's reply made no attempt to conceal his alarm. Dated 19 May 1971 and headed 'Confidential', it began, 'Dear Mrs Parry-Jones, Thank you for your recent letter with its disturbing contents. In view of your serious hints, as to the nature of the allegations and the connection with the gentleman you mention, I feel it is absolutely essential for you to provide me with further details and some evidence . . .'

In her letter back, Parry-Jones chose not to provide any further details. She did, however, write, 'Please tell Mr Peter Bessell that Mr Norman Scott is in a grave situation and if he has any decency he will fulfil his promise made to him immediately.' This was a sentence that struck Hooson as being loaded with hidden meaning. He suggested that she should come to see him in his constituency that weekend. Given the seriousness of the allegations, Parry-Jones felt it would be more appropriate if she and Scott went to the House of Commons. Hooson agreed and they arranged to meet the following week, on the afternoon of 26 May.

In New York, Bessell had embarked on a frantic round of meetings with various banks, trying to persuade them to keep the British arm of the Plastic Carton Corporation of America afloat. But in every case the response was the same – the company was finished and his only hope of escaping his creditors was to declare himself bankrupt.

After Bessell had been there a few days, David Holmes called him to say that he was also in New York. Why didn't they have lunch together? Feeling this might distract him from his own problems, Bessell eagerly accepted. They met, at Holmes's suggestion, at the Algonquin Hotel. In the 1920s this had been home to the Algonquin Round Table, an informal dining club at which some of the most notable literary figures of the day – Dorothy Parker, Robert Benchley and the playwright George S. Kaufman – would trade wisecracks.

Holmes and Bessell's conversation had rather less sparkle. They began by talking about how Thorpe's continued immersion in grief smacked of self-indulgence. 'He's wallowing in it,' said Holmes bluntly. Bessell wondered – possibly not without a twinge of hope – if Thorpe might be headed for a nervous breakdown. Holmes thought not, but did feel he was showing signs of becoming dangerously obsessive. In Bessell's absence, Thorpe had once again been on at Holmes to come up with a viable plan for murdering Norman Scott. What were they going to do?

As always, Bessell enjoyed Holmes's company. More importantly, he regarded him as respectable. With his heavy black glasses and his air of fastidious reserve, Holmes didn't look like the sort of person who would be mixed up in anything fishy. But, at the same time, Bessell found him almost impossible to read. Holmes's hobbies – Mozart operas and collecting small antiques – were as conservative as his appearance. There were times when Bessell wondered if this was all an elaborate front to conceal his true nature. Yet if Holmes was an enigma, he had never struck Bessell as being a particularly clever one.

Just as Thorpe and Scott had more in common than they would ever have wanted to acknowledge, so did Bessell and Holmes. Both of them idolized Thorpe. While Holmes was the more slavish in his devotions, Bessell had already proved that he was willing to put Thorpe's welfare above his own if the occasion demanded it. But why were they prepared to go to such lengths to help Thorpe? This was a question that Bessell often asked himself in later life. The only explanation he could come up with was that Thorpe had a remarkable capacity for inspiring not just loyalty in his friends but something far more than that – a willingness to endanger, even sacrifice, themselves on his behalf.

Without Thorpe's presence at the Algonquin, there was something ludicrous about discussing Scott's proposed murder. After all, Bessell hadn't made any attempt to lure him to America from Tal-y-bont. And, even if he had, it was highly unlikely Scott would ever have been given a visa. Thorpe, though, was under the impression that Scott was either on his way to the States – or else about to go.

By the end of lunch they had come up with what they felt was a viable plan. If the two of them could persuade Thorpe that they had done everything in their power to kill Scott – or have him killed – it was just possible he might conclude it was never going to work. But, in order for the plan to succeed, it was imperative that they should provide Thorpe with as much detail as possible. They needed to convince him that it had proved far too risky to hire a professional hitman. Instead, Holmes would do the job himself. Then they would say that something had gone wrong and they'd had to abandon the whole idea.

However distracted he was, Bessell could see that this wasn't a very good plan – it seemed to have almost as many holes in it as substance. But, unable to think of anything better, he decided to go along with it. In two days' time, he was flying to Florida – to talk to yet more banks – and Holmes said he would join him there to discuss it further.

As planned, they met outside the Howard Johnson Hotel in Fort Lauderdale. Before going inside, Holmes asked Bessell to have a look in the back of his rented car. Lying on the back seat was a gun.

Bessell stared at it in horror.

'But David, why?' he asked.

Holmes opened the door and told him to take a closer look. When he did, Bessell saw that it was a toy replica. In other circumstances he might have thought this was quite a good joke. Now, though, it just made him feel even more jittery. This sense only increased when they went into the café and Holmes unfolded a large map of Florida and laid it on the table. He pointed at a large, apparently uninhabited area in the middle of the state between Fort Lauderdale in the east and Naples in the west. Bessell saw it was called Big Cypress Swamp. Holmes said he was going to have a closer look at Big Cypress Swamp that evening so that he could describe it to Thorpe.

Bessell warned him to beware of rattlesnakes. Holmes shuddered and admitted that he had a phobia about snakes.

'David,' said Bessell. 'It's plain you were not cut out for murder.'

That night, Bessell decided that he too would go to look at Big Cypress Swamp. If Thorpe was to believe that they had done everything in their power to kill Scott, then he and Holmes were going to have to be able to withstand close questioning. As he drove into the swamp through the sticky night air, he saw in the beams of his headlights that there were deep ditches on either side of the narrow, unlit road. A body could be thrown into one of the ditches and lie there for weeks or months without being discovered, he realized. Either that, or it would be eaten by alligators.

Bessell found himself imagining what it would be like if Scott were really with him in the car. How he would stop in some prearranged spot in the middle of nowhere. Holmes would then step out of the darkness and shoot Scott through the head. 'I imagined heaving the warm body into the ditch where creatures of the night would gnaw and nibble at it like carrion.'

Driving back to West Palm Beach, where he was staying at the Holiday Inn, Bessell was overcome with a sudden sense of hopelessness. He thought about all the promises he'd made, all the women he had let down, all the financial disasters he had left in his wake. The sheer mess he had made of everything. After the oppressive gloom of Big Cypress Swamp, the neon signs and brightly lit streets of West Palm Beach felt like another world. But still Bessell's spirits did not lift.

In the hotel restaurant he sat and picked at his supper. A three-piece band began playing in one corner of the room and several elderly couples stood up and began to dance. On Bessell's table there was a candle burning in a red glass bowl. A moth kept flying round and round the bowl, getting closer and closer to the flame. Just before its wings caught fire, Bessell leaned over and blew out the candle. In that moment he came to a decision. He wasn't going to carry on like this. He wasn't going to carry on at all. He was going to kill himself.

20

A Death Unforeseen

Almost ten years earlier, in November 1961, when Norman Scott had first sat in St Stephen's Hall in the Palace of Westminster, he had looked up to see the grinning figure of Jeremy Thorpe bearing down on him with his arms flung wide. Now he watched as another figure walked across the black-and-white tiled floor to where he and Gwen Parry-Jones were sitting. Introducing herself as Helen Roberts, Emlyn Hooson's secretary, she explained that, regrettably, Mr Hooson had been called away on urgent business and wouldn't be back until that evening. Would they mind seeing David Steel, the Liberal Chief Whip, instead?

Scott suspected yet another ruse, another attempt to head him off at the pass. But they had already come this far – there wasn't much point going straight back to Wales. A few moments later the two of them were ushered into the Chief Whip's Office, where Steel, a dapper Scot, was sitting behind a large desk. As they were shown in, he stood up. Steel's first impressions of Scott were not favourable. 'He had a limp, clammy handshake, seemed to perspire profusely and spoke softly and hesitantly, giving the clear impression of having had some kind of nervous breakdown . . . In short he gave me the impression of being one of those rather inadequate drifters through life one meets from time to time who are always ready to blame their misfortunes on someone else.'

For his part, Scott, as he admits, was in 'a highly emotional state', while Gwen Parry-Jones was 'overawed and nervous'. Steel's immediate reaction was to dismiss Scott as a lunatic. Even so, he thought that he had better hear him out. Although Steel had already been briefed by Hooson on Parry-Jones's letters, he asked Scott to tell his story in his own words, hoping this might clarify matters. Scott duly plunged into a litany of the disasters that had befallen him, but, far from making anything clearer, Steel found himself becoming more and more confused. As Gwen Parry-Jones's second letter had mentioned Peter Bessell, both Steel and Hooson had assumed that he was the 'Liberal colleague' who had behaved so badly. Given Bessell's track-record, there was nothing surprising about that, but since he was no longer an MP any damage to the party was likely to be minimal.

Slowly the awful truth dawned on Steel. It wasn't Bessell that Parry-Jones had been referring to – it was Jeremy Thorpe. What's more, Scott apparently had letters to back up his claim. Lots of letters, which he proceeded to take out of a bag and hand to Steel. At this point Scott remembers Steel turning white. 'It was extraordinary; the blood literally drained from his face.' Steel saw that all of the letters were from Bessell and referred to a regular retainer that Scott had been paid – for what wasn't clear. One letter in particular stood out. It contained the line 'I have spoken to Jeremy Thorpe and put him in the picture regarding the present situation.'

There were others letters too, Scott claimed – love-letters, written to him by Thorpe. As Steel heard this, a single question kept resounding in his head. Could the sweaty, stammering Scott possibly be telling the truth? Like every other Liberal MP, Steel had heard rumours about Thorpe's private life, but he'd ignored them, assuming they were either untrue or irrelevant to his political career. But if Thorpe had actually been paying Scott a retainer, that changed everything. Although Steel was still disinclined to believe him, one thing Scott had said rang true. 'It was when he described how Jeremy had knocked on his door in the morning and asked how he liked his eggs boiled. I thought that was authentic Thorpe.'

Steel said that he would need to consult with his parliamentary colleagues. Could they have another meeting the next day? Scott told him he was happy to, but Gwen Parry-Jones had to go back to Wales. The moment Hooson returned to the House that evening, Steel called him into his office. Once again – according to Hooson – he was 'white as a sheet'.

'It's not about Bessell,' Steel explained. 'It's about Jeremy.'

They decided that the only thing to do was to speak directly to Thorpe – but he was away at the time, on a visit to Zambia. To complicate matters, the Whitsun recess was just coming up and Steel was due to go on a caravanning tour of Fife with his wife and two young children.

The next day, 27 May, Scott came back to face what was effectively a cross-examination conducted by Steel and Hooson. Again Scott mentioned the letters that Thorpe had sent him. Naturally Steel and Hooson wanted to see these letters, but Scott said they were no longer in his possession – he had given them to the police back in December 1962. Like Steel, Hooson's inclination was to dismiss Scott as a madman. 'I formed the strong impression that Norman Scott had a definite fixation about Jeremy Thorpe – somewhat in the manner of a jilted girl,' he said later.

Steel, though, wasn't so sure. Now that he had seen Scott again, he had revised his opinion. Steel could see that he was apt to be hysterical, but he didn't show any obvious signs of being mad. Before Scott left, Steel and Hooson asked if he could come back for a third time once the Whitsun recess was over. Feeling that he was at last getting somewhere, and being in no pressing hurry to return to North Wales, Scott agreed.

As an eminent barrister, Hooson had good contacts with the police. He managed to trace Edward Smith – formerly an Inspector, now a Detective Chief Inspector – one of the two policemen Scott claimed had interviewed him in 1962. Smith confirmed an interview had taken place, and that Scott had handed over some letters. These letters, he said, had been passed on to MI5. Hearing this, a tiny worm of doubt began to flex itself in Hooson's mind. As soon as Thorpe returned to London, Hooson called him up and demanded an explanation. Thorpe was quite frank about having met Scott, but insisted he had simply tried to help him out. In that case, Hooson asked, how had Scott been able to describe the décor of Thorpe's mother's house in Oxted as well as his old flat in Marsham Court?

Given that Thorpe had only just got off a flight from Zambia, he rode this pretty well. Yes, Scott had visited him on a number of occasions, he admitted, but nothing sexual had ever gone on between them. Hooson was not convinced. There would have to be an inquiry conducted by party grandees, he said. That was the only way of getting to the bottom of it. This, of course, was the last thing Thorpe wanted. He suggested they should meet the next day in his office in the House of Commons. Never lacking confidence in his persuasive powers, Thorpe felt sure he would be able to defuse the situation and talk Hooson round.

But Hooson proved more resistant than he had anticipated. The more he heard, the more he came to suspect that Thorpe was lying. Their meeting quickly erupted into a full-blown row. Hooson repeated that there would have to be an inquiry. Thorpe retaliated by threatening to use his contacts to destroy Hooson's career as a barrister – he didn't specify how. After a while they both calmed down, but Hooson still wanted assurances. What would happen if Scott's story was shown to be true? Would Thorpe resign as Leader?

'Of course,' said Thorpe brusquely. 'But it isn't and I won't.'

David Steel's caravanning tour of Fife proved a lot less restful than he had hoped. Every evening he would stop at a public phone box and call Emlyn Hooson to find out what was going on. He learned that Thorpe had given way over the inquiry – on condition that he could appoint the Chairman. This, he proposed, should be Lord Byers, Leader of the Liberals in the House of Lords. Byers had a distinguished war record and a prosperous business career. He was not, however, a man reckoned to possess enormous reserves of tact or subtlety.

At night, Steel lay awake in the caravan, worrying about what was going to happen. By the time he returned, a date for the inquiry had already been set. At two o'clock on the afternoon of 9 June 1971, Scott was shown into Lord Byers's office in the House of Lords. Facing him were Lord Byers, Emlyn Hooson and David Steel sitting at an oval oak table. Scott, by his own account, was very nervous. 'I had always been brought up to respect your elders and here were these three distinguished figures. It was extremely intimidating.'

Steel had hoped that Byers might adopt a conciliatory approach – he had already seen how easily Scott could flare up. But he knew too that Byers was not a man to use a nut-cracker when there was a sledgehammer to hand. Sure enough, Byers was aggressive from the moment Scott walked in, and only became more so as the meeting went on. When Scott had finished telling his story, Hooson asked him why he was pursuing this vendetta against Thorpe.

It wasn't a vendetta, Scott protested; he simply wanted his National Insurance card back. What's more, he said – in tears by now – he still loved Thorpe, even though he felt he'd been very badly treated by him. This was too much for Byers. Banging the table, he told Scott that he was nothing but a common blackmailer. He also said that he was mentally unstable and in obvious need of treatment. Where were these letters from Thorpe that Scott claimed to have? The letters that contained such damaging revelations? The reason he couldn't produce them was because they didn't exist.

Possibly Byers expected Scott to crumble at this point and slope off, never to return. If so he had hopelessly underestimated him. As Steel already suspected, Scott was made of much tougher stuff than he appeared to be. 'I'm the one who has been morally blackmailed!' Scott shouted. He went on to call Byers 'a pontificating old fart'. He did have evidence of his affair with Thorpe, he insisted, and he intended to get it.

Scott then stormed out, slamming the door behind him and leaving his three interrogators sitting in silence. All told, as Steel noted drily, 'The exchange had been less than useful.'

However angry Scott was, he had learned an important lesson: no one in authority was likely to believe him unless he could provide physical proof of his relationship with Thorpe. This meant getting hold of the letters he had handed to the police in 1962. And so, like Emlyn Hooson, he decided to track down Detective Chief Inspector Edward Smith.

When he went to Lucan Place Police Station in Chelsea, where the original interview had taken place, Scott learned that Smith had been transferred to Southwark Police Station. He left a message asking him to call, and went back to the flat where he was staying. Shortly afterwards, Smith called. They arranged to meet at Southwark the next day. When Scott arrived, he was taken to an interview room where Smith was waiting with another, more senior policeman – Detective Chief Superintendent John Perkins.

Scott had assumed that the meeting wouldn't take long, and that getting the letters back would be fairly straightforward. He was wrong on both counts. First, he was told that he would have to make a statement.

Why, he asked.

Smith wouldn't say, but claimed, 'It will help you in the future.'

Once again Scott went through the details of his relationship with Thorpe – in more exhaustive detail than ever. As the interview went on and the questions became increasingly pointed, he realized the police suspected him of trying to blackmail Thorpe.

After being quizzed for ten hours, Scott was asked to sign his statement – it ran to thirty-three pages – and then told he was free to go. It was now one o'clock in the morning. Detective Chief Superintendent Perkins drove him home. On the way Scott pointed out that he still hadn't got the letters back.

'Oh, I don't think you will ever see those again,' said Perkins.

The next day Scott headed back to North Wales, more convinced than ever that mysterious dark forces were massed against him. Meanwhile his statement ended up in the office of the Assistant Commissioner of the Metropolitan Police at Scotland Yard. There it was locked away in the iron safe that was used to store highly sensitive documents – the same safe that contained the statement Scott had given the police in 1962.

Much to Thorpe's annoyance, Emlyn Hooson was still sniffing about, trying to discover what had gone on. Hoping to kill off his investigations, Thorpe went to see Reginald Maudling, the Conservative Home Secretary. The two men had always got on well – both were members of an exclusive dining club, the Other

Club, which had been founded by Winston Churchill and met every fortnight in the Savoy Hotel. After giving Maudling a heavily doctored account of his problems with Scott, Thorpe explained that he was about to issue a statement to Lord Byers's inquiry. But, before doing so, he wanted to find out if the police were sitting on any further information about Scott.

Maudling advised him to go directly to Sir John Waldron, the Commissioner of the Metropolitan Police. Sir John Waldron was delighted to be of assistance. The police, he said, had no details of Norman Scott's psychiatric history – thus giving Thorpe a free hand to portray him as a deranged fantasist. Both Waldron and Maudling agreed to confirm that Thorpe's statement was accurate. Assuming that Waldron had read Thorpe's police file – and it's unthinkable that he wouldn't have done – he must have known that the statement was a ragbag of half-truths and outright lies. But, apart from making a couple of small changes, he raised no objections.

On 13 July 1971 Thorpe wrote a confidential letter to Reginald Maudling:

> *Dear Reggie,*
>
> *I am very grateful to you for your interest and help in the case of Scott. As far as Byers, Steel and myself are concerned, the case is closed. To the intense annoyance of all three of us, Hooson, whose motives are not entirely selfless, is intent to go on rummaging around, seeing if he can't stir up something. He's already suggested that I should have resigned from the leadership and possibly Parliament as well.*
>
> *Frank [Lord Byers] feels the only way to convince him that he is really muck-raking to no purpose is to set out the facts in a confidential letter from me to Frank, of which he would keep the letter but which Hooson should be shown. The enclosed is the letter which I propose to send Frank. Before I do so, I would want to be certain that it accurately reflects your own recollection of our exchanges and that of Sir John Waldron.*
>
> *In short, I would like to append to my private letter to Frank, a short note from you, and one from Waldron, or one from you on behalf of both,*

*saying that its contents are a fair summary. No more is required.
Needless to say it would remain in Frank's files and be treated as totally
confidential.*

*I am sorry to be a bother. But the first lesson in politics is that no one
can be as disloyal as one's own colleagues!*

*Yours ever
Jeremy*

Possibly Maudling suspected that Thorpe's account was neither
accurate nor comprehensive. At any rate his reply stopped some
way short of being a ringing endorsement:

Dear Jeremy,

*Thank you for showing me your letter to Frank Byers. I have shown it to
the Commissioner. Neither of us see any reason to disagree.*

R. M.

But, as far as Thorpe was concerned, it was more than enough. He
gleefully waved Maudling's letter in front of Frank Byers and Emlyn
Hooson, telling them it proved conclusively there was no substance
to Scott's allegations. After his own showdown with Scott, Byers
was only too happy to believe him. While Hooson still had his
doubts, there wasn't much he could do without any evidence – as
he wrote to Gwen Parry-Jones:

*Obviously my concern, and that of Mr Steel, is the very serious allega-
tions made against one of our colleagues in an eminent position which
are strenuously denied by that person. On the other hand, the young man
tells a very convincing story and is obviously in a very distressed state, so
that the question of corroboration is very important.*

Two days later, Gwen Parry-Jones replied. Only a month before she
had been only too eager to take up the cudgels on Scott's behalf.
But now something had changed. A measure of caution – possibly

even disillusion – had set in. 'The village at first accepted him,' she wrote of Scott,

> but later they all became suspicious and avoided him; as I do a lot of voluntary welfare work I felt it was my duty to try in my small way to provide him a meal and sit and listen to his troubles. At all times he was a perfect gentleman towards me and I saw no sinister motives, only in his mind about his guilty past, and it was a constant battle to him to try and prove that he wanted a more normal way of life – therefore no one can help him except himself to grow up and be a man.
>
> Don't if at all possible bring a case against him – he will not trouble you again.
>
> Thank you so much, sorry to have added more work to your already busy life.
>
> Yours sincerely
> L. G. Parry-Jones (Mrs)

Shortly after Norman Scott returned from London, he and Gwen Parry-Jones moved in together. Tal-y-bont looked on aghast. Hoping to take Scott's mind off Thorpe and the missing letters, she gave him £500 to help set up a pony-trekking centre. The trekking centre did well, with Scott teaching groups of children how to ride. But life at home proved much more fraught. Any dreams Parry-Jones had entertained that their relationship might work soon faded. It became painfully obvious that her feelings were much stronger than his. 'I think she was in love with me, but I wasn't in love with her,' he recalled.

She became increasingly depressed, and after a few weeks moved back to the house where she had been living before. A fortnight later, a letter arrived at Scott's house addressed to Parry-Jones. Thinking that it might be urgent, he opened it. The letter was from a woman who now ran the post office in Tal-y-bont. She had written to tell Parry-Jones that her aunt had been trying to contact her. Repeated attempts had failed and the aunt was growing concerned. Would Parry-Jones get in touch as soon as possible?

Immediately he read this, Scott felt that 'something was terribly wrong'. He phoned the postmistress and asked her to call the police. When the police went round to Parry-Jones's house and rang the bell, there was no reply. Breaking the door down, they found her upstairs in her bedroom. She was lying, dead, on her bed. The central heating was still turned on and her body was already badly decomposed, making it difficult to tell just when she had died, or how.

As far as Scott was concerned, Parry-Jones had killed herself, appalled by all the political corruption she had encountered. Throughout her life she had always had the highest respect for politicians, but after their visit to London her faith – so he maintained – had been shattered. It's possible that this had had something to do with her state of mind, although it hardly squares with her last letter to Emlyn Hooson. It's possible too that she had still been grieving for her husband, who had died less than a year earlier. But it's difficult to shake the suspicion that what Parry-Jones felt most of all was humiliated. She had very publicly taken up with a much younger man and then, not long afterwards, their relationship had fallen apart. In her own eyes – and the eyes of Tal-y-bont – she had made a fool of herself.

If the villagers had given Scott a wide berth before, now they literally turned their backs on him. Bookings for the trekking centre tailed off. There were even suggestions that Scott had murdered Parry-Jones. One man reported seeing a large object falling out of the side of Scott's van. Scott, he claimed, had got out and, apparently looking very shifty, had picked up this large object, then put it back in the van. The clear implication was that he had been trying to move Parry-Jones's body. The police investigated and found no evidence to connect him with her death.

None the less, Scott held himself responsible – 'I felt that disaster came upon all those with whom I had association,' he wrote later. At her inquest at Bangor Coroner's Court, in May 1972, he was called as a witness. Mrs Parry-Jones had been a 'very good woman, very moral', he declared. What's more, her death would never have happened if she hadn't met him. But he didn't stop there. Scott went on, unprompted, to describe how Mrs Parry-Jones had accompanied him to the House of Commons to try to sort out his problems – problems that resulted directly from the homosexual relationship he had once had with the Leader of the Liberal Party, Jeremy Thorpe.

Alarmed by this unexpected outburst, the coroner, Mr E. Pritchard-Jones, tried to shut him up: 'When he started to make his strange allegations against Mr Thorpe, I thought I don't want to know about this.' Reluctantly, Scott fell silent. Although traces of sedatives – Mogadon and Librium – were found in Parry-Jones's body, Pritchard-Jones concluded that she had died of alcohol poisoning.

'Mrs Parry-Jones did have mental troubles. But I am not satisfied that there is clear evidence of self-destruction and the safest course is to record an open verdict.'

By chance, a local journalist called Derek Bellis happened to be there that day. Bellis was no stranger to big stories – nine years earlier he had interviewed the Beatles when they played a six-night residency at the Odeon Cinema in Llandudno. Bangor Coroner's Court, however, was not normally a rich source of news. Bellis was only there because he was attending the inquest of a man who had died in a skiing accident. Having arrived early, he sat waiting in the back of the court, idly listening to what was going on. As soon as Scott launched into his speech, Bellis sat up, transfixed, quickly wrote a piece and then rushed out to ring every newspaper in London he had ever had dealings with.

21

A Simple Plan

Peter Bessell knew just how he was going to kill himself. First, he was going to take a Mandrax sleeping pill – he had been using these for several months and had found they not only made him drowsy; they also took away all his anxiety. Then he was going to drive to a secluded spot where there was a stretch of straight road, floor the accelerator and drive his car into a tree.

The likelihood was that a verdict of accidental death would be recorded at the inquest. As a result, his family would benefit from the life-insurance policy he had taken out some years earlier; if his death was classified as a suicide, the insurance company would never pay up. Also they would be spared the pain of knowing that he had taken his own life.

He knew too that he wanted to end his life in a place where he found the climate congenial. 'I wanted to feel the warmth of the sun, listen to the sound of the ocean and see a velvet night sky above me.' But, as Bessell drove around the backroads of Florida searching for a straight stretch of road and a suitably solid-looking tree, he realized there was one more thing he wanted to do before he died. Under the circumstances, it was an unusual last wish: he wanted to see Jack Hayward again.

The next morning Bessell called up to make an appointment and then booked himself a flight to Grand Bahama. Hayward met him at the airport in his Rolls-Royce with a Union Jack fluttering from the bonnet. Sitting on his terrace overlooking the beach, Bessell told Hayward all about his financial problems, and how he intended to kill himself the next day. While this must have come as quite a shock, Hayward doesn't seem to have been that surprised. Maybe he had already intuited that Bessell was someone whose morale was even more tightly pegged than most to the state of his bank balance.

But Bessell hadn't come to Grand Bahama to discuss his own difficulties, he explained. He had come because he wanted to do one last thing for Jeremy Thorpe. He gave Hayward a brief outline of what had gone on between Thorpe and Norman Scott. How their relationship had gone disastrously wrong and how he – Bessell – had been paying Scott retainers on Thorpe's behalf. After Bessell's death, Scott would need someone to turn to; otherwise he might try to tackle Thorpe directly. That must not be allowed to happen. Instead, he proposed telling Scott to go to Leonard Ross, his solicitor. But it was possible that, from time to time, 'small sums of money might be needed'.

Would Hayward consider providing them?

Yes, said Hayward, he would – as long as his identity was kept secret. 'You can count on me, Peter. I can't believe you won't find some way out of your difficulties, but whatever happens, don't worry about this fellow Scott. But if he finds out about me, he'll think he's found a bottomless well!'

Hayward then steered the conversation back to Bessell's problems. Couldn't he do something to help? Bessell was very touched by his offer. However, he said that he had reached his decision and nothing could deflect him from his course.

'Well, you know your own affairs, Peter,' Hayward said. 'But if you change your mind, you know where to find me.'

He insisted on driving Bessell back to the airport. As the two men parted, they shook hands. The last thing Bessell saw as he sat in the plane waiting to take off was Hayward standing on the tarmac, waving. Flying back to Palm Beach, he prepared himself for death. The next day, Bessell had decided, would be his last. But that night, in the sultry Florida heat, he was gripped by another, even stronger, desire. He longed to see Diane Kelly again. 'To touch her, feel her beside me, look at her beautiful eyes and to know the eager warmth of her arms around me – if only I could snatch from life one more weekend alone with her, death would be so much easier.' Hard on the heels of this vision, Bessell seemed to hear Jack Hayward's voice, as if from a long way away, reiterating what he had said earlier – 'If you change your mind, you know where to find me.'

First thing the next morning, Bessell headed back to the airport and booked another flight to Grand Bahama. This time he turned up unannounced. Had Hayward really meant what he had said, he asked. Absolutely, insisted Hayward. Why didn't they meet up again in New York the following week to discuss what he could do to help?

By the time Hayward came to New York, Bessell had spent a weekend with Diane Kelly and all thoughts of suicide had disappeared. Much of this was down to seeing her again – but not entirely. Kelly's father had also offered to help him. Keen to keep his daughter happy, Fred Miller, a wealthy accountant, was prepared to finance a New York office for Bessell and to set up an American subsidiary of 'Peter Bessell Ltd'. As for Hayward, he agreed to guarantee a £10,000 overdraft at Bessell's bank and to lend him another £25,000.

For months Bessell's creditors at the Plastic Carton Corporation had been angrily demanding their money. Now, armed with this new injection of funds, he was able to persuade them to accept an immediate down-payment to settle part of the debt, with the rest to come later. The storm had passed – or so it seemed. Once again, Bessell was able to lift his head and feel the sun beating down on his furrowed skin.

When Derek Bellis's story about Scott's outburst at Bangor Coroner's Court arrived in Fleet Street, Thorpe's office was asked for a statement. 'Mr Scott's allegations have been exhaustively investigated and there is not a scintilla of truth in them,' the statement said. 'He has a record of mental instability.' The moment news editors saw the words 'mental instability', they backed off. The story went unreported.

But Thorpe had already had some unwelcome press coverage to deal with. In May 1971, *The Times* reported: 'There is considerable surprise in Liberal circles about the life peerage which has been awarded, on Jeremy Thorpe's recommendation, to Simon Mackay, Joint Treasurer of the Scottish Liberals. Although he has fought three parliamentary elections at Galloway, many party members south of the Border have hardly heard of him. Some of them find it slightly puzzling that Mr Thorpe did not "nominate" a well-known party figure, such as Desmond Banks, the former Liberal Chairman, or Peter Bessell, who was MP for Bodmin.'

Bessell too was puzzled. When he asked what was going on, Thorpe explained that he'd had to change his plans. While Simon Mackay might be obscure, he was also very rich and had promised to give the Liberals £25,000. It was money the party badly needed after spending most of Jack Hayward's £150,000 on their election campaign. Any annoyance Bessell felt doesn't seem to have lasted long; the prospect of solvency meant much more to him than a peerage.

Thorpe decided to use some of Mackay's money on a new party political broadcast. He was keen that the party should connect with younger voters, and he cast around for a suitable format in which to put across his message. It's unclear who suggested that he should appear in front of an invited audience with the disc jockey Jimmy Savile, but it was an idea Thorpe eagerly embraced. By any standards they made a very peculiar couple: Savile clad all in black with his peroxide hair sticking out like mattress stuffing, and Thorpe in a dove-grey suit with an extravagant comb-over to conceal his bald patch.

At one point a member of the audience asked if it was ever permissible to break the law in this country. Both men vigorously shook their heads. 'I believe that this country is a democracy where people have no excuse to break the law,' said Thorpe. 'There are sufficient democratic outlets without having so to do.' Savile nodded his agreement.

Forty years on, Jimmy Savile was posthumously unmasked as the most notorious child abuser in British history. At the time of the broadcast, his sex-offending was at its most prolific. As for Thorpe, he had repeatedly discussed ways in which Norman Scott could be murdered. According to Bessell, he had also just sold a peerage in return for a political donation – an offence punishable by up to two years in prison.

Down in South Wales, Leo Abse had found another cause to campaign for. Increasingly concerned about the population explosion, he'd become convinced that one solution was a hitherto overlooked form of contraception: vasectomy. In the UK, the law to do with vasectomies was a muddle. Theoretically, surgeons who performed the operation could be prosecuted for impairing a man's ability to engage in hand-to-hand combat. When Phillip Whitehead, a newly elected Labour MP, announced that he intended to introduce a Private Members' Bill on legalization, Abse offered his support.

At first, Whitehead felt this was an offer he could happily refuse. Abse, inevitably, had his own theories as to why Parliament had fought shy of tackling the issue. He put it down to the 'Erotogenic Despair' that hovered over contemporary Britain. More specifically, it was a result of the 'Castration Complex' that apparently afflicted many – if not all – male Members of Parliament.

'There is, of course, a curious ambivalence in man's attitude to his sexual impulses and organs . . . Man's organs are regarded, in traditional Christian morality, as the source of impurity and sin, treated with contempt and attempted to be sternly controlled; yet, they can also be a source of pride, intimately connected with our self-esteem, dignity and power. And few are more prestigious, more concerned about power, than the politician.'

Not unreasonably, Whitehead felt that focusing too directly on a man's relationship with his sexual organs might do more harm than good. Abse's support for more readily available vasectomies also came with some awkward conditions attached. He felt it was vital that men who opted to have the operation should be carefully screened – to weed out those who wanted it not for contraceptive purposes, but because they 'neurotically desired self-abasement'.

Again, Whitehead felt that the number of men who wanted to have vasectomies in order to fulfil their masochistic fantasies was likely to be pretty small. But, at the same time, he knew his bill stood a much greater chance of success with an experienced campaigner alongside. Besides, Abse was on a roll by now; it wasn't going to be easy to stop him. If the issues were going to be properly aired, Abse felt that he needed to do something radical. At its Second Reading, in January 1972, he deliberately set out 'to steal the Bill and capture the headlines'.

Unlike Alasdair Mackenzie, whose concerns over Thorpe's rumoured homosexuality had so alarmed Bessell, Abse was not known for the brevity of his speeches – far from it. On this occasion, though, he excelled himself, giving the longest speech he had ever made in the House. In order that it should make the desired impact, he chose to vary the pitch of his voice, swooping from indignant barks to ominous rumbles. His language was equally dramatic and full of what he termed 'macabre illustrations'.

In the course of a wide-ranging address, Abse embraced subjects as diverse as 'the highly publicized perversions of the sad Lawrence of Arabia', the recently released film *A Clockwork Orange* and the business practices of the manufacturers of Durex, the London Rubber Company – 'a sinister monopoly'. He ended with a plea: 'Wisdom is what we men learn from our mistakes, and there is need for wisdom here.'

When Abse finally sat down, Laurie Pavitt, the Labour MP for Willesden West, congratulated him on his eloquence, which was 'matched only by his sartorial elegance' – even if, as Pavitt confessed, he had occasionally been unsure which side of the argument Abse was on.

Yet Abse's strategy paid off and in the end the bill was narrowly passed. After congratulating Phillip Whitehead on having achieved 'political maturation', a satisfied Abse went away hoping that the new legislation 'may perchance have added a little to family happiness in the land'.

In Manhattan, Peter Bessell was suffering from his own form of Erotogenic Despair. Having resolved to carry on living, he decided that he had better do something about his chaotic love-life. Although he was now having a full-blown affair with Diane Kelly, he was still married to Pauline. Things became even more awkward when Pauline landed a job with the United Nations in New York. Weighing up his options, Bessell decided that his only choice was to come clean. Any illusions that Pauline had once had about her husband had disappeared years earlier. None the less, she still loved him and was deeply upset by the news. In the end, they decided that Pauline would live in one rented apartment, while Bessell and Diane would live in another.

One afternoon in the autumn of 1972, Bessell was at home when the phone rang. It was Thorpe. He was in a state of great excitement. 'Take a deep breath, Besselli,' he said. 'I'm going to marry again, and this time it's royalty – well almost.'

'Good God!' exclaimed Bessell.

In fact, he had known for some months that Thorpe had been seeing Marion, Countess of Harewood. Born Marion Stein in Vienna, she had fled Austria with her parents just before the war. In England, Stein had gone on to become a successful concert pianist before marrying the Queen's first cousin, the Earl of Harewood. Not everyone in Harewood's circle had approved of the marriage – in large part because she was Jewish. One member of the Royal Family described her as having brought nothing to it except a Steinway piano. But she and the Queen always got on well – they were almost the same age – and they continued to see each other after her husband ran off with another musician, the violinist Patricia Tuckwell.

Now Thorpe was about to announce their engagement. 'Well,' he wanted to know, 'what'll that do for the image of the Liberal Leader?'

Not a lot, suspected Bessell – snobbery never having been one of the Liberals' besetting sins. He did, though, think it might finally signal the end of Thorpe's 'unhealthy sentimentality' over Caroline.

Thorpe's second marriage followed a similar pattern to his first. A modest wedding on 14 March 1973 at Paddington Register

1. An understandably pensive-looking Jeremy Thorpe
being squeezed out of his seat by his fellow
Liberal MP Cyril Smith.

2. Peter Bessell: the owner of a face like
'a badly tessellated pavement'.

3. Jeremy Thorpe and Caroline Allpass on their wedding day, May 1968.
'If it's the price I've got to pay to lead this old party, I'll pay it.'

4. David Holmes endeavouring to protect himself
from the coming storm.

5. Norman Scott: 'He was simply heaven,'
Thorpe told Bessell.

6. Andrew 'Gino' Newton: airline pilot,
gunman and dog-hater.

7. The public face of George Carman, QC: he was a very different man when he wasn't in court.

8. The indomitable Marion Thorpe, staunch as ever
in her husband's defence.

Office – this time with his financial adviser Robin Salinger as best man – was followed four months later by a lavishly immodest celebration. On gold-lettered cards bearing Thorpe's crest, almost a thousand guests were invited to attend a musical evening at the Opera House in Covent Garden. Once again there were criticisms that Thorpe was being too ostentatious. This time round Thorpe was more bullish. 'I don't care a damn,' he told the *Sunday Times*. 'One has to bloody well lead one's own life.'

The couple began their honeymoon in New York. During their stay, Thorpe and Bessell spent a day together. Still missing life in the House of Commons, Bessell was keen to hear all the latest news and gossip. Thorpe had plenty to tell him. The previous October the Liberal Party had pulled off a dramatic election victory in Rochdale in Lancashire, overturning a Labour majority of more than 5,000. Analysts were divided over what lay behind this victory. Some believed it was largely due to the unusual appeal of the Liberal candidate, an enormously fat, bluff Lancastrian called Cyril Smith, popularly known as 'Big Cyril'. Others, though, saw it as a more widespread indication that voters were growing disenchanted with the two main parties.

Six weeks later, the Liberals had another by-election victory: in Sutton and Cheam they won with a swing of 33 per cent. Now it was clear that something significant was going on. Thorpe believed there was a real possibility that the next General Election would result in a hung Parliament and that he – or rather the Liberal Party – would hold the balance of power.

After a while Thorpe and Bessell's conversation turned from politics to another, almost equally absorbing subject – their respective love-lives. Bessell told him all about Pauline and Diane. For his part, Thorpe said how happy he was with Marion. Not only was she well connected, but she shared his tastes in music, was fiercely loyal and had already formed a close bond with his son, Rupert. Not everything had changed, though. Thorpe admitted that he still had homosexual flings whenever he could.

'Does Marion have any inkling?' Bessell asked.

'Certainly not,' said Thorpe, and that was exactly how he intended to keep it. As he had done before with Caroline, Thorpe had brought up the subject in a vague sort of way, only this time the response had been far more extreme.

'She was shocked?' Bessell asked.

'Worse,' admitted Thorpe. 'She was disgusted.'

As always, Bessell adored being in Thorpe's company. Not only did it energize him; it made him feel valued. And he adored being with him even more now that Thorpe had given up his crazed plans to kill Norman Scott. Previously, David Holmes had told Bessell that Thorpe had believed their story of how they had tried – and failed – to bump off Scott. Holmes claimed that the two of them had endeavoured to lure him to Florida, intending to shoot him and dump his body in the big swamp. Unfortunately, Scott had failed to appear, and so they had given up. Of all the excuses ever offered for failing to kill someone, this must be among the limpest. Even so, it had apparently been enough to banish any thoughts of murder from Thorpe's mind.

Then, just before Thorpe went back to his hotel, he stopped and put his hand on Bessell's shoulder. 'By the way,' he said, 'we've still some unfinished business, you know.'

'What do you mean?'

'The Scottish Matter. I'll never feel safe while he's around.'

From New York, the Thorpes flew on to Grand Bahama, where they were the guests of Jack Hayward. While they were there, Hayward and Thorpe talked about a deal that they had first discussed some months earlier. Hayward had mentioned that he was thinking of selling several of his Freeport properties, and Thorpe had casually planted an idea. Why not have Peter Bessell broker the deal?

This wasn't an entirely altruistic suggestion. If the deal went through, Bessell and Thorpe would earn large slices of commission – possibly as much as a million dollars each. Hayward had agreed to the idea in principle, and Bessell had already spoken to a Director of the Mobil Oil Corporation. Assuming certain conditions could be met, Mobil were keen to come on board.

Then, with grim predictability, came disaster. Bessell had been convinced that a large property deal in Bronxville, a small town in New York State, would make his fortune – so convinced that he'd staked all of Diane's father's money on it. But the deal stalled and the banks threatened to pull out unless everything was signed within four weeks. Bessell was left in an all-too-familiar position – teetering on the edge of ruin. Once again his thoughts swung back to a long, straight stretch of road with a tree at the end of it.

On 12 December 1973, Bessell flew to London and went to see Thorpe at his new home in Orme Square – a large, stone-built Georgian house overlooking Kensington Gardens that Marion had received as part of her divorce settlement. After dinner, she left the two men alone. Bessell told Thorpe about his latest setback – if he didn't come up with close on half a million dollars by the beginning of January he was finished. What could he do? To begin with Thorpe couldn't think of anything. He asked Bessell to come back the following evening. In the meantime he would try to come up with something.

When Bessell turned up, Thorpe answered the door. He was grinning from ear to ear.

'Come in,' he said. 'I've got it!'

Thorpe had devised a plan. As he started to explain it, Bessell had to admit it was a very good plan. It was also startlingly bold. The plan involved Thorpe asking Jack Hayward for an advance on the commission from the sale of the Freeport property. Bessell would then be able to use his share of this money to pay off his debts from the property deal. There was only one possible snag. In order to get the money, they would have to pretend that the deal with Mobil was going ahead. While there was no reason to suspect it wouldn't, there was no guarantee at this stage that it would.

Bessell tried not to think about what would happen if this too went down the pan. But if, on the other hand, everything worked out, his life would be transformed once more. 'No more waking up in the morning, sitting on the edge of the bed, smoking cigarette after cigarette until I can force myself to face another day.'

'How much do you think we should ask for?' Thorpe asked.

'Four hundred and fifty thousand?' suggested Bessell.

'Make it five hundred,' said Thorpe. 'I need at least ten thousand pounds to settle the Scottish Matter.'

The next day he and Bessell went to the House of Commons. Sitting in his office, Thorpe picked up the phone and asked for an outside line. He began to explain to Hayward that he would need to pay the commission in advance. Admittedly, this was a little unorthodox, but there was nothing to worry about. Besides, he said, 'It's only five hundred thousand' – more than \$2.5 million today.

As Thorpe was speaking, it suddenly dawned on Bessell what was happening. 'The Leader of the Liberal Party, a politician respected for his integrity on all sides of the House of Commons and by millions throughout the country, was blatantly lying to a man who trusted him implicitly.' Nor was this the first time that Thorpe had engaged in financial chicanery. Only a month earlier the London and County Securities Group, a bank of which Thorpe was a Non-Executive Director, had crashed with debts of £50 million. The bank had previously attracted criticism for charging one borrower a punitive 280 per cent interest rate. Later, Thorpe would be censured for his role in the bank's affairs by a Department of Trade report.

Jack Hayward seemed quite unconcerned about having to pay the money in advance. Once he had run it past his lawyer, he would make the necessary arrangements, he said. The money should be in Bessell's account by the following morning. When Thorpe put the phone down, he stood up, grabbed Bessell by the shoulders and started waltzing him around the room.

'We've done it!' he cried. 'We've done it! We've done it!'

But after lunch the next day, when Bessell called in at his bank, the money had not come through. By the time he returned to his office, Hayward had called and left a message. Apparently there was a hitch. Would Bessell phone his lawyer? For a moment Bessell thought he might faint. After he had steadied himself, he called Hayward's lawyer and learned that the money would take another few days to arrive, as it was coming via the Channel Islands.

How long, Bessell wanted to know.

The lawyer couldn't say exactly.

Bessell had no choice but to go back to New York and wait. On the flight he chain-smoked, drank endless cups of tea and became increasingly convinced that something had gone wrong. Days went by and still the money did not appear. All that happened was that a business associate of Hayward asked him for more details about the Mobil deal. Bessell tried to reassure him everything was on track, but the man didn't seem convinced. The man also said that Hayward needed to consult further with his partners in the Freeport scheme.

Neither of these developments made Bessell feel any better.

On the phone Thorpe also sounded uncharacteristically edgy, telling him that he had to convince Hayward that the Mobil deal was going ahead. 'You've got to pull it off, Peter. Or we're both in the shit – and in a big way.'

But all Bessell's attempts to contact Hayward on the phone proved fruitless. As a last resort, he and Thorpe decided to fly out to Grand Bahama to talk to him face to face. Thorpe arranged for a private plane to fly them from Miami. On the way they ran into heavy turbulence, something Bessell took to be a bad omen.

In Grand Bahama, he prepared for their meeting by taking two Mandrax – he had recently upped his dose from one. When they arrived, Hayward was as welcoming as always, but a little reserved, Bessell thought. After the pleasantries were over, Thorpe did not equivocate.

'Jack,' he began, 'it's almost as if you don't trust us.'

For several seconds Hayward was silent. Then he turned towards Bessell and said, 'Now Peter can leave us.'

Bessell saw at once what had happened. Hayward didn't suspect Thorpe of trying to trick him – he hadn't gone that far. Instead, he had assumed that Bessell must be acting on his own. Standing up, he walked out of the room with as much dignity as he could muster and went back to his hotel. In a strange sort of way Bessell felt relieved. If anyone was going to have to take responsibility for the planned fraud, Bessell would rather it was him than Thorpe.

Before the meeting he had decided that he would have no choice but to kill himself if he didn't get the money. Now he realized there was an alternative. It was less drastic – but not by much. He could disappear. When Thorpe came back, Bessell told him what he had decided. Together with Diane, if she was willing, he was going to flee to some distant country – probably in South America, where he would be safe from his creditors and the police. Before he went, though, he intended to make it plain that any attempt to defraud Hayward was his and his alone.

Possibly Bessell hoped that Thorpe might object to this, however half-heartedly. If so, he was disappointed. Thorpe immediately agreed that under the circumstances it was the only realistic option. He told Bessell that as soon as he returned to London, he would ask his assistant to find out which countries in South America didn't have extradition treaties with the UK.

After that, there wasn't much left to say. Pleading tiredness, both men went to bed. On 2 January 1974, Thorpe caught a flight back to London from Miami. Bessell accompanied him to the airport. Watching Thorpe marching off splay-footed towards the departure gate, he felt sadness wash over him and wondered if they would ever see one another again. They would, but not for almost five years – and in circumstances that Bessell could never have dreamed of.

Two months earlier, in November 1973, the Manager of the Battersea Funfair had gone on trial at the Old Bailey accused of the manslaughter of five children. The children had been riding on the Big Dipper when the brake mechanism on their carriage failed and they slid backwards from the top of a one-in-three incline. The Manager – James Hogan – was represented by George Carman, QC, making one of his first court appearances in London. As far as the prosecution was concerned, the case was quite straightforward: the Manager of the funfair was responsible for ensuring the safety of all the rides and therefore culpable if something went wrong.

Carman's defence was not at all straightforward. He maintained that Hogan didn't know what the job entailed and should never have been given it in the first place. As he admitted, it wasn't much of a defence, but it was all he had. The night before his closing speech, Carman went out to dinner with a friend. After dinner they carried on drinking. Carman, who was never good at holding his liquor, became very drunk – so drunk that his friend had to help him home.

Before he left, he said, 'For Christ's sake, George, it's the biggest day of your life tomorrow, you'd better be on form.'

The next day, Carman addressed the jury. Also in court that day was Sir David Napley, perhaps the best-known lawyer in the country after Lord Goodman, and one of his partners, Christopher Murray. This was the first time either of them had seen Carman in action. Both of them were immediately struck by his manner. Whereas most barristers spoke as if they were addressing the back row of a packed theatre, Carman was much less showy and more conversational. But, while he plainly had an enormous facility with language and a knack for choosing memorable phrases, what made the most impression on Napley was Carman's effect on the jury – 'It seemed to me the jury were mesmerized.'

Murray too was enormously impressed. 'It was phenomenal, one of those spine-tingling episodes that happen very rarely in professional life, where suddenly you lift your head up and listen to an advocate for the first time and think gosh, this is something really special.'

After deliberating for four and a half hours the jury returned with its verdict. They found the Manager not guilty on all charges. As Napley left the court, he remarked to Murray that any barrister who could perform like that was worth keeping an eye on.

22

Things Fall Apart

When Bessell returned to England at the start of December 1973, he had been so preoccupied with his problems that he hadn't paid much attention to his surroundings. But even he couldn't help noticing that something very strange had happened in his absence. Hiring a car, he was told that he might have problems filling it up, as petrol supplies were running low. All over the country there were regular power cuts, because power stations were also short of fuel. Many factories had closed. Bessell arrived for one meeting in Mayfair to find the building in darkness. A secretary holding a torch led him through to a candlelit boardroom. It was like walking into a scene from a seventeenth-century Dutch painting.

For months the Prime Minister, Ted Heath, and the miners had been at loggerheads over the miners' demands for a pay rise in excess of 15 per cent. When the demand was turned down, the National Union of Mineworkers called a series of lightning strikes. At the same time, oil prices had shot up after the Arab-dominated Organization of Petroleum Exporting Countries (OPEC) imposed an oil embargo in protest at American involvement in the Yom Kippur War. By mid December the Central Electricity Generating Board warned that there were no longer enough fuel supplies left to last the winter. Floodlit football games were outlawed and television broadcasts turned off at half ten on weekdays. The country was shuddering to a halt.

In a desperate attempt to conserve fuel, Heath announced that from the beginning of January 1974 the working week would be cut from five days to three. But his hopes that public outrage might force the miners back to work proved unfounded. On 4 February, they voted for an all-out strike to start the following Sunday. Faced with such a blatant threat to his authority, Heath called a General Election, to be held on 28 February.

No other General Election of modern times has taken place against such a dramatic backdrop. Inflation was running at 17 per cent, while unemployment was at its highest level since the 1930s. But people weren't just frightened about losing their jobs; they were also frightened about losing their lives. The year before, the Provisional IRA had extended its bombing campaign to the British mainland. On the same day as the miners voted to strike, eleven people were killed when a bomb exploded on an army coach carrying soldiers and their families down the M62 near Leeds.

Thorpe was convinced that all this uncertainty would play in his favour. In an all-out bid to build on their by-elections gains, the Liberals decided to field more candidates than ever before – 517. When the election was announced, the Conservatives had a lead of around 7 per cent. But, as the campaign went on, the gap started to narrow. The closer the two main parties were, the greater the likelihood that the Liberals could storm through the middle and end up holding the balance of power.

This time, though, there were no helicopters to fly Thorpe around the country – the party's finances could no longer stretch to such expensive gimmicks. Once again, Jack Hayward dipped into his pocket, but not quite as deeply as before. Still convinced that Bessell had been acting alone when he had tried to defraud him, Hayward sent Thorpe a cheque for £60,000. Like its predecessor, it went not into the party's official account but into the unofficial one, to which only a select few had access.

As always, Thorpe made himself the centrepiece of the campaign. In the past he had done so – in part – because he was the only Liberal MP that voters would have been able to pick out in an identity parade. Now, though, he had a rival. No one who had ever seen Cyril Smith bearing down on them was likely to forget him in a hurry. As well as featuring prominently in the Liberals' publicity material, Smith fronted one of their two party political broadcasts.

'For goodness sake, let's get rid of all this hypocritical rubbish . . .' he declared in his homely, no-nonsense way. 'Let's cut the cackle and get on with it.'

The broadcast included a number of endorsements from celebrities, including Smith's friend Jimmy Savile, who sent a telegram of support: 'Jeremy, you built it up, now let it roll.' Like Savile, Cyril Smith would be posthumously exposed as a serial paedophile. In 2014 it was reported that there had been 144 complaints against him from boys as young as eight. Attempts to prosecute Smith had consistently been blocked, with police officers being told they would lose their jobs if they continued their investigations.

Jimmy Savile wasn't the only member of his family with close Liberal connections: his older brother Johnny was standing as the Liberal candidate in Battersea North. Fifteen years after his death in 1998, Johnny Savile was accused of sexually assaulting mentally ill patients at the hospital in Tooting, South London, where he worked as a recreation officer.

As the election campaign went into its final furlongs, Liberal morale was buoyed up by some remarkable opinion poll results. At the beginning of February, the Liberals had been on 10 per cent. Three weeks later, they had hit 28 per cent. This surge went straight to Thorpe's head and he declared that a 'Liberal landslide' was on the cards. His announcement appalled many of his fellow Liberals, but Thorpe was characteristically unabashed. The wind was at his back. Nothing, he felt convinced, could stop him now.

In Tal-y-bont, Norman Scott had become an outcast. Even his former friends there now shunned him. Closing down the trekking centre, he decided that the time had come for another move. But before Scott left Wales, he visited his son Benjamin. As Peter Bessell had predicted, Scott's hopes of winning custody of Benjamin had come to nothing. When his marriage was annulled in September 1972, he was awarded just four hours a year with him – on condition that a child protection officer was present throughout.

Scott travelled up to Lincolnshire, where Sue Myers was living with her parents. When he left, Benjamin gave him a present, a plastic Red Indian that had come in a cereal packet, and asked him to bring it when he next visited. But Scott went away feeling that the two of them could never have any sort of relationship under the circumstances. He never returned.

After leaving Tal-y-bont, Scott worked briefly on a stud farm in Sussex, and then two old friends of his, Jack and Stella Levy, told him that they had just bought a delightful old house in the small North Devon town of South Molton. Why didn't he stay there for a while? And so, in late 1972, Scott had moved back to Devon. As the Levys had promised, the house in South Molton was delightful. Unfortunately, it also happened to be next door to the local Liberal Club. With some money he had made, Scott bought himself a horse. One day, soon after he arrived, he was riding his horse through the centre of the town. On one side of the main square there was a gap through which only one car – or horse – could pass at a time. Approaching the gap, Scott saw a white Rover car waiting on the other side. Sitting behind the wheel was Jeremy Thorpe.

It was the first time Scott had seen him since 1964, eight years earlier. As he went past, he waved and called out 'Thank you!' in a loud voice. When he looked back several seconds later, the car had not moved. For Thorpe, this must have been proof that Scott was hell-bent on pursuing him, even going right into his heartland. In fact, Scott's main concern was trying to put his life back into some semblance of order, but once again circumstances had conspired to bring the two of them back together.

Maybe it was the shock of seeing Thorpe again, or maybe he was still upset over Gwen Parry-Jones's death, or maybe it was just his nature, but Scott soon slid downhill. He went to see a local doctor, Dr Ronald Gleadle, at the South Molton Medical Centre and poured out his life story – including his relationship with Thorpe. In case Gleadle thought he was a fantasist, Scott mentioned he had a number of letters from Peter Bessell, the former MP, which referred to retainer payments that Thorpe had sent him – the same letters Scott had shown David Steel in the House of Commons.

Gleadle was intrigued and asked if he could see these letters, and so Scott brought them along to his next appointment. Although Scott admitted that he was drinking heavily – as much as a bottle of gin a day – the doctor put him on a powerful anti-anxiety drug – Librium – and an equally powerful sleeping pill – Mogadon. But these only sent Scott into an even deeper spiral of shame and gloom. One evening, riven with guilt about his homosexuality, he took a razor blade and carved the word 'Incurable' on his arm.

After Dr Gleadle stitched him up, he suggested that Scott should go to see a friend of his, the Reverend Frederick Pennington. A man of unusually diverse interests, Pennington was a former bandleader and farmer who performed occasional exorcisms – both at his church in North Molton and, rather more unconventionally, at the health centre itself. According to another doctor who worked there, every Monday evening you could hear the moans and howling coming from upstairs.

The Reverend Pennington was also a keen amateur hypnotist. Both he and Gleadle thought that Scott might benefit from a course of hypnotherapy. Since two of the most powerful psychotropic drugs ever invented had failed to do him any good, Scott held out little hope that this would work. His suspicions were soon confirmed. But, once again, in various stages of consciousness, he trotted out his story about Thorpe.

Pennington was also fascinated – so fascinated that he decided to tape-record their hypnosis sessions. He then passed on the details of what Scott had said to an acquaintance of his, Tim Keigwin, Thorpe's Conservative rival in North Devon. At first Keigwin was inclined to dismiss the story as an elaborate fantasy, but Pennington convinced him there was something in it. Just what prompted Keigwin to take the word of a part-time exorcist and amateur hypnotist is not entirely clear. However, in January 1974 he was sufficiently curious to pay Scott a visit. Scott not only told Keigwin about his relationship with Thorpe, he gave him a written statement which went into even greater detail. Unsure what to do with this, Keigwin passed it on to Conservative Central Office.

There, no one else was sure what to do with it either and it flew up the chain of command, all the way to the Party Chairman, Lord Carrington. While Carrington didn't read Scott's statement – to do so would smack of prurience, he felt – he decided he had better tell the Prime Minister, Ted Heath. Both of them realized that Thorpe would be finished if Scott's allegations were found to have any substance. But Heath also knew that if he made political capital out of them, he would be broaching an unwritten code – one which held that politicians' private lives were their own business, however lurid they might be. He therefore decided to follow Carrington's advice: 'Don't touch them with a bargepole.'

It wasn't just the Reverend Pennington who felt that Scott's story deserved a wider audience – so did Dr Gleadle. If the doctor had any qualms about flouting his Hippocratic oath, they didn't stop him from going to see Thorpe's solicitor and friend, Michael Barnes. Gleadle told Barnes that he had a patient who was in possession of some compromising letters about his client.

By another strange coincidence, a mutual friend of both Thorpe and Barnes was staying there at the time – David Holmes. That night Holmes drove over to Thorpe's house. They met in the barn beside the house, where Holmes explained what was going on. 'It was decided that we had to have the letters. We could not risk publication with just a few days to go before polling.'

The next morning Holmes went to the South Molton Medical Centre, where he informed Dr Gleadle that he wanted to buy these compromising letters. Was the doctor prepared to act as an intermediary? Indeed he was. They then discussed money. Gleadle said he thought £25,000 would be a fair price. In his measured way, Holmes explained that this was impossible. After some light haggling, they settled on £2,500.

As the Levys wanted their house back, Scott had moved again – this time to an isolated bungalow on the edge of Exmoor. One night he had gone to bed at around half nine when he was woken by a loud knocking. Opening the door, he saw Dr Gleadle, who informed him that he must have Scott's letters immediately.

Catatonic from a cocktail of gin and Mogadon, Scott showed him the drawer where he kept them in a brown loose-leaf file. 'I was totally gaga. I said, "I don't understand what you're doing." He said, "It will all be all right. I'll leave a message on your kitchen table explaining what I've done. Come and see me tomorrow."'

After Holmes had paid Gleadle the £2,500, he and Michael Barnes drove back to Thorpe's house. The three men stayed up until three in the morning discussing what to do. Holmes and Barnes then drove to Barnes's house, where they threw the letters into the Aga and watched them burn. As far as Holmes was concerned, it was the culmination of a long but satisfactory day's work: another set of apparently incriminating letters had gone up in smoke.

The next morning, when Scott went into Lloyds Bank in South Molton, he found to his surprise that he now had £2,500 in his account. However, he was a lot less pleased when he learned that Gleadle had – as Scott saw it – stolen his letters. 'My main fear was that someone might use them to try to have me committed to a mental hospital. I walked straight over to the surgery and said, "What have you done with my file? I want it back." There was a terrible scene. I remember at one point a woman came in and said, "What's going on?" I said, "Dr Gleadle has stolen my letters!"'

Scott's fears turned out to be groundless. While Gleadle's behaviour may have been bizarre – baffling even – there's no suggestion that he wanted to have him committed. But it wasn't just Scott's fears that were groundless – so were David Holmes's. The only thing the letters proved was that Peter Bessell had been giving Scott a weekly retainer. Anyone reading them would have been far more likely to assume that Bessell – not Thorpe – was the one who had been trying to buy Scott's silence.

There was also another possibility, one that nobody seems to have considered. If Scott attached such importance to the letters, surely he would have made copies of them? In fact, that's exactly what he had done. In other words, Holmes had paid £2,500 for some worthless pieces of paper. However, he had done something far more stupid than that. Something that confirmed Peter Bessell's suspicions that, for all his urbanity and his love of small antiques, Holmes was a colossal chump. As he didn't have £2,500 on him in cash, Holmes had paid Dr Gleadle with one of his personal cheques – a cheque that was now sitting in a bank in South Molton.

For the first time, a direct line could be drawn from Scott, via Dr Gleadle, to David Holmes, Thorpe's oldest and closest friend. If anyone took the trouble to follow it, the paper trail now led right to Thorpe's door.

On election day, the final polls put Ted Heath ahead by as much as 5 per cent. By the time the counting began, Harold Wilson had all but abandoned hope and begun knocking back slugs of brandy. And then the results started coming in. At midnight, the result was too close to call. It stayed that way for much of the night. But by dawn the political landscape had undergone a dramatic change. The Conservatives had won the greatest share of the vote, with 37.9 per cent, while Labour had 37.2 per cent.

But none of this really mattered. All that counted was which party had the most seats – and that was Labour, with 301, four more than the Conservatives. The Liberals had won 19.3 per cent of the vote. If a system of proportional representation had been in place – something they had long campaigned for – this would have given them more than 100 seats. As it was, they had just 14, a gain of eight from the 1970 election. None the less, those 14 Liberal seats looked as if they might well prove crucial in determining which party formed the next government. While Thorpe's dream of winning outright may have been hopelessly pie-in-the-sky, his hopes of holding the balance of power were looking much more realistic.

For Thorpe personally the election had been a triumph. Having hung on to North Devon by a mere 369 votes four years earlier, he had increased his majority to more than 11,000. Never one to shy away from triumphalism, he and his supporters arranged to hold a candlelit rally through the streets of Barnstaple on the Saturday evening. In Downing Street, Ted Heath and his ministers sat glumly in the Cabinet Office trying to work out how to cling on to power. Meanwhile Harold Wilson, who had read the MI5 file on Thorpe and – like Heath – knew all about his affair with Norman Scott, thought seriously about leaking the file to the press. By destroying Thorpe's reputation, Wilson knew he would also scupper his chances of forming an alliance with the Conservatives. But in the end he took the advice of his Special Adviser, Bernard Donoughue: 'I said he should forget this muck-raking and not stoop to the gutter levels of the press.'

On the Saturday night the phone rang at Thorpe's cottage in Cobbaton. The babysitter answered and heard a man on the other end saying he was the duty officer at Number 10 Downing Street.

Could he speak to Mr Thorpe please?

The babysitter explained that Thorpe and Marion were still leading the candlelit parade in Barnstaple and wouldn't be back until half ten. The duty officer said he would call again later. By half ten Thorpe had returned home. At midnight, the phone still hadn't rung. Unable to stand the tension any longer, Thorpe rang 10 Downing Street and was put straight through to Ted Heath. It turned out that Heath had made several attempts to call, but the local exchange had broken down. After pointing out that the Liberals and the Conservatives had similar views on a number of subjects, Heath said he thought it would be a good idea if they met up.

Thorpe did not demur.

Heath had only one request: might they keep their meeting secret? Thorpe was happy to comply. The next morning he put on an overcoat and a pair of gumboots and left his cottage by the back door. A decoy car was parked outside the front of the house to throw reporters off the scent. Thorpe then walked across three muddy fields to where his assistant was waiting to drive him to Taunton Station. His date with destiny had finally arrived.

In New York, Peter Bessell had been busy planning his disappearance. Of the various countries he could flee to without running the risk of being extradited, he had decided that Nicaragua and Venezuela looked the most promising. Bessell knew that he couldn't tell anyone what he was planning, not even his children. Instead, he told them that if they hadn't heard from him in three days' time they should go look in his office safe. There he had left three letters – one for Paul, who was then twenty-one, one for Paula, who was twenty-four, and one for their mother, Pauline.

In the letters he admitted that he had lied about his financial situation, and described himself as a ruined, discredited failure. There was no money left, Bessell explained – nothing at all apart from the $200 in cash that he had put in each envelope. They would no longer be able to carry on living in the smart apartments he had been renting for them. All they could do was sell whatever assets they possessed and start again. He also wrote to his creditors, trying to explain how his property deal in Bronxville had come unstuck. Amid the chaos and the self-recrimination, one thing slipped Bessell's mind: he forgot all about the briefcase full of papers that he had hidden in his office in London in the summer of 1968.

He did, however, have some good news. Diane had agreed to go away with him, despite having just been given a new job. In January 1974, Bessell flew to Los Angeles – a trip Diane paid for. He had intended to stay in a cheap motel, but, to allay any suspicions, he felt he needed to keep up the pretence of being a successful businessman, so he decided to check into the Beverly Wilshire Hotel. Diane arrived the following morning, having left her new job without telling anyone where she was going. 'Everything was happening so quickly that there wasn't enough time for reflection. I went along because I loved him and it was the only way to dissuade him from committing suicide.'

To Bessell's dismay, she had brought their two dachshund puppies with her – 'I seriously doubted the wisdom of that.' After spending the night in the Beverly Wilshire, they hired a car the next morning and headed south, down Interstate 5, to Mexico. At three o'clock that afternoon, they crossed the border.

As they drove through the squalor of Tijuana, the implications of what they were doing hit Bessell more forcefully than ever. He had expected to feel some sense of relief at having left his responsibilities – and his debts – behind. Instead, he just felt desperately depressed.

They kept on driving until they reached the seaside town of Ensenada on the Baja California peninsula. There they stopped at a rundown motel and rented a cabin for $9 a night. While Diane had brought some travellers' cheques with her, Bessell now had $69 left to his name.

The following afternoon he sat on the beach gazing at Diane's dachshunds playing in the sand. Every so often, he would glance at his watch and wonder what was happening in New York. He imagined Paul and Paula reading the letters he had left for them. Bessell had always loved his daughter's hands – 'Pooh had small, exquisitely beautiful hands' – and he had very happy memories of holding them when she had been a child. Now he kept seeing them tearing open the envelope and finding what was inside. Both of them were bound to be worried sick: anyone reading his letters might well assume he was about to commit suicide. He wondered too how Diane's father, Fred Miller, would react when he discovered that all the money he had lent him had gone.

That night, Bessell took his customary two Mandrax and went to bed early. He woke up a few hours later feeling as if someone were sitting on his chest. He couldn't breathe. Although it was a hot night, he felt freezing cold. At the same time sweat was pouring off him. However excruciating the pain, Bessell was sufficiently aware to realize what was happening: he was having a heart attack.

23

Bessellised

From Paddington Station, Jeremy Thorpe went first to his house in Orme Square, where he changed into more formal clothes – clothes more befitting the occasion. He was then driven to Downing Street by Richard Moore, his friend and speechwriter. Although Thorpe was outwardly composed, Moore could tell how excited he was.

While Moore waited in the car outside, Thorpe went into Number 10. Emerging an hour later, he was unforthcoming to journalists, saying that he had better speak to his fellow MPs before saying anything. But his fellow MPs already knew about the meeting – a horde of press photographers had recorded Thorpe's coming and going – and they were furious. Not only did they think Thorpe had been disloyal by going to see Heath without telling them, but they suspected him of having struck a deal behind their backs. David Steel, the Chief Whip, only learned of the meeting on the lunchtime news – 'it was an extraordinary thing to do. A bizarre, but, I have to say, typical Jeremy act.' Even Eric Lubbock (later Lord Avebury), normally a staunch Thorpe supporter, felt that he had jumped the gun. 'The universal feeling in the party was that any sort of arrangement with the Tories was anathema.'

What, if anything, had Thorpe been offered in return for his support in a coalition? Thorpe himself later claimed that he could have become Foreign Secretary. According to Heath, he 'expressed a strong preference for the post of Home Secretary'. In fact, it's hard to imagine his being given either job. Heath was already wary of Thorpe. The idea of handing control of foreign policy to a man who had advocated bombing Rhodesia was never going to play well with the Tory faithful. And, knowing about Scott's allegations,

Heath would hardly have entrusted the country's security to some-one so vulnerable to blackmail.

As for the price of a deal, Thorpe insisted that nothing less than proportional representation would keep the Liberals happy. Desperate though he was to hang on to power, Heath found it impossible to agree to this. According to one Liberal, it was tanta-mount to inviting the Tories to sit in an electric chair, and then throw the switch themselves.

Over the weekend, Heath and Thorpe met again to try to ham-mer out a deal. The longer they went on, the less likely it became. Hovering over their negotiations was the knowledge that any coali-tion they managed to form would still be several seats short of a majority. On Monday morning, Thorpe went back to Number 10 for one last-ditch attempt. By six o'clock that evening they finally admitted it was hopeless. An hour later, Harold Wilson was driven to Buckingham Palace, where the Queen invited him to form a minority government. No one, least of all Wilson's closest allies, expected it to last more than a few months.

If there was to be another election soon, Thorpe wanted to be better prepared than before. That meant having more money, and so on 10 April he wrote to Jack Hayward. It was a letter that see-sawed uneasily between bluster and entreaty with the number of exclamation marks – high even by Thorpe's standards – offering some clue as to his embarrassment: 'Delicately, I would like to ask for two cheques! My reason is this: each candidate is limited to a total sum for his individual campaign. If he exceeds it by 1 penny he can be unseated! In my case I fought a national and a local cam-paign from Barnstaple. There is therefore an overlap on some expenditure which I would prefer not to have to argue about!'

It did, however, contain one brief, yet striking sentence about Peter Bessell. In the past Thorpe had described Bessell to Hayward as one of his most loyal lieutenants and trusted friends. But now the Mandarin Mask was more firmly set than ever.

'He is a bastard,' he wrote simply.

One of these cheques – for £40,000 – was to be made out to the

Liberal Party General Election Fund. The other – for £10,000 – was to go to a friend of Thorpe, a Parsee businessman called Nadir Dinshaw, who lived on Jersey in the Channel Islands. Thorpe was vague about why this was necessary, but implied that the cheque for £10,000 was to pay his own personal election expenses.

Three weeks later, after Hayward and his wife had been dinner guests at Orme Square, he sent Thorpe £50,000. Thorpe wrote again, this time adopting an even more servile crouch. 'It is difficult to tell you with any degree of adequacy just how grateful I – and through me the Liberal Party – have been for your munificent and magnificent help.' Then, just before he signed off, Thorpe rose off his knees to deliver another sharp jab: 'It was great to see you both at Orme Square. My only regret is that we both and in particular you should have been subjected to a dose of Bessellitis. Damn the man.'

Two days after he wrote this letter, on 16 May, Thorpe's older sister Camilla committed suicide at her home in Chester Square, Belgravia. Increasingly troubled by depression since the death of her husband five years earlier, Camilla had taken an overdose of barbiturates. She and her brother had been close since they were children, due in large part to their mother's blatant favouritism towards her son. None the less, Thorpe had to identify her body – as he'd done with his first wife, Caroline.

However upsetting he found this, he soon had something else to keep him occupied. As Thorpe – and just about everyone else – had anticipated, Wilson's government did not last long. After a summer spent stuttering from one crisis to another, the Prime Minister announced that there would be another General Election on 10 October, the first time there had been two elections in the same year since 1910. On this occasion the Liberals came up with an even more off-putting slogan: 'One More Heave!' Armed with Hayward's money, Thorpe promptly hired a hovercraft for £300 a day, a dynamic new form of transport that he felt was in keeping with the go-ahead image the Liberals were trying to project. Midway through the campaign it sank.

However, the British public proved reluctant to do any more

heaving on Thorpe's behalf. The party lost one seat, giving them thirteen MPs, while Thorpe's majority in North Devon was slashed by more than 4,000 votes. Wilson, though, was vindicated: Labour won a majority of three seats. As for Ted Heath, defeat marked the beginning of the end of his political career. No one – apart from Heath himself – had any doubt that he was finished. It was just a matter of when the axe would fall.

The doctor was adamant: Peter Bessell was suffering from a coronary occlusion. It was imperative that he should be taken straight to hospital. But Bessell refused to be moved. If he were going to die, he told Diane, he would rather do so in a rundown motel cabin than in a Mexican hospital. Reluctantly, the doctor agreed to let him stay where he was for the night. In the morning Bessell felt a little better. The pain in his chest had gone and, although he was unsteady on his feet, he was able to walk.

By now the idea of trying to disappear seemed more impractical than ever. Beset by intimations of mortality, all Bessell wanted to do was to turn round and drive back to America. 'I believed I was near the end; what had occurred in the night was similar to the first warning tremor of an earthquake.' Later that morning, they packed the car and, with Diane driving, headed north towards California. As soon as they reached San Diego, she wanted to take him to hospital, but again Bessell refused. While he didn't intend doing anything to hasten another coronary, he wasn't going to try to prevent one either. Instead, he asked her to call his daughter Paula in New York and reassure her that he was safe.

From San Diego they kept on driving until they reached the town of Oceanside. There they found another cheap motel on the beach. While Bessell rested up, Diane made another telephone call – to her father. There can't be many fathers who would be relaxed about their daughter taking up with a notorious philanderer – especially one with suicidal tendencies and a string of failed business ventures. From Fred Miller's perspective, Bessell's arrival in Diane's life must have seemed like a disaster: since she'd met him, her marriage had collapsed, she had walked out of a well-paid job, and apparently gone on the run.

Miller had also lost a lot of money by investing it in one of Bessell's doomed schemes. Under the circumstances he had every reason to want to fly out to California and finish Bessell off himself. But Miller was clearly a man with considerable reserves of forgiveness. He agreed to wind up Bessell's affairs and to do his best to keep his creditors at bay. He even paid Jack Hayward $10,000 of his own money in return for an unwritten promise that Hayward would take no further action against Bessell.

Among the other creditors were two banks – the Chase Manhattan in New York and the National Westminster in Plymouth. Due in large part to Miller's efforts, they both took a forgiving attitude to Bessell's misfortunes, the manager of the National Westminster in Plymouth writing to him in unusually philosophical tones: 'I am only too conscious of the frailties of man to have anything other than sympathy and understanding for you in the trauma you have experienced.'

By the time Bessell received this letter, he and Diane had decided to stay in Oceanside. They rented a tiny clapboard cottage overlooking the ocean – it had just one room and a bathroom. Although they had little money and scarcely any possessions, they were happy. Bessell found that the simple life suited him. He felt a sense of peace in Oceanside that he had seldom experienced before. He felt safe too, now that Fred Miller had pacified his creditors.

It was time, he decided, for another change of direction. In future, he wasn't going to engage in any more ambitious attempts to make his fortune. There would be no more plastic egg cartons or dodgy property deals. Instead, he was going to do something completely different: he was going to reinvent himself as a children's author. He discussed this plan with Diane and they decided that it should be a joint venture – with him writing the stories and Diane doing the illustrations.

Where had this idea come from? It's tempting to see Bessell's desire to live in a wooden cabin and write children's books as an attempt to escape into a world of innocence – a place where deceit, dishonesty and plans to dump dead bodies in Florida swamps had no place. It would be a way of purging himself of everything bad he had ever done, of finding peace before it was too late. What Bessell couldn't have known was that it was already too late. Once he had driven into the big swamp, there was no way out.

A month after the General Election, a builder and decorator named Anthony Johnson was working with his brother Donald and four other men doing up a suite of offices at 41 Pall Mall that had been hurriedly vacated by their previous tenant. As Johnson was working in the corridor of the suite, he noticed a glass-fronted door set into the ceiling. Only accessible by ladder, it had been painted over – 'so that it was not readily apparent'. Anthony Johnson showed this door to his brother and together they managed to force it open.

Inside were some old curtains and a leather briefcase. When they opened the briefcase, they found a large brown envelope fastened by a metal clasp. The envelope contained a number of black-and-white photographs of naked men, one of which had been inscribed on the back – 'To Jeremy, with love'. This was followed by some initials which they couldn't make out.

That night, Donald Johnson took the briefcase home and examined the contents more closely. As well as the photos, there were several letters bearing the House of Commons emblem and some bank statements in the name of Peter Bessell. Reading the bank statements, Johnson quickly deduced that this Bessell was in deep financial trouble. Another, much longer letter was addressed to Mrs Ursula Thorpe and signed by someone called Norman Josiffe.

The workmen had been told to dispose of everything in the office suite except for the carpets. But, rather than throw the contents of the briefcase away, they decided to call the *Sunday Mirror*. Later that day two reporters arrived at Bessell's old office and took away the briefcase. The next day the brothers called up to find out what had happened and were told they wouldn't be able to have the briefcase back. When they complained, they were invited to go to see the editor of the *Sunday Mirror*, Bob Edwards, that evening.

Over drinks in his office, Edwards explained that the letters belonged to Jeremy Thorpe, the Leader of the Liberal Party. That afternoon, said Edwards, he had been to the House of Commons, where he had personally handed them to Mr Thorpe. What Edwards omitted to tell Thorpe, or the Johnson brothers, was that – like Norman Scott – he had prudently photocopied all the documents before handing them over.

Several weeks later, the two brothers received a cheque for £200. With the cheque was a note explaining that this was a 'gratitude gift' and thanking them for having behaved in such a public-spirited fashion.

Having come so close to power and then seen it snatched away, Thorpe might have been expected to slip into the shadows for a while, perhaps even engage in some searching self-examination. But this had never been his style. In late November, he wrote to Jack Hayward asking for yet more money. The party needed it, he claimed, so that it could lobby for electoral reform – 'Once we get the system changed then we can go into coalition, since we'll have over 100 MPs and possibly 150.'

Once again he took a swipe at Bessell – or, rather, several swipes: 'I was *horrified* and shocked to hear of the extent to which that bastard Bessell landed you in the cart . . . The whole thing has sickened me . . . If with incredible generosity you felt disposed to close the [financial] gap I should be immensely grateful. But if as you say you think you have been Bessellised and that's that well I shall understand although will be bloody pushed! Damn the swine.'

By now it must have dawned on Hayward that nothing short of a selective meteor strike was ever going to give the Liberals 150 MPs. None the less, he agreed to send more money. The details of how much, and how it was to be sent, were outlined in a letter Thorpe wrote to him in March 1975. Again, he asked for two cheques. One for £7,000 should be made out to 'Liberal Election Funds', he wrote, and another, for £10,000, was, once again, to go to Nadir Dinshaw in the Channel Islands.

As he had been before, Thorpe was vague about why this was necessary. However, it was all perfectly above board, he assured Hayward. Ultimately, the money would go towards the same cause, namely 'keeping the Liberal Party alive'. But Thorpe had another, quite different plan in mind for the £10,000 – one that had nothing to do with keeping anything, or anybody, alive. After six years of talking about it, he had finally decided that the time had come to get rid of Norman Scott.

It's impossible to say just when Thorpe made up his mind that Scott should be killed. Nor does there seem to have been any one factor that pushed him over the edge. Perhaps it was the discovery of the cache of letters in Bessell's study, and the knowledge that the editor of the *Sunday Mirror* had seen them. Perhaps his sister's suicide had left him even more fixated with death than usual. Or perhaps he had just had enough of wondering where the next blow would fall.

Fifteen years after they had first met, he and Scott were locked in a macabre gavotte, with each one blaming the other for blighting his life. As long as Scott was alive, Thorpe lived in a perpetual state of fear. The only way of removing the fear was to shut him up for good. In the past, of course, Thorpe would have turned to Bessell. Instead, he told David Holmes what he wanted done – the £10,000 was to be used to pay someone to kill Scott. It was up to Holmes to sort out the details.

Holmes went away and thought about it. Then he called a friend of his in South Wales called John Le Mesurier. Widely known as 'John the Carpet', Le Mesurier was a genial 41-year-old who ran a cut-price carpet business near his home in Bridgend. It was their shared interest in carpets that had first brought him and Holmes together – Holmes had once been a Director of a company called the Magic Carpet Company. On this occasion, though, Holmes did not want to talk about carpets. He had something else to discuss.

*

In the summer of 1975, shortly after he had asked David Holmes to find someone to kill Norman Scott, Jeremy Thorpe appears to have had some sort of nervous breakdown. He suddenly cancelled all public engagements, left London and spent six weeks in his cottage in Devon. According to his mother, Ursula, Thorpe was suffering from stress. Apparently this had been brought on by his campaigning for the Referendum on whether Britain should stay in the EEC – he was staunchly pro membership. But Thorpe was not someone who normally suffered from stress, least of all when he was campaigning. In the light of what happened later, it seems likely that there was another reason why he shut himself away. A decision had been taken, a line crossed. For Thorpe, as well as for Holmes and Bessell, nothing would ever be the same again.

While Thorpe was holed up in his Devon cottage, a small-time crook and dealer in antique firearms called Dennis Meighan was phoned up by a man who described himself as 'a representative of Jeremy Thorpe', and asked if they could meet as a matter of some urgency. They had lunch together in an Italian restaurant in west London where the man eventually came to the reason for their meeting. Would Meighan consider killing a man called Norman Scott – described as 'a nuisance who had to be silenced' – for the good of the Liberal Party? Meighan was sufficiently taken with the idea to drive down to Devon to have a look at his potential victim. But once there he got cold feet and drove back to London. 'It's a big step, shooting somebody,' he later recalled. Meighan did, however, agree to ask around in case anyone else might be interested.

The 1975 annual Showmen's Dinner, a men-only charitable event to raise money for fairground workers, was held at the Savoy Hotel in Blackpool. Tickets cost £15 each, but included in the price was a bottle of spirits – whisky or brandy. Not surprisingly, the evening soon got out of hand. While all the guests were in high spirits, one of them was particularly boisterous. His name was Andrew Newton, and he was a 29-year-old commercial pilot with British Island

Airways – an airline based in Blackpool. Although he liked to be called Gino by his friends, they had another nickname for him: 'Chicken-brain'.

At some point during dinner – accounts are hazy – Newton was approached by a friend of his, George Deakin. Known in South Wales as 'The King of the One-Armed Bandits', Deakin was a small, sandy-haired man of thirty-one who had made a small fortune renting out slot machines. A few days earlier, Deakin had been asked if he knew anyone who might want to do what was described as 'a frightening job'. Might this be of any interest to Newton, Deakin wondered. Hearing that the fee involved would be between £5,000 and £10,000, Newton did not hesitate. 'I'm your man,' he told Deakin.

After dinner there was a mock-auction of topless women, during which Newton tried to stick meringues on the nipples of one of them. The woman's boyfriend, who was also among the guests, asked him to stop. But by this point Newton was swigging brandy straight from the bottle and had long passed the point of no return. A fight duly broke out and the two men had to be prised apart. As Newton later told police, 'That evening became fairly hectic as far as I was concerned and I had a lot to drink . . . I remember seeing a strip show and a comedian but I cannot really remember much more about that night.'

At the end of the dinner Newton was barely capable of walking, let alone driving, so Deakin drove him back to his flat in St Anne's. Before Deakin left, they agreed to speak in a few days' time about the proposal that he had mentioned earlier. Later that night, Newton was violently sick all over his bed.

24

The Man from Canada

Shortly before Christmas 1974, Norman Scott moved out of his isolated bungalow on Exmoor. He had begun to feel increasingly frightened there. One incident in particular had left him badly shaken. By his own account, Scott was about to go into the house for lunch one day when he heard the heavy rattle of a helicopter overhead. As he looked up, the helicopter began to descend. Sensing danger, he ran into the house and locked the doors. Two men got out of the helicopter – one smartly dressed in a grey suit, the other wearing an anorak. First, they banged on the front door of his house, then on the windows.

Meanwhile Scott was cowering on the other side of the front door. 'I was in a frightful sweat. I just had this strong feeling that they meant to do me harm.' The men went round the back and tried the door there. Then Scott heard the gate clanging outside. A few minutes later the helicopter took off, made a circuit of the house and disappeared off in the direction of Taunton.

After moving out, Scott spent Christmas with some friends of his, Janet and Christopher Lawrence, at their home near Barnstaple. Like him, the Lawrences were great animal lovers and had just bought a boisterous Great Dane puppy. They decided to call her Rinka, a Japanese name traditionally given to baby girls who were thought to possess unusually trusting temperaments.

In the New Year, Scott moved again, to stay with other friends. Having lost all faith in Dr Gleadle, he went to see another doctor, a consultant psychiatrist at the Exe Vale Mental Hospital in Exeter called Douglas Flack. After examining him, Dr Flack pronounced Scott sane, but suffering from a severe anxiety condition. During his examination, Scott told Flack about his experiences with Dr Glea-dle, and the sale of his letters. Concerned about a possible breach of ethics, Flack thought he had better inform the Medical Defence Union. As soon as they heard that Scott was claiming to have had a homosexual affair with a prominent politician, the Union told the Treasury Solicitor's Department – now the Government Legal Department. The Treasury Solicitor's in turn passed the details on to MI5, where they joined an already bulging file on Jeremy Thorpe.

Then came a number of other incidents which confirmed Scott's suspicions that something very strange was happening. One even-ing, he was drinking in his favourite pub in Barnstaple – the Market Inn – when he was told there was a phone call for him. Speaking with a thick German accent, the caller identified himself as a 'Mr Steiner' who worked for the magazine *Der Spiegel*. Steiner explained that he was doing a story on Jeremy Thorpe and asked if they could meet up. He'd heard that Scott had had an affair with Thorpe, and wondered if he had any evidence of this.

Yes, said Scott, he certainly did – he had photocopies of the let-ters for which David Holmes had paid £2,500. Would he mind bringing them with him? They arranged to meet two days later at the Imperial Hotel in Barnstaple. Scott took along some – but not all – of the photocopies in a folder. It was only after he got there that he realized he had no idea what Steiner looked like. Sitting in the lounge, Scott saw a silver Mercedes pull into the car park. 'I thought that's a German car; it must be him.' But the next thing he knew he was being paged by one of the staff – a Mr Steiner was on the phone for him.

Scott went out to the pay phone in the lobby, leaving his folder on the chair. The thickly accented Steiner apologized and explained that he had been called away to write a news story. It was a big story, Steiner explained. A huge story, in fact, one that was bound to be of interest to his readers – the Conservative Party had just chosen a 49-year-old mother of two called Margaret Thatcher to be their new Leader. Unfortunately, this meant they would have to meet up another time.

'When is that likely to be?' Scott asked. Instead of answering, Steiner rang off. Puzzled as well as a little fed up, Scott went back into the hotel lounge. It was only after he had sat down that he realized his folder had disappeared.

Partly in order to have a record of what was happening – and partly because he thought someone might publish it – Scott began to write a kind of memoir. In it, he recalled as much as he could of what had happened since he had first met Jeremy Thorpe. He also told several people that he was hoping to sell his story to a newspaper. Eight days after Steiner's non-appearance, Scott was walking through the covered market in Barnstaple late one night when he was beaten up. First, several men beat him to the ground, then they repeatedly kicked him – he lost two teeth and was knocked unconscious.

After coming round, Scott managed to stagger to the North Devon Infirmary. While he was being tended to, he tried to piece together what had happened. At first he assumed it was a random attack. Then, as his head cleared, he remembered what one of the men had said. 'He asked, "Are you Norman Josiffe?" I said, "Yes, I was" – even though it was a name I hadn't used for more than six years.' As soon as he said that, they started hitting him.

The £2,500 that Dr Gleadle had put in his bank account had all gone by now, and so Scott began sleeping rough. 'I used to spend the night in the public toilet at Rock Park in Barnstaple. I would drink myself into a stupor on rough cider and sleep on the floor in one of the cubicles. Then I did a stupid thing. I've always been a very clean person and I had never been down and out before. As I needed a bath, I went to a hotel – the Fortescue – and booked a room for the night. I didn't even stay there because I felt guilty; I just had a bath and then went back to the public loo.'

After he had been sleeping rough for about six weeks, a couple took pity on him and invited him to stay. While he was there, he had another mysterious phone call. A man called Ian Wright told Scott he had been trying to track him down, as he wanted to hire him for a modelling job. 'What he actually said was, "Can you get your arse up to London in a hurry?"'

The man claimed to work for a company called Pensiero Fashions and said he would pay him £800 for two weeks' work. Scott was immediately suspicious. 'I said, "There are at least five hundred good-looking models in London. I haven't been seen in a magazine for years. Why on earth do you want me?" ' Wright, however, was adamant that Scott was the one he wanted, and said he had booked a room for him at the Royal Garden Hotel in Kensington for the following night. He also left a contact number.

When he rang off, Scott called Directory Inquiries and found that there was no company called Pensiero Fashions. As for the number Wright had left, it turned out to be a public phone box in Trafalgar Square. Soon afterwards, the landlady of the Market Inn, the aptly named Mrs Edna Friendship, offered Scott a room in return for helping her with some chores. As the two of them were coming out of a folk concert in early September, two police officers grabbed Scott by the elbows and frogmarched him to a police car. When Scott protested that there was no need for them to be so rough, one of the officers said, 'Oh, yes, there is. We want to hang on to you.'

At Barnstaple Police Station, he was charged with leaving the Fortescue Hotel without paying his bill – 'obtaining a pecuniary advantage by deception'. But it soon became clear that the police weren't really concerned about the unpaid hotel bill. Instead, they wanted to know about some documents they believed Scott possessed. Scott said that any documents he had were private, whereupon the tone of the interview – fairly polite up to this point – changed.

One of the police officers, Detective Sergeant Furzeland, told him that they were taking orders directly from the Lord Privy Seal, the Prime Minister's unofficial representative in the House of Lords. Apparently someone from the Lord Privy Seal's office was coming down later that night. Scott was also told that if he didn't cooperate, he would be locked up and wouldn't 'see the light of day for fourteen years'.

Feeling that he didn't have much choice, Scott agreed to take the police to the Market Inn, where he gave them the remaining photocopies of his Bessell letters. They also wanted to see the manuscript of the memoir that they had heard he was writing. The police then escorted him back to the police station, where – quite deliberately, he thought – he was locked in one of the women's cells for the night. In the morning, he was taken to the Magistrates' Court and fined £58. After he had been sentenced, his papers were handed back.

Even then Scott might have dismissed these incidents as empty threats had it not been for a letter he received from his solicitor, Jeremy Ferguson, a few days later: 'Dear Mr Scott . . . I do think you are in very real danger of being badly hurt by some person who wishes to prevent your story from being published . . .' the letter began. 'He [Detective Sergeant Furzeland] told me that, like me, he feared if you stayed in this area too long and your views and intentions get publicly known, you are likely to suffer severe injury. Indeed it was for this reason that he asked that you should keep in touch with him if you do make any attempt to publish because he wants to be quite sure that if you are in danger, he will be able to afford you some protection.'

Fond though they were of animals, Scott's friends, the Lawrences, had begun to find Rinka rather a trial. She wasn't aggressive, not remotely, but she was now the size of a small pony and needed a lot of exercise. They wondered if Scott would be prepared to take her for a daily walk. Coincidentally, Mrs Friendship also had a Great Dane and Scott used to walk the two dogs together. One evening in early October 1975, he had just dropped the dogs off with their respective owners and was having a drink in another Barnstaple pub, the Three Tuns, when he noticed a man standing at the bar. The man was wearing a navy-blue donkey jacket and a polo-neck sweater.

However, it wasn't his appearance that made the most impression on Scott: it was his pipe. He was smoking a large Meerschaum with a curly stem and a silver ring around the bowl. It was the sort of pipe that Scott had seldom seen outside of a Sherlock Holmes film. Clouds of noxious-smelling smoke were coming out of the top of it. 'He looked totally incongruous. He was also staring at me.' Scott, who had always hated the smell of pipe tobacco, asked him if he would mind moving a little further down the bar. 'I wasn't rude or anything. I just explained I couldn't stand the smell. He moved to the other end of the bar, where he puffed away and glowered.'

Another week went by, and then, on Sunday, 12 October, at around midday, Scott was taking Mrs Friendship's dog back to the Market Inn when he saw the same man. Now he was standing beside a yellow Mazda wearing a red rally jacket. As Scott approached, he stepped forward and introduced himself. His name, he said, was Peter Keene. Scott nodded at him and was about to move on. But what the man said next stopped him in his tracks. 'He told me that I was in danger – very grave danger. Apparently some-one was coming from Canada to kill me, and was being paid more than a thousand pounds to do so.'

Keene claimed that he had been hired to protect Scott. Although he wouldn't say who had hired him, he offered to drive Scott to meet the person. For all sorts of reasons, Scott felt this was not a good idea. When he refused, Keene started to get annoyed. 'He said, "I wish you would fucking well come with me." ' Still Scott said no. He did, however, agree to have a drink with him in the hope of learning more about his mysterious protector. But first of all, he explained, he had to take the dog back to its owner.

Running into the Market Inn, Scott told Mrs Friendship to note down the number of the yellow Mazda. Then he and Keene went down the road to the Fortescue Hotel – the same hotel that Scott had booked into without paying the bill. In the bar, Keene had a bitter lemon while Scott, trying to steady his nerves, had a double Scotch. But they hadn't been there long when Keene complained that the barman was giving him peculiar looks and insisted they go somewhere else.

As they moved on again, this time to the Imperial Hotel, it

occurred to Scott that Keene was even more nervous than he was. When he asked Keene what exactly he did, he said that he was a 'Special Investigator', but wouldn't be drawn on what this involved. Clearly curious about Scott's relationship with Jeremy Thorpe, he made a great show of writing down his answers on sheets of pink paper, which he had brought with him. He also repeated that Scott was in mortal danger – apparently he had been 'within a hair's breadth' of being killed when they had last seen one another.

Scott still had no idea what to make of Keene. He was not the sort of man who naturally inspired confidence: 'He had this particularly off-putting estuarine whine when he talked.' But by now Scott was so confused that he didn't know who to trust. However shifty Keene might seem, Scott found it reassuring that someone apparently had his best interests at heart. They parted, with Keene saying he would be in touch again – just as soon as he heard that 'the man from Canada' had arrived in England.

When Scott told the Lawrences about this meeting, they made a suggestion – one they felt might be in all their interests. Since Scott and Rinka had formed such a close bond, why didn't she live with him? However docile the dog was, she made an undeniable impression and anybody intending to do him harm would be likely to think twice as soon as they saw her.

Nearly two weeks later, Scott went to house-sit for a friend in the village of Combe Martin and took Rinka with him. There was no phone at the house, but he told Mrs Friendship that if anyone wanted to reach him they could always leave a message at the local pub, the Pack of Cards. He was drinking in there on the evening of 23 October when the landlord said there was a call for him. Picking up the phone, Scott heard a voice say, 'Hello, is that Norman?'

'Yes,' he said.

'This is Andy.'

'Andy who?' Scott asked.

'I'm sorry . . .' said the voice. 'I meant Peter.'

Scott realized it was Keene. He noticed that he sounded breathless. Also that he was speaking from a pay phone – every so often the pips would go.

'He's here,' Keene said.

'Who is?'

'The man from Canada.'

'Are you sure?'

'He's arrived,' said Keene. 'And he's already in Devon.'

'What should I do?' asked Scott.

'Meet me tomorrow at six o'clock at the Delves Hotel in Combe Martin,' Keene told him, and then rang off.

25

Death on the Moor

The next evening Scott arrives at the Delves Hotel with Rinka trotting obediently behind him. Walking up to the hotel, he can see Keene waiting in a public phone box opposite the entrance. No longer in his rally jacket, Keene is now dressed in a black polo-neck sweater and a khaki-coloured anorak. Nor is he driving the yellow Mazda; instead, he's in a beaten-up blue Ford Cortina. Keene explains that he has to go to visit a client in Porlock about twenty miles away. Scott should go with him, he says. That way he will be able to protect him in case the man from Canada suddenly appears. It's only as they approach the car that Keene catches sight of Rinka for the first time. Abruptly, he stops. All his life Keene has had a phobia about dogs; the larger they are, the more he loathes them.

'I don't want that in the car,' he says, pointing at Rinka.

'If she's not coming, neither am I,' Scott tells him.

After much grumbling, Keene relents. But getting Rinka into the Cortina is not easy. As the car's back doors no longer open – they appear to have rusted to the chassis – she has to climb in through the driver's door. Once inside, she just about manages to lie down on the back seat. With Keene glancing suspiciously in the rear-view mirror, they set off for Porlock. By now it is already dark. It has also started to rain. Despite everything, Scott is feeling peculiarly relaxed. 'I just had this strange feeling that no harm was going to befall me.'

Shortly after leaving Combe Martin, Keene asks Scott to look in the glove compartment and find some matches. He wants to light his pipe, he explains. Although the thought of inhaling his pipe smoke makes Scott feel queasy, he reaches inside. There, he finds a matchbox, but it seems much heavier than it should. Sliding it open, Scott can see there are several small cylindrical objects inside. They make a light clicking sound when they knock together. For some reason it crosses Scott's mind that they might be pearls.

Brusquely, Keene tells him to put them back and have another look. This time Scott finds some matches. Keene passes him his pipe – the Meerschaum – and asks him to light it. The smell of the tobacco is even worse than Scott remembers, but the weather is so foul that he doesn't like to open the window.

At around half seven, they arrive in Porlock. Keene tells Scott to wait for him at the Castle Hotel – he will be back by eight o'clock. After half an hour he still hasn't appeared. Scott waits another twenty minutes. Thoroughly fed up and thinking he will have to pay for a taxi to take him home, he goes outside. The rain is so heavy that it's bouncing off the tarmac. Scott is about to go back in when he sees a car on the other side of the road flashing its lights at him. His first reaction is to ignore it – all this subterfuge is getting on his nerves. But the car keeps flashing its lights, so he runs over with Rinka beside him.

Keene winds down the window of the Cortina.

'I thought we were supposed to meet inside the pub,' Scott says.

'Oh, no,' says Keene. 'I can't possibly be seen with anyone.'

He then offers to drive Scott back to Combe Martin.

'But what about the man from Canada?' Scott wants to know.

Keene says that he doesn't know exactly where the man from Canada is. But there's no need to worry; he will look after him. Scott and Rinka get back into the Cortina. Shortly after half eight the car starts to make its way up Porlock Hill, towards the open moorland above. As they drive up the hill, visibility worsens. Along with the rain, fog has started coming down. Keene drives very slowly, rarely exceeding 20 mph. To Scott's surprise, he starts weaving the car back and forth from one side of the road to the other, all the while staring through the windscreen as though he's looking for someone, or something.

Despite Keene's driving, Scott is still feeling oddly relaxed, secure even. But there is something about Peter Keene that he doesn't know. His real name isn't Keene at all. It's Andrew Newton, and he hasn't been sent to protect Scott, but to kill him. As Newton peers through the windscreen, he's trying to find a cardboard box he had put on the verge earlier to mark a suitable spot where Scott's body could be buried.

When Scott asks if he is feeling all right, Newton admits to being tired. Even though he's never held a licence in his life, Scott offers to take the wheel. Newton agrees this is a good idea, and suggests they should change places as soon as the road levels out. They carry on in silence. While the fog is lifting a little, the rain is still pelting down. Scott can hear it drumming on the car roof.

Having reached the top of the hill, Newton pulls over. Ahead of them, in pitch-darkness, lies Exmoor, with miles of uninhabited moorland before the nearest village. To their right, Scott can see the lights of Cardiff on the horizon. Opening the passenger door, Scott runs through the rain to the other side of the car. Newton too has got out – and so has Rinka, apparently under the impression that she's about to be taken for a walk. As soon as Rinka sees Scott, she starts jumping excitedly up at him. Scott takes hold of the chain around her neck and starts to explain to Newton that there had been no need for him to get wet – he could simply have slid across on to the passenger seat.

But Newton just says, 'Oh, no, this is it.'

Scott never hears the shot. The next thing he knows Rinka has slumped against his body and slid to the ground. Reaching down to touch her head, Scott finds that his hands are sticky. Although it's too dark for him to see anything, he feels certain that the stickiness is blood.

'What have you done?' he cries.

As Scott kneels on the ground, he feels something hard press against his head. Then he hears Newton say, quite distinctly, 'It's your turn now.'

Without thinking, Scott jumps up and runs away – across the grass verge and on to the moor. But as he runs, he realizes that he's heading straight towards the lights of Cardiff. Backlit by a bright orange glow, he could hardly have presented an easier target if he tried. All at once he stops. Convinced now that he's about to be killed, Scott decides he would rather die with his dog than by himself. Soaking wet and covered in Rinka's blood, he turns and starts running back towards the car.

As he approaches, Scott sees Newton in the headlights behind a curtain of rain. In his hand he's holding a revolver. Bending down, Newton begins shaking the gun about. Scott can hear him shouting 'Fuck it! Fuck it! Fuck it!' over and over again.

Suddenly, Newton jumps in the car, slews it around with the wheels spinning in the mud and drives off, back down Porlock Hill. Scott kneels by Rinka's body, worried that if he moves he might never find it again in the darkness. Several minutes later, he looks up. In the distance he sees a pair of headlights.

Scott watches as the lights approach. When at last the car comes over the brow of the hill, he rushes out into the road, waving his arms. At first he thinks the car isn't going to stop, but then it slows down and pulls over. Inside are an off-duty AA patrolman called Ted Lethaby, his wife and two friends.

'Please help me,' gasps Scott, close to fainting now. 'Someone's shot my dog and tried to shoot me.'

PART THREE

26

Vive les trois mousquetaires!

Norman Scott was covered in so much blood that at first the police thought he must have been shot. He was driven in the back of an ambulance to Minehead Hospital, where a doctor ascertained that he was uninjured – though plainly in a state of shock. From there he was taken to Minehead Police Station. 'It's all the fault of that bloody man Thorpe,' Scott told the police officers who interviewed him. 'He has destroyed me completely and now he has involved my animal.' Yet again he ran through what had happened: his seduction by Thorpe, the National Insurance card, the mysterious incidents of the last few weeks. In passing, he mentioned the book he was writing about his life.

The police duly noted this down, then drove him back to Combe Martin. The next day another policeman, Detective Sergeant McCreery, came to the cottage. Whereas the police the night before had been sympathetic, McCreery was more sceptical. Scott's story sounded 'a bit too fantastic', he said. He went on to imply that Scott had shot Rinka himself in order to publicize his book. Although Scott didn't know much about publishing, he thought it highly unlikely that anyone, even an author, would go to such lengths for the sake of publicity. Still McCreery was not convinced.

Then came the first real lead. Mrs Edna Friendship walked into Barnstaple Police Station with the number of the yellow Mazda which Scott had asked her to note down. The car turned out to belong to a hire company in Blackpool. From there it was simple enough to find out who had hired it on the day in question. But Newton had vanished – he and his girlfriend had gone on holiday to Karachi.

When the two of them returned, on 18 November 1975, he was arrested at Heathrow and taken for questioning. Asked to account for his behaviour, Newton decided, not for the first – or last – time to let his imagination run wild. He claimed that Scott had been blackmailing him over some compromising photographs that he had obtained. Apparently these had appeared in a contact magazine where Newton had advertised for a 'lady of leisure'. But instead of a lady of leisure, Scott had turned up, threatening to send the photographs to Newton's employers.

While Newton admitted shooting the dog, he denied ever intending to kill Scott – 'I wanted to frighten him, but the gun wouldn't go off.' After being questioned for two days, he was charged with possession of a firearm with intent to endanger life and then released on bail. However fantastical this story was, the police were inclined to give it more credence than Scott's version of events. When they questioned him again at Minehead Police Station, they took a much harder line than before. According to Scott, they banged his head repeatedly against the wall and denied him his medication. They also made it clear that they considered homosexuals to be more prone to hysterical fantasizing than heterosexuals. Perhaps they thought this might shame Scott into silence. If so, they too had underestimated him. 'I wonder what deviations you get up to in your own bed,' he shot back. The atmosphere in the interview room did not improve.

Thus far the press hadn't got wind of any of these developments. But all that changed on 31 October 1975, when the *West Somerset Free Press*, a small family-owned newspaper with a circulation of less than 10,000, ran a story under the headline 'The Great Dane Mystery: Dog-in-a-Fog Case Baffles Police': 'Police are believed to be still investigating at press time, a mystery as impenetrable as moorland fog, in which a self-described political writer is said to have claimed that an attempt was made on his life. Police at Bridgwater refused to confirm or deny a story that has gained circulation – that the killer of the pet also tried to shoot the man, but that the gun jammed. Neither would they say whether the dog owner is a Mr Norman Scott of Park Lane, Combe Martin.'

It would soon become the most famous story in the newspaper's history.

Among Peter Bessell and Diane Kelly's few possessions at their tiny beach-house in Oceanside was a television set. On New Year's Eve 1975, they watched a live broadcast from Times Square in New York City. The screen showed a huge illuminated ball on top of the Allied Chemical Building. As the countdown to midnight began, the ball started moving down the front of the building, hitting the ground just as the chimes of midnight rang out. Diane and Bessell embraced with tears in their eyes. 'I have a feeling this is really going to be our year,' she said.

Bessell too was feeling optimistic. He had now written three drafts of his children's book. It was about a small extra-terrestrial being called Moon who lands on Earth and is looked after by a man with a marked resemblance to Bessell himself – a well intentioned if occasionally misguided man with an abiding faith in human nature. He had also started doing some consultancy work in Los Angeles, which brought them in a modest income. And in three weeks' time he and Diane were going to be entertaining their first visitor from England. Both of them felt this was going to mark an important step in their social rehabilitation, even if their visitor wouldn't necessarily have been top of Bessell's guest-list. David Holmes was coming to stay. He had called at the end of December to say that he was going to San Francisco on holiday and asked if he could drop in.

'How is Jeremy?' Bessell asked.

'He sends you both his love. He's well, but a bit worried,' Holmes told him.

When Bessell asked what he was worried about, Holmes said he would rather not say over the phone. He arrived bearing a gift from Thorpe – a copy of a book about Lloyd George. Inside Thorpe had written:

For Peter, from Jeremy with affection

From one Liberal to another Liberal about a third Liberal.
Vive les trois mousquetaires!
New Year 1976

After the pleasantries were over, Holmes asked if they could speak in private. As there was no spare bedroom in their house, Bessell had booked Holmes into a local hotel – the Bridge Motor Inn. He suggested that they could talk on their way to the hotel.

'The problem,' said Holmes as soon as they had set off, 'is Norman Scott.'

It had been so long since Bessell had heard Scott's name that for a moment he didn't realize who Holmes was talking about.

'Oh, you mean Josiffe. Don't tell me he's still around?'

'Very much so,' said Holmes stiffly.

He proceeded to tell him a story – a story that to Holmes's dismay soon had Bessell snorting with amusement. According to Holmes, Scott had been blackmailing a promiscuous airline pilot called Andrew Newton. One night, as they were driving across Exmoor, an argument had broken out during which Newton had shot Scott's dog. Bessell, who had always liked dogs, asked what breed it was. Even more stiffly than before, Holmes said that he didn't know, but it was big – very big. The problem, Holmes explained, was that the pilot had been arrested. When Newton appeared in court, Scott would be called as a witness. Judging by his past behaviour, he was sure to repeat his allegations about Jeremy Thorpe.

Still Bessell couldn't see what any of this had to do with him. But he didn't have to wait long to find out. If Scott could be shown to have a previous history of blackmail, Holmes said, no judge would believe a word he said.

'What do you mean, a previous history of blackmail?' Bessell asked.

'Well . . .' said Holmes. 'Let's say that you were to write a letter saying that Scott had also tried to blackmail you.'

It was at this point that Bessell realized that Holmes's visit might not be entirely social.

Had he talked this plan over with Thorpe, he asked. Holmes admitted that he had – as a matter of fact it had been Thorpe's idea. Bessell said he would need to think about it. The more he did so, the worse an idea it seemed. What if he was ever asked to prove that he had been blackmailed by Scott? Then he could be accused of perjury.

'No, no, that will never happen,' Holmes assured him. 'Really the letter is only an aide-memoire.'

That evening Holmes came to dinner with Bessell and Diane. Although the dinner went well, one incident gave Bessell pause for thought. The three of them had been having coffee when he glanced over at Holmes. To his surprise, he saw that Holmes was staring straight ahead of him with a strange expression on his face. 'His eyes had a hunted expression and for a moment I sensed something I could not understand and it made me uneasy.'

After Holmes had gone back to his hotel, Bessell mentioned his proposal to Diane. She made her feelings quite clear: he would have to be crazy to agree. Bessell suspected she was right. Then, in the middle of the night, he woke up with a disturbing memory going round and round in his head. Years earlier, he had been in Cornwall with his wife Pauline when she had said, 'That Josiffe business is going to bring Jeremy down one day. And when it does – Jeremy'll drag you down with him.'

'Nonsense,' Bessell had retorted. 'In any case how could Jeremy drag me down?'

'I don't know. But you mark my words – he will.'

The next morning Bessell went round to Holmes's hotel to drive him to the airport. In his hand he was carrying a portable typewriter.

'All right,' Bessell told him. 'I'll do it.'

Of all the many crackpot things Bessell did, this is the hardest to explain. His instinctive reaction had been to refuse Holmes's request. Diane, whose judgement he trusted completely, had left him in no doubt about how she felt. And he had even had an ominously prophetic memory in the middle of the night. Yet still he went ahead. The only explanation Bessell himself could offer is that he was flattered to be asked. Despite everything, he yearned to feel the warmth of Thorpe's approval.

The moment he agreed, Holmes took some sheets of House of Commons notepaper out of his pocket. This turned out to be a draft that Thorpe had already written, in effect telling Bessell what to say. Although he altered a few passages, Bessell basically did what Thorpe wanted. He wrote that, when they'd first met, Scott had been 'extremely polite and grateful for the help I was trying to give him'. But then Scott's behaviour had changed. 'He came to see me and threatened to expose the fact that I was having a relationship with my private secretary. Naturally this alarmed me since an exposure of this kind would have been disturbing to my wife and children and damaging to my political career . . . I submitted to his demand in part, gave him a few pounds and promised to see him again on my return. Of course, this was the wrong thing to do, but under the pressure of the moment I took the wrong course.'

All this of course was nonsense. So too was Bessell's claim that he had paid Scott money to keep him quiet. After he had signed the letter, Bessell looked at what he had written, then added a postscript – one that seemed intended to convince himself as much as anyone else that he was a virtuous man: 'PS I should add that it was my practice to help people in serious difficulty during the time I was an MP. What I did for Scott was not unique, as many of my former constituents would confirm.'

Afterwards Holmes took Thorpe's draft into the bathroom, tore it into little pieces and flushed it down the toilet. He then dialled Thorpe's number in London. Marion answered and told him that Jeremy was out. 'Just tell him – mission accomplished,' Holmes said.

Once again Bessell felt suspicious. On the way to the airport, he asked Holmes if he was holding something back. At first Holmes didn't answer. Then, when at last he did, he spoke so softly that Bessell had to ask him to speak up.

'The pilot was hired to kill Scott,' said Holmes.

Bessell realized he should have thought of this earlier. But how had Thorpe found a hitman, he wanted to know.

There was another pause.

'Jeremy didn't,' Holmes told him. 'I did.'

'Oh, Christ, David!'

Holmes went on to say that the pilot was going to be paid £10,000, but the plan had gone wrong. After Newton had shot the dog, his gun had jammed and he had driven off into the night. Listening to this, Bessell wondered if he were dreaming – 'it was like an excerpt from a badly written detective novel.'

When they reached the airport, he dropped Holmes off at the terminal and went to park his car. As he was doing so, he had a thought. Now that Holmes had admitted he had hired Newton to kill Scott, Bessell couldn't allow him to go off with his letter. Apart from anything else, it suggested that he, rather than Thorpe, had a motive for wanting Scott dead.

In a panic, Bessell began running towards the terminal. But he soon became breathless and had to slow down. Although Holmes had promised to wait for him, by the time Bessell got there he had gone. Bessell rushed to the departure gate. Through the window he could see Holmes's plane on the runway. As he watched, the plane door closed and the mobile staircase started to move away.

27

A Bloody Mess

The moment Jeremy Thorpe learned that Norman Scott was going to be called as a witness at Andrew Newton's trial, he knew he had to do something – anything – to minimize the likely damage. He decided to pay a visit to the Liberals' newly appointed Chief Whip, Cyril Smith. As Chief Whip, Smith was responsible for ensuring that Liberal MPs fell into line when it came to a vote.

But there was more to the job than that. The Chief Whip was also the unofficial custodian of the party's morals. If there were any possible scandals or embarrassments hovering on the horizon, he needed to know. It's hard to conceive of a more blatant case of the blind leading the blind than this – even if Thorpe is unlikely to have known anything about Smith's sexual proclivities.

As Smith later recalled, 'I was totally unprepared for the conversation that followed as Jeremy sat down on a small stool, crossed his legs and asked, "Have you heard about my hot head?"

' "No," I said, "what hot head?"

' "I think I will have to tell you about it – it could lead to some publicity." '

Thorpe told Smith that a deeply unstable man would soon be appearing in court, where he would almost certainly claim that the two of them had once had a homosexual relationship. Once he had got over his surprise, Smith gazed pensively at the Himalayan reaches of his waistband, then said that he didn't think there was anything to worry about. If this man was as unstable as Thorpe claimed, no one was likely to believe him.

But after Thorpe had gone away, Smith decided to do some investigating of his own. For the first time he learned about Scott's visit to David Steel in 1971, and about Peter Bessell's payments. He also went to see the Home Secretary, Roy Jenkins. Happy to help a fellow MP who was in difficulties, Jenkins – as Smith put it – offered to 'draw the attention of the police to Scott's background'.

Already the danger was much closer than Thorpe had realized. In Somerset, Auberon Waugh, son of the novelist Evelyn Waugh and the author of a column for the satirical magazine *Private Eye*, had seen the story about the mysterious case of the dog in the fog. Although Waugh had never met Thorpe, he had always detested him from afar – partly because he felt there was something deeply suspect about the double-breasted waistcoats he wore, and partly because of Thorpe's 'general air of a public school show-off'.

In early December 1975, Waugh wrote a piece for *Private Eye* about how 'West Somerset is buzzing with rumours of a most unsavoury description . . . Mr Norman Scott . . . who claims to have been a great friend of Jeremy Thorpe, the Liberal statesman, was found by an AA patrolman weeping beside the body of Rinka, his Great Dane bitch, which had been shot in the head.' His piece ended with a vintage piece of Waugh double-speak. 'My only hope is that sorrow over his friend's dog will not cause Mr Thorpe's premature retirement from public life.'

The *West Somerset Free Press* was not widely read in the Palace of Westminster. *Private Eye*, however, was. So too was the *Sunday Express*, which on 2 November had run a story headlined 'Exmoor Riddle of a Frightened Man and a Shot Dog':

The strange story of the body of a pet Great Dane, shot through the head, a terrified man found wandering across Exmoor at night and police secrecy over the case is puzzling the local inhabitants. The man, a Mr Norman Scott, who was living in the North Devon village of Combe Martin, is claiming to be a former friend of the Liberal Party Leader, Mr Jeremy Thorpe.

The tale he has told police and the people who picked him up on the moor nine days ago is a sinister one. He says that a man he took to be a private detective drove him from an hotel in nearby

Porlock. They stopped in a lay-by in a desolate spot when the man suddenly pulled a gun and shot the dog. He then pointed the gun at Mr Scott but it jammed. Scott ran off and the man drove away. Police are refusing to discuss the background to the case and are saying officially that they are investigating the case of a shot dog. But local people are asking: Why has the case of a shot dog been taken over by the deputy head of the Avon and Somerset CID, Detective Superintendent Michael Challes? Superintendent Challes told me: 'I am in charge because of the ramifications of the affair.' He refused to explain further.

In the tea rooms and corridors, people began to talk. And, as the gossip swirled, so did half-remembered rumours from years before. Then came another blow. Norman Scott didn't have to wait until Andrew Newton's trial to publicly denounce Thorpe. Another, equally golden opportunity presented itself beforehand. On 29 January 1976, Scott appeared in court at Barnstaple accused of dishonestly obtaining £58.40 worth of Social Security benefits. He had deliberately committed the fraud knowing he could say whatever he wanted in court without any risk of being sued.

From the dock, he launched his carefully primed missile. 'It has been fifteen years,' he began in a quavering voice. 'I really would like to get this matter cleared up. It has become so sick. I am being hounded all the time just because of my sexual relationship with Jeremy Thorpe.'

Within minutes, the missile had landed in Fleet Street. After issuing a terse statement – 'It is well over twelve years since I last saw or spoke to Mr Scott. There is no truth in Mr Scott's allegations' – Thorpe disappeared into his house in Orme Square, locked the door and instructed his housekeeper to tell all callers that he wasn't at home. In his absence, Cyril Smith had to fend off inquiries.

The next day he begged Thorpe to give him more information. If Scott was as unstable and unscrupulous as he maintained, didn't he have any evidence to back this up? Evidence that could be leaked to the press. Thorpe thought about it. As a matter of fact, he said, there might be something.

This time it wasn't the sensation of someone sitting on his chest that woke Peter Bessell. Nor was it a disturbing memory from years earlier. It was the sound of the phone ringing. Picking up the receiver, Bessell looked at his alarm clock. It was three o'clock in the morning.

'Peter, it's Charles.'

Charles Negus-Fancey was Bessell's solicitor.

Bessell was still wondering why Negus-Fancey was calling him in the middle of the night as he tried to make sense of what he was saying. 'Every newspaper in the country has been phoning me,' Negus-Fancey went on. 'Reporters were here in the office before I got in. What do you want me to do?'

'Do about what?' asked Bessell, more confused than ever.

'This Jeremy Thorpe Affair,' said Negus-Fancey impatiently. 'They all want to see a copy of your affidavit about Norman Scott.'

'Hold on,' said Bessell. 'What affidavit?'

'The affidavit you wrote that Cyril Smith, the Liberal Chief Whip, has just leaked to the press.'

Bessell was wide awake now. His first reaction was disbelief. After David Holmes had left, Bessell had written to him asking him to destroy his letter about being blackmailed by Norman Scott. Holmes wrote back promising that he would. Clearly that hadn't happened. Thorpe also had promised – via Holmes – that the letter would never be seen by anyone apart from his solicitors. There was only one explanation as far as Bessell could see. Both of them had lied to him.

He had to talk to Thorpe as soon as possible, Bessell decided. The trouble was, his finances were so rocky that he could no longer afford to make transatlantic phone calls. He asked Negus-Fancey to pass on a message asking Thorpe to phone him urgently. But two days went by and still Thorpe didn't call. Bessell busied himself with doing bits of DIY around the house. One of Diane's dachshunds, Thurston, had developed arthritis and he made it a special carriage so it could pull itself along by its front legs.

As Bessell took Thurston – literally – for a spin on the beach, he wondered what was going on in London. Cut off from British news – the papers normally took two days to reach Oceanside – he had an unpleasant sense that the scenery was being shifted behind his back. He worried too what people might be saying about him. Although he was only too aware that he no longer had much of a reputation, he was anxious to preserve what shreds there were.

When at last the phone did ring, it wasn't Thorpe. It was Gordon Greig, the political correspondent of the *Daily Mail*, who had managed to track him down. Would he answer a couple of questions on the record? Bessell hesitated. If he didn't try to put his side of the story, he might be completely sunk, he realized.

'All right,' he said.

'Is there an affidavit?'

'No . . .' said Bessell. 'No, there is no affidavit in existence.'

This was quite true – an affidavit is a formal statement sworn in front of a solicitor.

'Is it true that you were making regular payments to Scott to keep him quiet about an affair you were having with a woman?'

'No.'

'Then where did that story originate?'

'I simply don't know,' Bessell replied. 'I would obviously not have paid blackmail money for that. Why the hell would I have done so? Too many people would know about that sort of thing.'

'Then you were making the payments for Jeremy?'

It had been some time since Bessell had clambered on to his high horse. None the less, he managed it easily enough. 'That statement is ridiculous,' he said huffily.

Instead, he insisted he had been paying Scott out of the goodness of his own heart, helping an unfortunate who had fallen on hard times. This, as Bessell knew, was woefully threadbare stuff; it wasn't going to fool anyone for long. Before he rang off, Greig told him that the *Mail*'s Los Angeles correspondent was already on his way to Oceanside. Putting the phone down, Bessell found that his hands were shaking. For two years he had successfully kept the outside world – and reminders of his past behaviour – at arm's length. Now all that threatened to be swept away.

Before the *Mail*'s correspondent arrived, Bessell told Diane there was something he needed to tell her. They sat down at the kitchen table.

'There was far more to David's visit than you knew . . .' he began.

He was aware of her tensing up in anticipation.

'Go on,' she said. 'You know I'm used to taking it.'

He admitted that he had ignored her advice and written a letter for David Holmes – a letter that had now been leaked to the press in London.

Not surprisingly, Diane didn't take this well.

'So it's a cover-up for attempted murder?' she said incredulously.

That was very much how it looked, Bessell admitted.

When he finished explaining what he had done, Diane didn't say anything for a while. Then she looked him in the eye and said simply, 'You've got some terrible decisions to make.'

Then the telephone rang again. This time it was Thorpe. Acting as if nothing strange was going on, he began by asking after Bessell's health. Rather testily, Bessell told him that it had hardly been improved by the events of the last few days. They then moved on to the so-called affidavit. How had the press got hold of it? That was all Cyril Smith's fault, Thorpe said. After Scott's outburst, he had shown it to Smith, who had leaked it without his knowledge.

Despite everything, Bessell was inclined to believe him. He suggested that he should issue a statement through his solicitor – a statement which stuck as closely to the truth as possible. Bessell would say that Scott had originally gone to Thorpe for assistance, then Thorpe had passed him over to Bessell because he needed help with a lost National Insurance card. While Scott was in the process of trying to sort things out with the Department of Health and

Social Security, Bessell had given Scott some money – £5 a week – as he was virtually destitute. It was an act of charity, nothing more. Bessell also told Thorpe that he intended to deny that Scott had ever blackmailed him, or had any knowledge of his private life.

For the first time, Thorpe sounded panic-stricken. 'You can't do that,' he said. 'It'll ruin everything. I am begging you, Peter, give me time – time to get this thing under control. I promise afterwards we'll issue a joint statement.'

Hearing the note of fear in Thorpe's voice, Bessell gave in. 'The last thing on earth I want to do is cause you additional problems, but you have to understand that I have to protect myself too.'

In the end they agreed that the two of them would draft a statement, which Bessell would then release through Charles Negus-Fancey. But, before he rang off, there was one thing that Bessell needed to know. He'd already heard it from one Musketeer. Now he wanted it straight from the one who really counted.

'I want it in plain language. Did David hire the pilot?' he asked.

This time it was Thorpe's turn to hesitate.

'Yes,' he admitted eventually. 'That's the worst danger of all.'

'Oh, Christ,' said Bessell. 'What a mess.'

As soon as he had finished talking to Thorpe, Bessell started writing his statement. He then dictated it over the phone to Negus-Fancey, who, in turn, relayed it to Thorpe. After a lot of quibbling, Thorpe finally approved the wording. That afternoon, Bessell's statement was released to the press:

> I have been asked to make a statement with reference to Mr Norman Scott . . . First, the retainer which I or my company, Peter Bessell Ltd, paid to Mr Scott many years ago over a period of several months amounted in total to no more than £200–£300. The sum involved was solely intended to help Mr Scott to establish himself at a time when he was destitute. No further significance should be read into those payments. In particular, I reject utterly the suggestion that they were made for or on behalf of a third person.

Secondly, I have no knowledge whatsoever of any payment to Mr Scott of £2,500. At the time when it is reported this payment was made, I was recovering from a very serious illness, was totally penniless and out of communication with everyone including my immediate family.

I am also informed that it has been suggested that my continued absence from Britain is being attributed to a fear on my part that if I return I might be bankrupted. There is no truth in this suggestion. About a year ago, with the exception of one contested claim, the generous co-operation of my personal creditors enabled a settlement to be made that I believe precludes such a possibility.

By the time this was released, the *Mail*'s correspondent, Douglas Thompson, had arrived at Oceanside. Bessell told Thompson that he couldn't say anything about Thorpe, but was happy to talk about his disappearance and his life in California. The following morning – 3 February – the *Daily Mail* ran a front-page story: 'My Part in the Thorpe Affair'. In the story, Bessell denied that he had been blackmailed by Scott and reiterated that his motives had been entirely philanthropic.

His former Liberal colleagues were still digesting this the next day when they questioned Thorpe at their regular weekly meeting. Although Thorpe appeared tense to begin with, he soon relaxed and dealt with each of the allegations in turn. No, he repeated, he had never had a homosexual relationship with Norman Scott. By the end most of the people there were inclined to believe him. None the less, the Liberals were left in a quandary. The longer the story went on, the more of an electoral liability Thorpe was bound to become. Yet they could hardly dump him on the basis of what – so far – were unsubstantiated allegations.

As Emlyn Hooson wrote in a document he circulated to the twelve other Liberal MPs – 'It would be an appalling injustice and a condemnation of our democratic society if Jeremy were to resign merely because the party is embarrassed by allegations that were untrue.' However, Hooson wasn't a lawyer for nothing. 'On the other hand,' he went on, 'if there is a sound basis of truth in the allegations, Jeremy Thorpe owes it to the party, which he has led so well and so ably, not to lumber us with the stark choice between apparent disloyalty and engagement in a kind of cover-up.'

Liberals were no strangers to ridicule – they had long ago become used to being caricatured as a bunch of quixotic featherheads. But, after Norman Scott's outburst, the jibes had a much sharper edge to them. In Strasbourg, David Steel hosted a reception for the Liberal group on the Council of Europe Assembly in his hotel suite. Purely to save money, Steel had always been in the habit of sharing a bedroom with his male assistant. Seeing the twin beds, one of his guests – a Tory MP – roared with laughter and said, 'We know what you Liberals get up to.'

Steel was furious. Taking the MP aside, he said, 'You can make crude jokes about me, but you have no right to insult my assistant. I expect you to apologize to him.'

As he soon realized, though, Steel was trying to stem an unstoppable tide. By now the press had tracked down Dr Gleadle and found out about the £2,500 that he had been paid for Bessell's letters: 'Male model and the £2,500 present: Riddle of gift to Thorpe's accuser' ran a headline in the *Daily Mirror*. Meanwhile, Bessell's clapboard cottage was effectively under siege by journalists trying to beat him into submission with bundles of cash.

So far the press, while riveted by the whole affair, had taken a broadly sympathetic line. At the same time, they regarded Scott with undisguised revulsion. The *Sunday Mirror* on 8 February dismissed him as 'nauseous'; the *News of the World* doubted if anyone would 'hang a cat' on his word; while the *Sunday Times* described him as 'an erratic and desperate man seemingly bent on character assassination'.

Later that day, Thorpe was questioned again – this time by Detective Chief Superintendent Proven Sharpe, Head of the CID for Devon and Cornwall. Thorpe told him that he was in the process of preparing a comprehensive account of his relationship with

Norman Josiffe, aka Scott, which he would let him have just as soon as he'd shown it to his solicitor, Lord Goodman.

Throughout all this, Thorpe, on the surface, remained his usual urbane self. He and Marion continued to attend dinner parties, where he was as amusing and charming as ever. The only sign that the pressure might have been getting to him was when he launched an uncharacteristically sharp attack on someone he suspected of having been rude to Marion.

Several days after Sharpe had questioned Thorpe, he telephoned to ask what had happened to his account of his relationship with Scott. Thorpe said that unfortunately Lord Goodman had caught a cold and been unable to read it.

What about the payment to Dr Gleadle, Sharpe asked. Did he know anything about that? While Thorpe admitted that he had heard – indirectly – about the payment, he denied having authorized it.

Sharpe also questioned him about Andrew Newton. Here Thorpe was on safer ground. 'I have never met the accused, Mr Newton,' he declared confidently. 'I have never seen him or had any contact with him, direct or indirect. In respect of his incident I again know no more than I have read in the press.'

But all this begged an obvious question: if Thorpe hadn't paid Dr Gleadle for Bessell's letters, who had? It was a question that might have remained unanswered for some time if it hadn't been for David Holmes. In late February, Holmes did something that Bessell had long suspected he might – he cracked. Terrified that he was about to be exposed, Holmes went to see the Director of Public Prosecutions, Sir Norman Skelhorn, and told him that he had bought the letters. He'd done so, he said, in order to protect the Liberal Party. His solicitors subsequently issued a statement in which Holmes emphasized that he had acted 'entirely on his own initiative, and in particular without the knowledge of Mr Thorpe'.

If Holmes thought this would dampen things down, he must have been even more of a chump than Bessell thought. The moment the press learned that Holmes was Rupert Thorpe's godfather, they broke into an ecstatic war-dance. 'I paid £2,500 to Norman Scott, says the godfather' ran the headline in the next day's *Daily Mirror*. The night before, Thorpe had called Holmes from Orme Square. The conversation began with Thorpe saying bitterly, 'David, how could you?'

The Mandarin Mask was starting to slip. For the first time there was open speculation that Thorpe would have to go. Emlyn Hooson now thought he had reached the end of the road. So did Richard Wainwright. As for David Steel, he couldn't decide what to think. 'It might *just* be believable that Holmes had made the purchase as he said without Jeremy's knowledge; but it seemed to me inconceivable that once the fact of that payment by somebody had become public, he would not have told his old friend that it was he who had done it.'

Later that night Thorpe called Cyril Smith to ask where all this press coverage left him.

'In a bloody mess,' said Smith.

In Oceanside, Peter Bessell had come to another decision. He told Diane that he intended to perform a manoeuvre she must have become all too familiar with: a complete about-turn. As his earlier statement had done nothing to take the heat off Thorpe, he was now going to assume full responsibility for Norman Scott's behaviour. In short, he would shoulder the blame for everything that had happened. His own reputation had been hopelessly damaged, he reasoned. But if Thorpe had to resign the leadership of the Liberals, that would cause the party irreparable damage.

'It's really Jeremy you care about, isn't it?' said Diane shrewdly.

He realized she was quite right – 'my decision was purely emotional.' As was often the case, Bessell's emotional surges came decked out in a full range of Churchillian accessories.

'Yes,' he declared. 'If his ship is going down – then, by God, my little guns will be firing for him!'

Even by Bessell's standards, this was a bizarre reaction. What was he thinking of? Despite everything, it seems he was still more concerned with protecting Thorpe than with saving himself. That at least is one explanation. Another is that he simply couldn't bear the thought of being written out of the drama.

So convinced was Bessell that he was doing the right thing that he decided to call Thorpe and tell him the news – despite the cost of a transatlantic phone call. But it wasn't Thorpe who answered the phone. It was Marion.

'He's not available,' she told him coldly.

Stung by her tone, Bessell wondered if she could ask Jeremy to call him as soon as possible.

'I could,' said Marion, then put down the phone.

Within half an hour Thorpe called back. What on earth was the matter with Marion, Bessell wanted to know. 'It's just the strain, Pedro,' said Thorpe. 'I'm sure she didn't mean it. We're going through hell here, you know.'

In fact, Marion had fully intended to be frosty. However tense she may have been feeling, she never wavered in her loyalty to Thorpe. Nor, at this stage, did she attach any credence to the rumours about his homosexuality. But she'd finally made up her mind that Bessell was a bad lot, holding him responsible for the story having broken in the papers.

When Bessell told Thorpe what he intended to do, Thorpe hardly seemed to take it in. Far from being disappointed, this only made Bessell feel even more sympathetic. 'Jeremy, I know what you must be going through.'

'Yes,' said Thorpe in an exhausted voice. 'Every morning I wake up with a terrible sick feeling.'

'Jeremy, I'll do my best,' Bessell told him. 'I'll be thinking of you all the time. Remember you can phone me at any hour, day or night. Keep your chin up. The old team won't be beaten!'

The next day, on 19 February, Thorpe wrote to Bessell thanking him for his loyalty and urging him to stand firm. 'You need say nothing more,' he wrote – just in case Bessell felt tempted to do so.

'Bless you. Take care of yourself + remember LG [Lloyd George]. Ever yours affectionately, Jeremy.'

Bessell's reply suggested he had been doing some more brooding, and that he was still smarting over his earlier phone call. 'You know that I have done all I can to be helpful over many, many years . . . For these reasons I am mystified about Marion's attitude. She treated me like excrement on the 'phone and this is wholly unjustified.' But by the end of the letter, he'd come round again. 'You must trust me to handle this in a way that ensures I do no harm to you, to myself, or to the Liberal Party. *You need have no uneasiness at all* – but if you are worried telephone me. Diane sends you her love and loyal sympathy. Sometimes I wake up and think of the hell you are going through and ache for you.'

Two weeks after Bessell had written this, Leo Abse was summoned to see his old friend and fellow Welshman, George Thomas, Speaker of the House of Commons. The two had been friends for years, and Abse had always found Thomas to be a witty and urbane companion. Now, to his shock, he saw that Thomas was in a terrible state. His face was grey, and he was trembling so much he could hardly speak. When Thomas finally calmed down, he told Abse that he had just been contacted by a BBC television crew who were making a programme about Jeremy Thorpe. In particular, they were looking into an incident thirteen years earlier, when the Barnstaple Police had investigated allegations that Thorpe was having a homosexual relationship.

He paused. With some inkling of where this was going, Abse asked him to carry on. Thomas explained that Peter Bessell had told him that Thorpe had written some compromising letters – letters which he had been anxious to prevent the Barnstaple Police from seeing. Thomas had arranged for Bessell to see the then-Home Secretary, Sir Frank Soskice. As far as he knew, the story had been discreetly buried. But now the BBC had requested an interview to discuss his role in the incident.

On the face of it, Thomas had nothing to worry about. Abse,

however, was one of the few people who knew that Thomas was homosexual, and terrified this might come to light. What Abse didn't know was that Thomas was one of a number of senior MPs, including Cyril Smith, who were also suspected of being involved in child abuse – allegations that didn't surface until after Thomas's death.

Abse saw straight away how dangerous it would be for Thomas to give an interview. 'It was clear to me that if he submitted to an interrogation by the investigative journalists, he was in danger of betraying himself.' Typically, he suspected that Thomas might be undone by his own subconscious. 'I doubted if, under pressure, he would successfully control the nascent guilt-ridden self-castigations that were just beneath the surface and forever waiting to be released.' He advised his friend to adopt a tone of lofty detachment. He should get his secretary to write back saying that it was inappropriate for the Speaker to give a private interview. That, Abse confidently predicted, would be the end of it. As it turned out, he was right. Thomas took his advice and the BBC went elsewhere.

But Thomas wasn't the only one who was feeling the pressure. At the beginning of March David Steel went to have dinner with his old friend Nadir Dinshaw, at the Chesterfield Hotel in Mayfair. As soon as he arrived, Steel saw that something was wrong. Dinshaw was also in a state. He began by swearing Steel to secrecy. Wondering what could be going on, Steel solemnly gave his word.

Dinshaw was worried, he said. So worried that he'd gone to see another old friend, the Dean of Westminster, that afternoon. He went on to tell Steel about the £20,000 that Jack Hayward had sent him. As Thorpe had asked him to, Dinshaw had sent the money on to David Holmes. At the time, Thorpe had told him this was because Hayward wished to preserve his anonymity – apparently he didn't want to become known as a soft touch. But now Dinshaw was having his doubts about the whole business. What if the £20,000 hadn't gone to pay election expenses, as Thorpe had claimed? What if it had actually been used to buy the Bessell letters?

As Dinshaw was telling him this, another, far more disturbing thought occurred to Steel. Could the money have been used for something else entirely – paying Andrew Newton? The implications of this beggared belief. Was it really conceivable that the Leader of a major political party could have effectively stolen a large sum of money from party funds to pay someone to threaten – perhaps even try to kill – his former lover?

Whatever the truth, Steel found himself in a very awkward position – 'I remember I went away with a sense that the ground had shifted beneath my feet. It was the beginning of the end for me.' Steel had given his word to Dinshaw that he wouldn't mention anything they had talked about. But now he was in possession of information that had finally convinced him Thorpe couldn't stay on as Liberal Leader.

And then came a development that no one could have foreseen.

28

Damned Lies

On Tuesday, 9 March 1976, at Prime Minister's Questions, Harold Wilson stood up, rested his hands on the dispatch box and told a stunned House of Commons, 'I have no doubt at all that there is a strong South African participation in recent activities relating to the Leader of the Liberal Party.'

It wasn't just South Africa that was hell-bent on bringing Thorpe down, Wilson claimed. Apparently other dark forces were also at work, including 'private agents of various kinds and various qualities'. There were those, even in the Prime Minister's own party, who thought that he must have gone mad. Why would anyone in South Africa be remotely interested in discrediting the Leader of a political party with just thirteen MPs, they wondered. And who on earth were these 'private agents of various kinds and qualities'?

One of the few people not left baffled was Thorpe himself. Two weeks earlier the Prime Minister had asked Thorpe and his wife Marion to come to his office at the House of Commons. The three of them had stayed there until the early hours of the morning discussing what Wilson had become convinced was a plot by the South African Bureau of State Security (BOSS) to destroy both him and Thorpe.

What grounds did Wilson have for believing this? In retrospect, hardly any. There was no hard evidence of any South African involvement, only a swirl of conspiracy theories, and strange, apparently sinister coincidences. Wilson's house had been burgled on several occasions and some of his personal papers stolen. Some years earlier, Norman Scott had also become friendly with a South African journalist called Gordon Winter, who supplemented his income by working part time for BOSS. Eager to curry favour,

Winter passed Scott's story back to BOSS. To complicate matters still further, Scott and Winter began sleeping together.

All this was enough to convince Wilson that he and Thorpe were the victims of some carefully orchestrated plot to discredit, or even topple, political leaders in the UK. Again, with the benefit of hindsight, Wilson's paranoia may have been one of the first symptoms of the dementia that would soon engulf him. For Thorpe, though, it must have seemed like a divine intervention. The more talk there was of secret agents swarming around Whitehall, the more confused people would become – and the less likely to come after him.

Thorpe wrote several letters to Wilson in which he did everything he could to fan the flames of his paranoia, suggesting that BOSS were using Scott as a kind of gay Mata Hari. For good measure, he claimed that Scott's friends, the Levys – whose house Scott had stayed in when he moved back to Devon – 'might be running some sort of vice ring'. Apparently, wrote Thorpe, they had a bath 'big enough for six people'. But not everyone was fooled. Detective Chief Superintendent Proven Sharpe wrote a report for the Director of Public Prosecutions expressing scepticism about any South African connection and concluding, 'There is some doubt as to whether the truth of this incredible affair has so far been discovered.'

Meanwhile journalists were still camped out in Orme Square, hoping that Thorpe might emerge. So far he had kept his head down and refused all interview requests. But on the Friday after Wilson's speech in the Commons, the editor of the *Sunday Times*, Harold Evans, did manage to get through on the phone. Although they weren't friends exactly, Thorpe and Evans had always got on well. 'I liked him enormously,' Evans recalls. 'If I went to a reception and saw him there, I would feel a sense of relief because he was always such fun to talk to.'

Thorpe told Evans that he could come round and said that he should use the tradesmen's entrance at the back so he wouldn't be seen. When Evans arrived, the two of them went into Thorpe's study. 'He wasn't as exuberant as usual, but I wouldn't say he seemed stressed or downcast. I remember he sat at a small antique desk by a tall window. Through the window I could see this mass of pressmen outside.'

Evans urged Thorpe to make 'a full and frank statement'. At first he refused to answer any direct questions, but after a while he began to relent. It was possible that there might be one or two letters between him and Scott, Thorpe conceded, but they were purely formal. Once again, he denied that there had been a homosexual relationship and put the whole thing down to the occupational hazards of being a public figure: 'There is a woman called Joan who is in a mental hospital at the moment who claims that I married her, and I am also said to be the father of three children by another woman.'

Evans went away, not entirely convinced that Thorpe was telling the truth, but prepared to give him the benefit of the doubt. That week's edition of the *Sunday Times* led with the banner headline 'The Lies of Norman Scott'. What followed was a statement by Thorpe refuting each of the main claims. He had never slept with Scott, nor had he stolen his National Insurance card, nor had he – or anyone else – paid Scott what he called 'subventions' to keep him quiet. The statement finished up, 'In addition, it is alleged that I was acquainted with or involved in a correspondence between Scott and Bessell and that I knew of, or was involved in, the purchase of the Bessell letters from Scott for £2,500. All these allegations are totally false.'

Peter Bessell was in Los Angeles when he read this. In LA, he always stayed at a motel on Sunset Strip, where he booked in under the name of Dr Paul Hoffman, just in case there were any stray creditors hanging about. It seems entirely typical of Bessell that he should go in for this sort of subterfuge. It also seems entirely typical that he should award his alias a doctorate.

The motel was at the sleazier end of the Strip, surrounded by topless bars and hippie boutiques – among the specialities on offer at the café opposite were 'Edible Urine Cakes'. There was also a shop that sold British newspapers. Bessell bought a day-old copy of the *Sunday Times* and took it back to his motel room. For a while he just stared at the front page in disbelief. Of the six points that Thorpe refuted, two – to Bessell's knowledge – were absolutely true: Thorpe clearly had had an affair with Norman Scott, while 'subventions' had been paid to keep Scott quiet. Inside was another piece, written by the paper's Insight Team, in which Thorpe went into greater detail.

As he read it, Bessell's disbelief quickly gave way to fury. The whole thrust of the piece was to shift blame from Thorpe to him. Apparently Bessell had allowed Scott to 'hang around' his London office; indeed he had 'more or less a free run of the place'. But there was worse to come. Bessell's earlier claim – in the so-called affidavit – that Scott had been blackmailing him over his sex life was dismissed as lacking any credibility: 'A threat to expose heterosexual behaviour is not usually regarded as being particularly lethal.' Instead the Insight Team had come up with another reason why Bessell – and not Thorpe – might have wanted to keep Scott quiet: embarrassment over his business affairs. They brought up the disastrous Bronxville deal, as well as the plastic egg carton catastrophe, but what hurt most of all was their description of Bessell as a 'runner' – as if he were nothing more than a glorified errand-boy. The general impression was that he was, at best, a gullible idiot and at worst a priapic crook.

It wasn't just the manner in which Bessell was portrayed that infuriated him; it was also the way in which Thorpe laid into Norman Scott – 'incorrigible liar', 'elaborately woven mendacity and malice', 'pure moonshine', and so on. While Bessell had no reason to feel protective towards Scott, he felt Thorpe had gone way too far. This was not the man that he had once idolized, someone whose dynamism had won the votes of six million electors. Rather it was the snarling of a cornered beast trying to save his skin.

Meanwhile, Norman Scott was still in Devon, where his life had undergone yet another upheaval. He had drifted into an affair with a woman called Hilary Arthur, who was now pregnant – she later gave birth to a daughter, Bryony, in May 1976. When Scott read the *Sunday Times*, he had an even more extreme reaction than Bessell: he tore it to pieces. He then issued his own statement, a deliberate echo of Thorpe's in its brusqueness.

> Yes, there was a homosexual relationship between us. No, I never said Jeremy Thorpe stole my National Insurance card: he simply retained it because he was stamping it for me. No, I have never said the Liberal Party was paying me money to keep quiet. Peter Bessell was paying me £5 or £7 a week to enable me to live at my mother's place.
>
> Finally, Mr Thorpe's statement denies that he was acquainted or involved in correspondence between Peter Bessell and myself. My only answer is that I have a letter dated August 27th 1969 in which [Bessell] states that he has spoken to Jeremy Thorpe and put him in the picture.

But this wasn't the only proof Thorpe had known what was going on. There was far more conclusive evidence. Evidence that made it quite obvious that he and Scott had had an affair – namely the letters they had once exchanged. In particular, the letters that the police had taken off Scott back in December 1962 when he had threatened to kill Thorpe. On 1 May 1976 Scott would issue a summons against the Commissioner of the Metropolitan Police, Robert Mark, demanding they be returned.

By the time Bessell read Scott's statement he was back in Oceanside. There he went for long walks along the beach, brooding over the way he had been treated. He kept half expecting Thorpe to phone and explain his behaviour, perhaps even apologize. But the phone didn't ring and in the silence that ballooned around him Bessell grew more and more aggrieved.

29

Judas

Shortly after the trial of Andrew Newton began at Exeter Crown Court on 16 March 1976, a man came in, walked over to the press bench and began whispering to a colleague. Soon all the journalists were whispering. News had just arrived through on the wire from London – news that overshadowed anything happening in court. Harold Wilson had done something even more unpredictable than blaming Thorpe's misfortunes on South African spies: he had resigned.

Wilson later claimed that he had been intending to resign for the last two years, but at the time his announcement caught almost everyone by surprise. Faced with the prospect of yet more political uncertainty, the stock market went into free-fall. Then, three days later, came another bombshell – this time from Buckingham Palace: Princess Margaret and Lord Snowdon were separating, the first time a royal marriage had been publicly acknowledged to have broken down.

One by one the pillars of state seemed to be toppling. The effect of all this was to push the Andrew Newton trial off newspaper front pages. Compared with everything else going on, the whole business had taken on the air of a distasteful sideshow. In court, Newton stuck to his story that Scott had been blackmailing him over some compromising photographs. As he was still hoping to be paid for trying to kill Scott, he was careful not to say anything about Holmes. Newton insisted that he had never pointed the gun directly at Scott, but had deliberately aimed away in order to frighten him. He had then pulled the trigger, but nothing happened: 'I could see there was a spent cartridge inside which was jamming it.'

Scott, duly called as a witness, repeated his story about his affair with Thorpe – a story which Newton's barrister, Patrick Back, QC, dismissed as an absurd fantasy. Back described Scott as unbalanced and obsessed – at the same time as noting that he was a self-confessed homosexual. 'Let us be charitable, very often a man cannot help if he is born homosexual.'

That said, he went on, homosexuals were afflicted with 'a terrifying propensity for malice'. Back also accused Scott of hamming it up in the witness box. 'Do you remember how he started with a soft effeminate voice and a sort of false humility?' he reminded the jury.

The court heard that police inquiries had not uncovered any link between Newton and a member of the Liberal Party – or anybody 'mentioned by this man Scott'. It didn't take the jury long to conclude unanimously that Newton was guilty. Passing sentence, the judge adopted a waggishly reproving tone, telling Newton that he couldn't go around brandishing guns at possible blackmailers, no matter how great the temptation. He then gave him two years for intent to endanger life – to run concurrently with another sentence of six months for damaging property. To begin with, no one knew what property the judge was referring to; then they realized he meant Rinka.

At this point, Thorpe still believed he was in the clear. The former Prime Minister had thrown him an unexpected lifeline – two lifelines, in fact: Norman Scott had had his day in court; and Andrew Newton was safely in prison. Peter Bessell was five thousand miles away; and, as for his fellow Liberals, Thorpe was confident of being able to quell any concerns they might have.

But he had underestimated just how sore Bessell was feeling – if he had stopped to consider it at all. He had also underestimated how appalled the Liberals were. Not only was their Leader apparently mixed up in a murder plot, but there was also the possibility that he had misappropriated party funds. Several senior figures in the party had already called Bessell to discuss Thorpe's future. Although Bessell insisted that he knew nothing about any murder plot, he talked more freely to them than he'd done before about his dealings with Scott.

Still he'd had no contact with Thorpe. Increasingly, Bessell began to suspect he was being set up. As a precaution, he bought himself a tape recorder that he attached to his phone. When it rang on Tuesday, 20 April, and he heard David Holmes on the other end, Bessell pressed the record button.

Holmes (in his now customary doleful voice): 'Well, it goes on.'

Bessell: 'Really? You mean it hasn't ended?'

Holmes: 'No, it hasn't ended.'

Bessell: 'Oh my God! I thought with the dog thing over that would be the end of the whole thing . . . How is Jeremy?'

Holmes: 'Bearing up, but the strain is telling, of course, as we expected it would . . .'

Bessell: 'Tell him that I would like to hear from him and if he does have a chance to drop me a line . . . I do love to hear from him.'

After another few minutes, Holmes came to the reason for his call. Apparently Jack Hayward had been asking for Bessell's address. While Thorpe had been trying to hold him off, he wasn't sure if he'd be able to for much longer. In other circumstances, Bessell might not have read too much into this. Now with his antenna on full alert, he was pretty sure he knew exactly what was going on. Thorpe – through Holmes – was sending him a coded message: if Bessell didn't stop talking about Scott, Thorpe would put Jack Hayward on to him. This had all sorts of awkward implications. As well as landing Bessell in yet more financial trouble – he still owed Hayward money – he might well end up accused of fraud.

In the days that followed Bessell kept poring over this conversation. He wasn't especially concerned about Thorpe passing on his whereabouts to Jack Hayward – he suspected he would be able to wriggle out of any fraud charges. The sense of betrayal, though, was another matter. He was no longer in any doubt that his friend had turned his back on him. As Bessell had found before, there was something peculiarly chilling about being frozen out by Thorpe; it made the world a bleaker, emptier place. It also made it more dangerous. He knew only too well how readily Thorpe tried to destroy anyone who threatened him. In the past Bessell had been a willing accomplice, eager to do almost anything to win his master's approval. But now the camaraderie, the helpless giggling, the waltzing around Thorpe's office had all gone.

Again, Bessell felt that if he did nothing, he might end up more vulnerable than ever. Even so, it took him another two weeks to take a step that he knew would be as drastic as it was irrevocable. By 5 May he had made up his mind. He called up Douglas Thompson, the West Coast correspondent of the *Daily Mail*, and asked if they could meet the following afternoon at a West Hollywood coffee shop – not the one that sold edible urine cakes. When Thompson arrived at the café, Bessell announced that his previous accounts of what had happened had been untrue. Scott had never blackmailed him. As for the retainers that Bessell had paid Scott, they had all been on Thorpe's behalf.

That evening, Thorpe attended a white-tie gala at the Royal Academy. By then Harold Evans had got wind of the *Mail* story and asked Thorpe to meet him beforehand. As they stood in the courtyard by the Royal Academy entrance, Evans immediately noticed there was a marked change in Thorpe's behaviour. 'He was no longer as relaxed, as assured, as he had been before. I could see the nonchalance was wearing thin. And my willingness to believe him was also wearing thin.'

Evans's earlier inclination to give Thorpe the benefit of the doubt had been prompted – in large part – by his not wanting the *Sunday Times* to appear homophobic. But now he too had begun to suspect that he had been set up. His suspicions were confirmed when he quizzed Thorpe about the meeting between Bessell and Holmes in California – a meeting that Thorpe had previously denied knowing anything about. Now, Thorpe implied that he had known about it all along.

'I realized then that he had lied to me.' And if Thorpe had lied about this, what else had he lied about, Evans wondered.

As he was leaving, Evans mentioned Bessell again. Before, Thorpe hadn't reacted to his name, but now he did.

'Bessell,' he said simply, 'is a Judas.'

*

The next day, the headline on the *Daily Mail*'s front page read 'I Told Lies to Protect Thorpe'. While Bessell didn't confirm there had been a homosexual relationship between Thorpe and Scott, he didn't deny it either. As he must have anticipated, this did nothing to still the clamour. Instead, it simply cranked up the volume. In an effort – so he insisted – to set the record straight, Bessell agreed to give one more interview, to Tom Mangold at the BBC. He wanted to do a TV interview, he said, so that people would be able to look him in the eye. As soon as he heard about this, David Holmes phoned. Once again, Bessell switched on his tape recorder.

Holmes began by imploring him not to talk to anyone else.

'Have you forgotten we three are the only ones who know everything?' he said.

Bessell, of course, had not forgotten. But it was too late now for any appeals to friendship or to loyalty. The secret they had shared for more than a decade had taken on a life of its own.

'I'm sorry, David,' he said wearily. 'The time has come to tell the truth.'

For a moment Holmes stuttered, then he asked Bessell to wait a moment. In the distance, Bessell thought he could hear muffled voices, as though Holmes had put his hand over the mouth-piece. When he came back on, Holmes sounded gloomier than ever.

'There's nothing more to be said, is there?'

'No,' said Bessell. 'I'm afraid there isn't.'

Then he put down the phone.

Knowing that Scott had issued a summons to try to get his letters back, Thorpe now took drastic action of his own. His solicitor, Lord Goodman, obtained copies of the letters from the police and, in an attempt to wrest back some of the initiative, offered two of them to the *Sunday Times* for publication. Harold Evans was asked to go to a meeting at Goodman's office. Thorpe was there too – even more subdued now than he'd been outside the Royal Academy, Evans noticed. Goodman said that the paper could publish the letters as long as they didn't do so in an unduly hostile way. Thorpe's friend Robin Salinger was also present and asked if only parts of them could be published. Evans, though, wasn't having it. Either they published the letters in full or not at all.

Throughout the meeting Thorpe barely spoke beyond asking, plaintively, for assurances that there was nothing damaging in either of them. When Evans asked him if he could explain why he had written the sentence 'Bunnies can (and will) go to France', he said that he couldn't remember.

On the night before the paper came out, a group of senior Liberals – including his friend and fellow MP Clement Freud – asked if they could come and see Thorpe. They wanted, they said, to discuss a personal matter. Thorpe invited them round to Orme Square for a drink. There, he ushered them into his study and shut the door.

Having heard that the letters were going to be published the next day, Freud and his colleagues felt there was something Thorpe needed to do before it was too late. If there was any truth to these persistent rumours about his homosexuality, he ought to come clean to Marion. It's often been thought that Marion knew all about Thorpe's homosexuality and was quite relaxed about it. After all, she was close friends with the composer Benjamin Britten and his long-term lover, the tenor Peter Pears. But, as Thorpe had told Bessell in New York, she didn't know anything – or, if she did, she chose to blank it out.

'We felt it would be terrible if Marion read it in the papers,' one of those present recalls. 'Up until then I didn't know anything about Jeremy's sexual history, or about his being gay. It came as a big surprise. We all spoke very frankly. Jeremy certainly didn't want to tell Marion, but he didn't try to make any secret of his sexual inclinations. In a rueful sort of way, he said that in the past he had been completely promiscuous and couldn't stop himself. At the same time you could tell how tense he was; he was desperate and looking for a way out. My understanding is that he did talk to her that night.'

Although she was clearly shocked, Marion doesn't seem to have been that distressed. 'I believe her attitude was simply that they had both done things in the past that they might wish to alter, but that was the past and she wasn't interested in it.' While she was prepared – privately – to accept that her husband had once been homosexual, there's nothing to suggest that she ever entertained the possibility that he had tried to have Scott killed.

The headline on the following morning's *Sunday Times* read 'What I Wrote to Scott by Jeremy Thorpe'. Printed underneath were the two letters. One of them – about Scott's dog, Mrs Tish, having to be put down – was pretty innocuous. The other one, however, wasn't. This was the handwritten letter that Thorpe had signed off 'Bunnies can (and will) go to France. Yours affectionately, Jeremy.' Across the breakfast tables of the country, one subject dominated conversation – bunnies. Even the staunchest of Liberals couldn't pretend this was how MPs normally addressed members of the public. What, then, did it mean?

The *Sunday Times* continued to give Thorpe the benefit of the doubt, although their support was losing conviction by the hour: 'They [the letters] are clearly [written] in terms more affectionate than most men would use to another man; but they are also wholly consistent with the record of Thorpe . . . trying to revive the spirits of a man in distress. But are they the record of a love-affair? If the letters are imagined as passing between a man and woman in an unequivocally heterosexual context, it is immediately clear they do not constitute proof of a physical relationship.'

That night David Steel caught the night train down from Scotland. As soon as he arrived in London, he went round to Clement Freud's house in St John's Wood. 'The atmosphere was very sombre. There were just the three of us. We sat down and Jeremy handed me an envelope.' Inside was his letter of resignation.

When Bessell had told Holmes that the time had come to tell the truth, he wasn't being strictly accurate. There was still one crucial piece of information he intended to keep back – the link between Newton, Holmes and Thorpe. Bessell knew that if he said anything about this, Thorpe could be accused of conspiracy to murder. However bitter he was, he wasn't prepared to go that far.

On the Sunday morning, Tom Mangold began recording his interview for the BBC in Bessell's living room at Oceanside. At one point he stopped filming and said, 'Are you willing to say anything about the Newton affair – the shot dog?'

'No,' said Bessell. 'That's not among the relevant matters.'

They carried on filming for the rest of the day. The next morning, when Mangold arrived at the cottage at eight o'clock, Bessell could tell from the set of his face that he had important news.

'He's resigned,' said Mangold.

In a way, this was hardly unexpected. Yet the news still left Bessell feeling shattered. Why now, he wondered. What had finally made up Thorpe's mind? He doubted if it was the Bunnies letter. Embarrassing though this was, it hardly proved anything. The more Bessell thought about it, the more he thought he knew what had happened. When he had said on the phone that he meant to tell the truth, Holmes – and Thorpe – must have assumed that he was going to talk about the connection with Andrew Newton. That was why Holmes had sounded so appalled. It was also, Bessell suspected, why Thorpe had felt he had to quit.

All this left Bessell with even more mixed feelings than before. However relieved he was that Thorpe had finally resigned, he had never wanted to be the one who pushed him over the edge. He remembered Thorpe's promise that he would blow his brains out if his past was ever exposed. He remembered too that Thorpe's sister Camilla had killed herself.

Later that day, Bessell drove Mangold back to the airport. By now he was feeling physically and emotionally exhausted. So was Mangold, who sat half slumped in the seat beside him. On the way Mangold asked casually why he hadn't answered any questions about Newton and the dead dog.

'Because we agreed to exclude all matters that were irrelevant,' Bessell repeated.

'And there was no connection between Jeremy and the shooting incident?' said Mangold in the same casual voice.

Bessell paused.

Among the papers that Mangold had brought with him from London was a copy of the *Daily Mirror* which carried Scott's statement in the witness box at Andrew Newton's trial. One quote in particular had stood out: 'Mr Bessell, you will find, in the end, will tell the truth.' Any testament to his moral values always made a big impression on Bessell, especially one coming from somebody he had previously accused of blackmail. Now he thought back to all the conversations he and Thorpe had had about how Scott could be killed: the fast-setting concrete, the tin-mine, the poisoned hip-flask, the big swamp . . . As revulsion and guilt rose up inside him, prudence, yet again, fell away.

'Yes,' he said slowly. 'There was a connection.'

Beside him, Mangold immediately sat up.

'What connection?'

Bessell kept his eyes on the road and took his time before replying. 'Jeremy persuaded David Holmes to hire Andrew Newton to murder Norman Scott,' he said.

When Mangold next spoke, he sounded as if he were talking more to himself than to Bessell. 'Yes, of course, it all fits now . . . But how can we prove it?'

'We can't,' Bessell told him. 'David Holmes will admit nothing and it's only my word against Jeremy's.'

This time it was Mangold who took his time before replying.

'No, it isn't,' he said. 'It's not just your word against Jeremy's. There's Newton. When he gets out of jail he can be made to talk.'

30

Ice Cold in Minehead

Andrew Newton emerged from Preston Prison in April 1977 with one thing on his mind: how to make as much money as possible. Having been convicted of possession of a deadly weapon, his chances of resuming his old job as an airline pilot were not looking good. And after the mess he'd made of trying to kill Scott, it also seemed unlikely that there would be much of a rush to employ him as a hitman.

Three weeks later, John Le Mesurier paid him £5,000, hoping this might be enough to keep him quiet. But Newton had already decided that he stood to make far more by selling his story to a newspaper. Realizing that he didn't have much actual proof of a conspiracy to kill Scott, Newton, like Bessell, began to record his phone conversations – with David Holmes, George Deakin and Le Mesurier.

The race to secure Newton's story was won by Stuart Kuttner of London's *Evening News*. While Newton was in prison, Kuttner had become friendly with his girlfriend, ensuring he was ideally placed to pounce as soon as Newton was released. But, before doing a deal, he wanted to be sure that Newton was telling the truth. First, Kuttner showed him a number of photographs and asked him to pick out David Holmes. 'He did so without a moment's hesitation.'

Then Newton offered to play him one of his tape-recorded conversations with Holmes. 'I remember there was one of those moments that make any journalist's blood run cold. Holmes was in the middle of saying, "You and I know there was a bloody conspiracy to . . ." I could tell he was just about to say "murder" when Newton interrupted. I could have throttled him.' But even without a direct admission, the fact that they were talking at all was incriminating enough. However, Newton's hopes of making his fortune came to nothing. He had started off by asking for £75,000 for his story, with another £25,000 in the event of his being rearrested and charged with a more serious offence. In the end he was paid just £3,000 for allowing Kuttner to listen to his tape.

Kuttner and his co-writer, Joanna Patyna, spent the next four months trying to unpick the tangle of threads that they were now convinced linked Jeremy Thorpe to Andrew Newton. On 19 October 1977 the headline on the *Evening News* read: 'I Was Hired to Kill Scott. *Exclusive*. Gunman Tells of Incredible Plot'. Asked for a statement, Thorpe said, 'I know nothing about an alleged plot, but welcome any inquiries the police might make.'

As he must have known, this was unlikely to keep anyone quiet for long. The wolves were closing in. However untroubled a face Thorpe tried to present to the world, in private he had started to fray. He was drinking heavily and becoming increasingly maudlin. At a reunion at his old Oxford college, he broke down and confessed that his life was ruined. Friends worried that he might indeed be suicidal.

Eight days after Newton's story had appeared in the *Evening News*, Thorpe gave in to unrelenting pressure and called a press conference. More than eighty journalists gathered in the Gladstone Library of the National Liberal Club. They all fell silent when Thorpe came in accompanied by Marion and a lawyer from Lord Goodman's office, John Montgomerie.

A gaunt-looking Thorpe began by reading a statement. 'I must stress that anyone expecting sensational revelations is likely to be disappointed . . . Not a scrap of evidence has been produced to implicate me in any alleged plot to murder Norman Scott.' He admitted that he had tried to help Scott and that 'a close and even affectionate friendship' had developed. However, 'no sexual activity of any kind took place.'

In a clear swipe at Bessell, Thorpe went on, 'It is my considered opinion that if he [Bessell] had credible evidence to offer, he should have gone to the police rather than the press.' As for David Holmes's purchase of the letters that Scott had exchanged with Bessell, this had been done without his knowledge. 'Had I known of these negotiations, I would have stopped them at once.'

He ended by saying, 'It would be insane to pretend that the re-emergence of this story has not placed an almost intolerable strain on my wife, my family and on me. Only their steadfast loyalty and the support of many friends known and unknown from all over the country has strengthened my resolve and determination to meet this challenge. Consequently, I have no intention of resigning [as an MP], nor have I received a single request to do so from my constituency association.'

Putting a hand on Marion's shoulder, Thorpe then took a drink of water and sat down. A few fairly innocuous questions followed before Keith Graves, a BBC reporter, dared ask the one that was uppermost in everyone's thoughts. 'The whole of this hinges on your private life. It is necessary to ask if you have ever had a homosexual relationship.'

If Thorpe had ever had any doubts about his wife's loyalty, they were about to be swept away on a wave of hauteur. So far Marion had been silent, but now she let rip. 'Go on – stand up,' she snapped. 'Stand up and say that again.' Graves repeated what he had said. 'Would you comment on rumours that you have had a homosexual relationship?'

Before Thorpe – or Marion – could say anything else, John Montgomerie broke in. 'I cannot allow him to answer that question. I do not propose to say why. If you do not know why it is improper and indecent to put such a question to a public man, you ought not to be here.'

Amid continuing uproar, the Thorpes slipped out by the back staircase.

On 12 December 1977, Detective Chief Superintendent Michael Challes and his deputy, Detective Superintendent Davey Greenough, flew out to Los Angeles. Travelling with them were two journalists, Barrie Penrose and Roger Courtiour, who were writing a book on the Thorpe Affair. Known professionally as 'Pencourt', Penrose and Courtiour were in the unusual position of being trusted both by Peter Bessell and by the police. Challes had asked them if they would be prepared to smooth his path towards what he suspected was going to prove a difficult encounter. In return, Penrose and Courtiour would be allowed to sit in on Bessell's interview.

The four of them met Bessell in his lawyer's office in Beverly Hills. Once the pleasantries were over, Challes came to the reason for their visit. Was Bessell prepared to cooperate in bringing a case against Jeremy Thorpe? More specifically, was he prepared to be a witness if the case came to court?

Bessell said he needed time to think it over. As usual, he turned to Diane for advice. 'We mulled over the conflicting arguments. Peter struggled with what was the right thing to do.' Next morning he asked them all to come to their home in Oceanside. They spent the next four days cloistered together, with Diane bringing them sandwiches and cups of coffee. Challes may have been a long way off his usual beat, but he'd been a policeman since he left school and knew all about chipping away at people's resistance. While he made it plain that he couldn't force Bessell to come back to England, he emphasized how vital he was to any chance of making a prosecution stick.

Although nothing had been decided by the time Challes and Greenough flew home, both felt their trip had not been wasted. A few days later, Bessell received an unexpected phone call. It was Jack Hayward. The two men had not had any contact for four years. After their last meeting Bessell had every reason to suppose that if Hayward was ever going to speak to him again it would be through gritted teeth. Instead, he was affability itself. Perhaps they could meet up sometime if Bessell was going to be in England, Hayward suggested.

Warily, Bessell said this sounded like a delightful idea. In the same friendly tones, Hayward went on to say that if Bessell could see his way to repaying some of the £35,000 he still owed him, he'd be extremely grateful. But he made it clear that he wasn't in any hurry and had no intention of pressurizing him.

When he put the phone down, Bessell did some more pondering. What did this mean? Once again, he thought he detected a coded message. The more he replayed the conversation in his head, the more sure he was what it was. It was the reference to England that convinced him. In his veiled way Hayward appeared to be saying that if Bessell chose to testify against Thorpe – something that would clearly entail his returning to England – then he had nothing to fear from him. That could mean only one thing: Hayward no longer thought that Bessell had acted on his own over the Freeport fraud. Now, it seemed, he suspected Thorpe too.

In March 1978, Challes and Greenough were back in California. This time they brought copies of the papers that had been found behind the hidden door in Bessell's old office. Among them was the letter that Scott had sent Thorpe's mother and various letters from Scott to Bessell about his retainers. Although these didn't prove that Thorpe and Scott had had a homosexual relationship, they made a nonsense of Thorpe's claims that he hadn't known what was going on. Again, Challes asked if Bessell would be prepared to testify.

Still Bessell's feelings were deeply divided. The friendship with Thorpe was clearly beyond repair. Any shreds of loyalty Bessell may have felt had vanished after reading the *Sunday Times* article in which Thorpe had tried to shift the blame on to him. As far as he was concerned, this had signalled a final parting of the ways. But Bessell also knew that if he went back to England, he would be branded a Judas. What's more, he was sure to be vilified for his role in the murder plot.

'They'll pelt me with rotten eggs,' he said glumly.

Adroitly Challes played his trump card. 'We don't have a case without you,' he told him. 'As we see things, at present you're our principal witness.'

As Challes had clearly deduced, nothing was more likely to break down Bessell's resistance than flattery. Whenever he faced a moral quandary, Bessell always liked to believe his conscience was his guide. Invariably, though, there was more to it than that. However much he liked being in Oceanside with Diane, part of him found the seclusion – and the obscurity – hard to bear. Having spent a good deal of his life in one pulpit or another, silence was almost as foreign to his nature as prudence. Appearing in court would give Bessell the chance to be a somebody again – not just another middle-aged dog-walker on a Californian beach.

That evening Bessell and Diane had another talk. The next day he called his lawyer and told him what he had decided. He was prepared to go back, but only on certain conditions. Chief among them was his insistence that the case against Thorpe should be 'vigorously prosecuted'. Even at this stage Bessell suspected that the British Establishment would close ranks to protect Thorpe and make sure he never came to trial.

When Challes and Greenough boarded their flight that afternoon, Challes had a signed statement in his briefcase. With it was a single sheet of paper, also signed: 'I, Peter Joseph Bessell, agree that, if necessary, I will visit England to give evidence in accordance with the statement I have this date made to Chief Superintendent Michael Challes at a trial . . . of any person specifically referred to in said statement who may be prosecuted in regard to the matters mentioned in that statement.'

It had been a long, difficult and expensive campaign, but in the end they had netted their fish.

As Jeremy Thorpe's solicitor, Lord Goodman, didn't handle criminal work, Goodman had asked Sir David Napley if he would take on the case. On the morning of 4 August 1978, Thorpe was picked up from his home in Orme Square by Napley and driven down to Minehead Police Station. Arriving shortly after midday, they were met by Napley's partner, Christopher Murray. The three of them were shown into an interview room, where Thorpe was asked if he would like to sit down. To Napley's surprise, a small, nondescript man was standing in the corner, 'looking for all the world as though the teacher had put him there'. When he asked who this man was, Napley was told it was the Chief Constable of Somerset, Kenneth Steele.

Chief Superintendent Michael Challes then informed Thorpe that he had obtained a warrant for his arrest. 'I showed him the warrant and read the contents over to him and invited him to read it if he so wished. I told him that in accordance with the warrant I was arresting him and cautioned him.'

The enormity of the occasion was not lost on anyone. 'I remember having this very strong sense that history was being made,' recalls Christopher Murray. 'Thorpe himself was totally under control. He was ice cold. It was quite astounding. I remember talking about it with David Napley and we decided that he had had so much experience of waiting for election results that he had become used to the tension.'

After he had been cautioned, Thorpe replied, 'I hear what you say. I am totally innocent of this charge and will vigorously challenge it.' He was then offered coffee and sandwiches before being taken to Minehead Magistrates' Court a few hundred yards away. In the courtroom Thorpe was charged with conspiracy to murder as well as incitement to murder – the most serious charges ever levelled against a sitting Member of Parliament. Once again he insisted that he was totally innocent. 'I will vigorously defend them [the charges] and plead not guilty.'

Earlier that morning Challes had arrested David Holmes. Unlike Thorpe, he had said nothing after being cautioned. The ever loyal Holmes had previously been questioned for two days by police at Bristol Police Station – much to his distress, he caught bed bugs in his cell – but had refused to implicate Thorpe. He hadn't even protested when Thorpe had suggested that he could shoulder the blame for everything and take whatever punishment he was given. As he later recalled, 'Jeremy had thanked me for keeping his name out of it all. He consoled me, saying, "I've made inquiries and if things go wrong you shouldn't get more than seven years. With good conduct you'd be out in four and a half – and you must agree that there doesn't seem much point in both of us going down." '

But it had all been for nothing. Now they had both been arrested. Holmes was charged with the single offence of conspiracy to murder, as were George Deakin and John Le Mesurier. Once all four men had been charged, they were remanded on bail of £5,000 each.

Peter Bessell was 3,000 miles away in a hotel room in New York when Tom Mangold phoned with the news. Just as Mangold told him that Thorpe had been charged, there was a sudden flash of lightning. This was followed almost immediately by a tremendous clap of thunder. Looking out of his window on the twenty-fifth floor of the Wellington Hotel, Bessell could see the skyscape of Manhattan lit up with bright blue flashes. It seemed a suitably dramatic backdrop to what he was hearing.

31

Waiting in the Wings

In October 1978, the Liberal Party Conference got under way in Southport on the Lancashire coast. When Jim Callaghan's Labour government had lost its majority eighteen months earlier, the Labour Party and the Liberals had formed an unofficial coalition – the 'Lib–Lab Pact'. Now, after all the disappointments and embarrassments they had suffered, it looked as if the party's fortunes might once again be on the rise. As a result, the atmosphere at the conference was unusually tense; the last thing the Liberals needed was any more bad publicity.

For a day and a half, everything meandered placidly along. Then, just as a debate on foreign affairs was about to start, the doors at the back of the hall were flung open. With his wife Marion by his side, Jeremy Thorpe marched down the aisle towards the stage. Liberal Party conferences were not renowned for moments of high drama, but this was unquestionably one. Nobody was quite sure how to react. Some of the audience stood up and began to clap. Others stayed conspicuously in their seats.

Following his resignation, Thorpe had been given a consolation job as the Party Spokesman on Foreign Affairs. When his successor as Leader, David Steel, heard that Thorpe had been charged with conspiracy and incitement to murder, he begged him to step down. Reluctantly, Thorpe agreed. He had also given Steel his word that he would resign as an MP if he was arrested, but following some carefully orchestrated pleading from his local party, he changed his mind and decided to stay on.

Thorpe had made another pledge – to save the Liberals any further embarrassment, he would stay away from the party conference.

Now, as an appalled Steel watched Thorpe striding towards him, he realized that he had broken this promise as well. 'Of course, it was all done in his usual dramatic fashion – he didn't just come in through a side-door. It was typical Jeremy.' Some quick thinking was required. 'I had to put a brave face on it; there was no point trying to snub him.'

Jumping to his feet, Steel thrust out a hand. Thorpe grasped it and grinning wildly the two men shook hands in a far-from-convincing show of unity. As one watching journalist wrote, 'Mr Steel shook him [Thorpe] warmly by the hand while looking as if he would rather have gripped him warmly by the throat.' Later on, Steel was more frank about his feelings. 'Jeremy virtually wrecked the conference and the rest of us just had to put up with it.'

However, there was one important lesson to be learned from Thorpe's behaviour. If anyone thought he was going to vanish meekly into the shadows, they couldn't have been more wrong.

That autumn, police on the M60 motorway in Manchester observed a new Mercedes swerving erratically and colliding with a number of traffic bollards. When they stopped the car, the driver refused to take a breathalyser test or to provide a urine sample. Taken to Platt Lane Police Station, he said to the Police Sergeant, 'Do you know who I am?'

The Sergeant admitted he had no idea.

'I'm Standing Counsel to the Chief Constable of Greater Manchester,' the man declared. 'I am George Carman.'

He then told the Sergeant to get the Chief Constable on the phone. It turned out that the Chief Constable, James Anderton, was at a formal dinner with some senior colleagues. As soon as he heard what had happened, Anderton sent a Superintendent to investigate. When the Superintendent arrived, still in his dinner jacket, he found Carman sitting in a cell with the door open. He was being served tea by another of the policemen.

Although Carman never needed much – indeed any – encouragement to drink, he had had ample reason to celebrate. A few weeks earlier, he and his son, Dominic, had been staying in the Tresanton Hotel, St Mawes, when they heard on the news that Jeremy Thorpe had been arrested and charged.

This was the moment that Carman had been waiting for all his life. Turning to his son, he said, 'I can do it. I can get him off.'

After Sir David Napley agreed to take on Thorpe's case, he and Lord Goodman had several meetings to discuss tactics. Knowing how intense press interest was, Goodman proposed that they should give themselves aliases in case anyone overheard what they were saying. They decided to call themselves after types of fruit: Napley was 'loganberry' and Goodman 'gooseberry'. But the idea was soon abandoned after Napley's partner, Christopher Murray, told him that he had received a call from 'gooseberry' – whereupon the two of them collapsed in helpless giggles.

The biggest decision of all was who was going to represent Thorpe in court. Whoever they picked would need particular strengths. As Murray recalled, 'Thorpe had, in effect, already been tried and convicted by the media, so it was crystal clear that this case was going to rely on tremendous powers of cross-examination and, above all, an excellent jury speech.' They would also need someone who could cope with the publicity. 'When David and I discussed it, we were fully aware that whoever was retained would become a household name.' As they talked, both of them thought back to the Big Dipper case of 1973 and the electrifying effect that George Carman had had on the jury.

Thorpe, who remembered Carman from Oxford, was willing to be guided by Napley. An approach was made, and instantly accepted. As Napley had anticipated, the news caused a sensation. In the Inns of Court and the bars around Fleet Street, everyone was asking the same question: who was George Carman? It was like one of those old backstage dramas where the understudy is suddenly pushed into the spotlight.

Carman wasn't just an unknown quantity; he didn't even have much experience of doing criminal cases. Although people who had seen him in court testified to his brilliance, rumours drifting down from Manchester about his private life added to the general disbelief. Not only did Carman apparently drink with hectic abandon and blow vast amounts of money in Manchester casinos, but, to cap it all, his second wife had left him for the legendary Manchester United footballer George Best.

For Carman, all this incredulity made his triumph even sweeter. But if he thought he was going to get rich as a result, he soon had a shock. Knowing how much the case would mean to him, Napley set his fee accordingly. Carman was to get £15,000 – rather less than he would have got for doing legal aid cases. When his clerk protested, Napley said simply, 'It will be worth more than £100,000 in publicity to Mr Carman.'

And it wasn't long before Carman's delight gave way to frustration. While he would act for Thorpe if the case came to court, Napley – far from a recluse himself – decided that he would represent Thorpe at the pre-trial committal hearing in Minehead. Under English law as it then stood, any charge, however serious, had to be heard first in a local magistrates' court. If the magistrates decided the defendants had a case to answer, then, and only then, would they be sent for trial.

For Carman, never a patient man, this was a kind of agony. As Napley wrote later, 'I detected and understood his great desire to be in the fray at the earliest moment.' The starring role may have been his, but he was going to have to wait in the wings until the time came for his entrance.

On Sunday, 19 November 1978, Sir David Napley and his wife Leah drove down to Devon in their brown Rolls-Royce – a car whose boot was reputed to be always well stocked with champagne. Along with Christopher Murray, Napley would be spending the next month staying in Jeremy Thorpe's guest cottage. The first thing he saw when he pulled open his bedroom curtains on the Monday morning was a photographer with a telephoto lens pointed at his window.

After breakfast, Napley and Thorpe left Cobbaton in Thorpe's white Rover 3500 and drove across Exmoor to Minehead. Normally, there are few places more dispiriting than an English seaside resort out of season. But now, as they approached the town's courthouse, they saw that the place resembled a film set. The trees all around were festooned with arc lights, and cameramen perched among the chimneys on specially erected gantries. In the field opposite the courthouse, local primary schoolchildren gazed through the railings, enthusiastically cheering each new arrival.

It wasn't just the national press that was riveted by the Thorpe case. The story of the only murder plot ever – allegedly – hatched in the House of Commons played well in any language. Journalists and television crews from Canada, Australia and the USA had descended on Minehead, booking out every room for miles around. As the court could only accommodate around a hundred people, most of the journalists present had to mill about outside frantically trying to work out what was going on inside. Those who had managed to gain admission were met by a very strange sight. The Clerk of the Court, Frank Winder, had been instructed to keep a meticulous record of proceedings. To do so, he wore a portable dictation machine strapped to his face like a black oxygen mask into which, with great deliberation, he repeated every question and answer.

The first surprise came when Gareth Williams, QC, counsel for George Deakin, stood up and asked the three presiding magistrates to lift reporting restrictions, saying that his client 'welcomed the fullest scrutiny'. Beforehand, almost everyone – Napley included – had assumed that reporting restrictions would remain in place throughout, severely limiting what any of the journalists could write. But if just one barrister applied for restrictions to be lifted, everyone else had to comply. This was particularly unwelcome news for Thorpe, who'd been hoping to keep the more lurid details of his relationship with Scott out of the papers.

The second surprise came at the end of the opening address by Peter Taylor, QC, the prosecuting counsel. Physically imposing, he was regularly likened to a second-row rugby forward – Taylor tended to steer clear of theatrical tricks. However, he had a knack for delivering speeches which rose, almost imperceptibly, to quietly devastating climaxes.

Taylor described how Thorpe had tried to persuade Jack Hayward to threaten Peter Bessell with a writ if he – Bessell – came back to England. 'But Mr Hayward would have nothing to do with that. Despite that attempt to keep Mr Bessell away, and despite threats last week of what might be in store for Mr Bessell by way of cross-examination, Mr Bessell is here. And,' Taylor concluded, 'I propose to call him now.'

A ripple of excitement went through the courtroom. All eyes turned towards the door. Six days earlier, Peter Bessell had arrived back in England – the first time he had set foot in the country in nearly five years. That morning a Police Constable had picked him up from his hotel in Taunton and driven him to Minehead Magistrates' Court twenty-five miles away. There Bessell was shown into a small room containing nothing but two hard chairs, an ashtray and an electric fire, and asked to wait. By the time he heard his name being called nearly two hours later, the ashtray was full.

For Bessell, returning to the UK was full of risks. It wasn't just the risk of being pelted with rotten eggs; there was also the possibility that he might face criminal charges. His solicitor, Lionel Phillips, had strongly advised him to seek immunity from prosecution before agreeing to testify. At first, Bessell refused, insisting that he'd done nothing wrong, but in the end prudence, or self-preservation, won out. Phillips drafted a proposal – later described as the most sweeping immunity ever granted to a witness – and presented it to the office of the Director of Public Prosecutions. To his amazement, they didn't raise a single objection.

Hearing that Bessell might testify against Thorpe, the *Sunday Telegraph* approached him with an offer. If the case came to trial, the paper would pay him £50,000 for a series of six articles about his role in the affair. However, there was a caveat. If the defendants were acquitted, Bessell would only get half this amount. Lionel Phillips told Bessell he would have to be mad even to consider this. 'The defence will have a high old time with that. They'll say it's an incentive for you to exaggerate your evidence to obtain a conviction.'

But £50,000 was a lot of money, especially for someone in Bessell's financial straits. He didn't want to let the opportunity go without putting up a fight. Phillips agreed to sound out the office of the Director of Public Prosecutions to see what they thought. Having done so, he wrote to Bessell outlining their response. 'I have told the ADDP [Assistant Director of Public Prosecutions, Kenneth Dowling] that a contract of this kind was in the offing and he did not seem unduly concerned mainly, if I understood him aright, because you would be attacked on so many grounds that one more really would not make much difference.'

This was an extraordinary decision. The DPP's office, it appears, failed to realize how damaging any deal would be – both to Bessell's credibility as a witness and to the outcome of a trial. Possibly, no one thought through the implications of what had been agreed. It wouldn't be long, though, before they became all too clear. Three days later, with any bumps in the *Sunday Telegraph* contract apparently ironed out, Bessell signed a deal with the paper's editor. As he wrote later, 'It was to prove the most disastrous document to which I had ever given my assent.'

Accompanied by another policeman, Bessell walked down a narrow corridor and into the courtroom. His entrance certainly caused a stir, but not necessarily for the reasons that Peter Taylor had expected. People who had known Bessell before were shocked by how much he had changed. Although he was only fifty-seven, he appeared much older, despite his deep mahogany tan. He was wearing one of his old mohair suits, and the sheen it now gave off seemed almost ghostly. He had also dyed his greying hair chestnut-brown. In daylight, this wasn't too obvious, but under the courtroom strip lights it turned a peculiarly orange colour. The overall effect made him look as if he had been pickled in iodine.

In silence, and with some difficulty, Bessell made his way between metal boxes of documents and the extra chairs that had been crammed into the courtroom and took his place in the witness box.

In his drawling, lounge-lizard voice, he took the oath. Before Peter Taylor began his questioning, Bessell looked around him. He saw that instead of sitting in the dock, the four defendants were dotted about the court.

First of all he spotted David Holmes, sitting by himself on one of the pale oak benches. He was staring straight ahead with the same haunted expression that Bessell had last seen almost three years earlier when Holmes had come to dinner in Oceanside. Then Bessell spotted Thorpe. He too was on his own, sitting on a large blue cushion, busily scribbling notes with a gold pen. Next, Bessell noticed the Clerk of the Court, waiting expectantly with his portable dictating machine clamped to his face. For a moment a mad thought struck Bessell. He imagined catching Thorpe's eye, nodding towards the Clerk and his ludicrous black mask, and the two of them dissolving into helpless laughter.

Suddenly Thorpe turned and stared at him over the top of his gold-rimmed reading glasses. But there was no look of amusement in his eyes. There was nothing but hatred.

Every day Napley would return to Thorpe's guest cottage in Cobbaton. As he had been when Thorpe was arrested, Napley was amazed by his sang-froid. Having hit rock bottom a year earlier, he had now recovered his poise. 'He possessed far more resilience than, I believe, any other person I have met . . . Although under the inevitable stress and strain of the experience there were times when he looked drawn or haggard, he never failed to bounce back to his customary vitality and exuberance.'

After they had all had dinner together – Thorpe, Marion, Rupert, Napley and Christopher Murray – they would watch the television news to see how the case had been reported. Then Napley would call George Carman in London to tell him what had happened. But, far from reassuring him that he was being kept in the picture, these calls only added to Carman's sense of frustration. Increasingly, he became convinced that Napley was making a terrible mess of the committal hearing.

It was absurd, Carman thought, that the other three defendants should be represented by barristers, while Thorpe was represented by a solicitor. Then there was the decision to lift reporting restrictions; plainly that had caught Napley unawares. Carman also felt that Napley's Rolls-Royce – widely reported to be gold-coloured, even gold-plated – sent out a quite inappropriate message, suggesting Thorpe was the sort of swanky, privileged figure who could buy himself out of a tight corner.

Far more crucial, though, was Napley's handling of the main witnesses. Despite having been in the witness box for eight hours, Peter Bessell had emerged effectively unscathed. True, Napley had said that 'when you looked at his demeanour, mendacity was oozing out of every pore of his body', but Bessell had heard people say far worse things about him than this. As for Napley's claim that the murder plot had been cooked up by Bessell and the journalists Barrie Penrose and Roger Courtiour, for their own warped ends, that left almost everyone baffled.

Napley had had even less success with Norman Scott. Beforehand, it had been widely assumed that Scott would fly into a frothing rage at the slightest provocation. Instead, for the most part, he was composed and quick-witted – even though someone had poisoned seven of his eleven cats on the night before he first gave evidence and laid them out neatly on his back doorstep. When Napley accused him of carrying around a copy of Penrose and Courtiour's recently published book, *The Pencourt File*, presumably to make sure his story tallied with theirs, Scott pointed out that the book had actually been a volume of Anglo-Saxon poetry. When Napley quoted William Congreve's lines: 'Heaven has no rage like love to hatred turned/Nor Hell a fury like a woman scorned,' Scott blasted back an unplayable return – 'I am not a woman.'

As far as the watching press were concerned, Scott had clearly come out on top. Later, Napley admitted that he might have made mistakes, but on the whole he didn't feel he had anything to reproach himself for – 'My conscience was clear.' And whatever grounds Carman had for thinking that Napley was making a mess of it, there's little doubt that jealousy played a part in his feelings. As he saw it, Napley was stealing his thunder. Stuck in London, there was nothing Carman could do except crack open another bottle of gin, stay out of his car and wait for his daily phone call.

At the climax of the committal hearing, the elements once again played their part. The night before the magistrates announced their verdict, Napley was woken in the middle of the night by rain beating on the window. Going outside in the morning, he found that his Rolls-Royce had been struck by lightning.

On 13 December 1978, four weeks after the proceedings had begun, the Chairman of the magistrates, Edward Donati, a retired architect, told the four defendants to stand in line in front of them. 'We find there is a *prima facie* case in respect of each of the four of you,' he declared. 'There is also a *prima facie* case in respect of you, Thorpe, of inciting Holmes to murder Norman Scott . . . You will all be committed to trial.'

When she heard this, Marion Thorpe put her hand to her mouth, looked quickly at her husband, then away again. Thorpe himself blinked rapidly and moved his jaw slowly from side to side. As the journalists spilled out of the tiny courtroom and into the glare of the arc lights, one of them turned to a colleague. 'That was the out-of-town run,' he said. 'Just wait for the West End premiere.'

32

Overture and Beginners

The trial of Jeremy Thorpe, David Holmes, John Le Mesurier and George Deakin – 'The Trial of the Century', as the press had already started calling it – was due to begin in Court Number One at the Old Bailey on 30 April 1979. But at the beginning of the year that still seemed like a long way off. Once again, the country stood on the brink of chaos. Amid runaway inflation and further strikes, an epidemic of panic buying had taken hold. People began hoarding tinned food, fearful that there might be nothing fresh to eat in the shops. There were even reports in the papers that pigs, starved of feed by a lorry drivers' strike, had turned to cannibalism.

In London, the bin men had also gone on strike. Leicester Square had been turned into a giant rubbish dump. As cinema-goers walked past an eight-foot-high mound of swollen bin bags, they heard a strange rustling coming from within. It was the sound of rats scurrying through the polythene.

Returning sun-tanned and beaming from a summit meeting in the Caribbean, the Prime Minister, Jim Callaghan, denied that he was about to declare another state of emergency. He had considered doing so, he admitted, but decided there was no point. A new phrase was on everyone's lips – or, rather, an old phrase reminted for the occasion: 'The Winter of Discontent'.

Propped up by the Liberals, the government limped from one seemingly insoluble crisis to the next. Then, at the end of March, the Conservative opposition led by Margaret Thatcher called for a no-confidence debate in the House of Commons. The debate itself took place in an unusually gloomy atmosphere – aptly enough, the

Palace of Westminster catering staff had also gone on strike. Having lost all faith in Callaghan, the Liberals decided to switch their allegiance to the Conservatives. Shortly after ten o'clock at night, on 28 March, the vote was taken and the Speaker, George Thomas, rose to announce the result. 'The Ayes to the right [the Opposition] three hundred and eleven. The Noes to the left [the Government] three hundred and ten.'

Later that night, several Conservative MPs – not including Mrs Thatcher – danced a conga through the Palace corridors. The next morning, Callaghan announced there would be a General Election in five weeks' time, on 3 May. Under the circumstances, it had been confidently assumed that Jeremy Thorpe would not be putting himself forward for re-election. But, to general disbelief, Thorpe declared that he had every intention of standing. Not to do so, he reasoned, would imply that he had something to be ashamed of. David Steel was furious – 'I needed Jeremy as a candidate like I needed a hole on the head.' However, Thorpe's constituency association had no hesitation in adopting him as their candidate. 'I am grateful and very proud to have been asked to stand again,' Thorpe announced. 'This will be my eighth election and I am delighted to be back in the fray. The adrenaline really starts pumping. My wife is also delighted,' he added.

In order to give himself time to campaign, Thorpe applied to have his trial postponed by a fortnight. A postponement was granted – prompting complaints that he was being given preferential treatment – but for only eight days. Even if there were rats jitter-bugging down the Strand, the trial would start on Tuesday, 8 May, just five days after the election.

While the rest of the country was gripped by election fever, George Carman had other things on his mind. He had spent months working out how he was going to fight the case, obsessively talking over strategy with his son, Dominic. Now, finally, he was in charge. He began by making this abundantly clear to his client. Carman invited Thorpe to come to Napley's firm in Clerkenwell, Kingsley Napley, where he had been given an office. Also at the meeting was

Graham Boal, a young junior barrister who had recently started work there. Thorpe, a qualified barrister himself, turned up holding an out-of-date legal handbook and immediately started talking about how the case should be fought.

'At the beginning he was very cocky,' Boal remembers. 'He was very confident, knew it all, wanted to argue the toss on the law and used silly Latin phrases. I think he thought that the two of them would have some sort of partnership, but he discovered very quickly that it wasn't going to be like that.' Politely, Carman informed Thorpe that he was going to do exactly what he was told. And, if he had problems with that, he would have to find himself another barrister.

All along, Thorpe had assumed that he would be appearing in the witness box. Far from dreading the prospect, he seemed to be actively looking forward to it, apparently convinced that his powers of oratory could win over a jury. But from the start Carman felt that an over-confident, garrulous Thorpe might well do himself more harm than good. A few weeks before the trial began, Carman ran into a fellow QC, John Macdonald, who asked how his preparations were going. 'I can't possibly let Jeremy go into the box,' Carman told him. 'He wouldn't be able to answer the first three questions.' The implication was that Thorpe would be torn to pieces as soon as he opened his mouth. Macdonald walked away convinced that Carman would put up a ferocious fight on Thorpe's behalf, but far from certain he believed in his client's innocence.

The other big issue facing Carman was what to do about Thorpe's homosexuality. He knew that the prosecution had lined up a number of men who claimed to have had sex with Thorpe and were prepared to give evidence. It was unlikely that all of them were lying. But, if Carman admitted Thorpe had been gay, that would clearly undermine Thorpe's insistence that he'd never slept with Scott.

Carman also had to work out how to cross-examine the main witnesses. Detailed biographies were drawn up by Napley's staff, along with notes on how best to deal with them. Norman Scott, it was suggested, should be treated with great caution. 'Counsel will have no difficulty in establishing that this man is a miserable, weak, unprincipled and spineless individual who considers that not only the world, but that anyone he meets with whom he has the slightest friendship owes him a living.' That said, 'His cunning is not to be underestimated.'

Witnesses had also been tracked down who described how extravagantly Scott had embellished his past. A woman called Betty Jones recalled how he had claimed to have once been a ballet dancer, but apparently had to stop when a piano fell on his foot. Another woman, Janet Harthill, for whom Scott had briefly worked, said he had told her that his wife and child had been killed in a car accident. Then there were examples of Scott's behaviour. A man called Christopher Matkin claimed that Scott had told a mutual friend, Cat Oliver, that Matkin didn't want to have an affair with her because she smelled and had ginger hair under her arms. 'I confronted him [Scott] with the false allegation he had made against me and he took umbrage and said I was one of the most evil people he knew.'

But Scott wasn't the only one whose past was being raked over. The same thing was happening to Peter Bessell. Among those who testified to his deficiencies was a former secretary called Christine Downes. She gave a statement saying that Bessell was 'a nasty, conspiratorial little man as well as an incorrigible liar . . . It was so bad that if he said it wasn't raining, I think I would probably check because I couldn't believe him.'

As far as Carman was concerned, it was Bessell, rather than Scott, who was the key figure. If Bessell, the chief prosecution witness, could be broken in court – not just dented but smashed to pieces – the whole case against Thorpe might collapse. The big challenge for Carman was identifying Bessell's Achilles heel and working out just how to attack it.

The choice of the trial judge may not have caused quite as much astonishment as Carman's appointment as Thorpe's barrister, but it still came as a surprise. Like Carman, the Honourable Sir Joseph Donaldson Cantley was from Manchester. But that was just about all they had in common. Far from having a rackety private life, Cantley was rumoured to have been a virgin until the age of fifty-six, when he had married the widow of a former judge.

Marriage had done nothing to dispel his air of unworldliness. Cantley had once tried a case in which a 23-year-old man had applied for damages after being badly injured in a bulldozer accident. Told that the injuries had affected the man's sex life, he asked if he was married. Learning that he was not, a puzzled Cantley said, 'Well, I can't see how it affects his sex life.'

At sixty-eight, he was so little known outside legal circles that not a single news agency possessed a photograph of him. Hesitant of manner, fond of laughing at his own jokes and looking like a startled dormouse in his ermine robes, Cantley was not considered to be an intellectual heavyweight. He was also reckoned to be a crashing snob. Even Carman thought him a strange choice. But for Thorpe this came as a rare piece of good news. The more snobbish and unworldly the judge, the less likely he was to believe the allegations against him.

Was Cantley's appointment just a happy accident? Perhaps – but then again perhaps not. The Lord Chancellor, Lord Elwyn-Jones, was responsible for deciding which judges should officiate at which trials. An Establishment stalwart, Elwyn-Jones had been friendly with Thorpe for a number of years. Both of them had been original Trustees of the Amnesty International Prisoners of Conscience Appeal Fund, and in 1964 Thorpe and Elwyn-Jones had been co-sponsors of a bill to regulate the placing of advertising contracts on television. They had also sat on the House of Commons Committee of Privileges together – the body which oversaw MPs' business interests at the time. Elwyn-Jones, it seemed, had done his old friend a favour.

With the election looming, Thorpe now spent most of his time in North Devon, desperately trying to save his political career. It soon became clear that the Liberal leadership had cut him adrift.

David Steel recorded a lukewarm message of support, but stayed well away. To raise funds for his election expenses, Thorpe's mother, Ursula, sold off the top floor of her house. At the start of the campaign Thorpe seemed as wolfish and as upbeat as ever, but people soon began to notice that the old spark had gone. So too had his rapport with his constituents. At one point he addressed an audience of just three people – two of whom turned out to be journalists.

Auberon Waugh, keen to cause Thorpe as much embarrassment as possible, decided to stand in North Devon, representing the 'Dog Lovers Party'. Just as Waugh was about to distribute his election manifesto calling on anyone who'd been moved by the death of Rinka to vote for him – 'Rinka is NOT forgotten. Rinka lives. Woof Woof, Vote Waugh to give *all* dogs the right to life, liberty and the pursuit of happiness' – Carman secured an injunction preventing him from publishing it on the grounds that it might prejudice the trial.

Carman had been active elsewhere too. In Rochdale, the local paper didn't dare risk Cyril Smith's wrath by investigating the allegations of sexual abuse against him that had been circulating round the town for some time. But a student free-sheet, the *Rochdale Alternative Paper*, did report the claims – whereupon Carman wrote to every national newspaper editor warning that if they repeated them, they too would be prejudicing the trial. No one chose to argue, and the story effectively stayed buried for the next twenty years.

Four days before election day, Thorpe celebrated his fiftieth birthday. Like his campaign, it was a subdued affair. At half three in the morning on election night, he stood on stage in the Queen's Hall, Barnstaple, with the other candidates, waiting for the result. He looked terrible, his skin waxy, his face frozen, his eyes barely seeming to focus. As the result was read out, his expression did not alter. The result was a humiliation – every bit as bad as anyone had feared. Thorpe's majority of nearly 7,000 had been overturned and the Conservative candidate had won by almost 8,500 votes. At the other end of the scale, Auberon Waugh had polled 79 votes – not bad considering that no one had been allowed to read his election address.

When Thorpe left the hall shortly afterwards, he was asked for a comment. In a dazed voice he said simply, 'The gap was much wider than I thought.' But, however dramatic all this was, it was only a sideshow. No one had any doubt about who was topping the bill. In Finchley in North London, another election result had just been announced. Standing on the stage with the other four candidates was a 53-year-old woman wearing a dark blue suit and clutching a handbag.

By now it was clear that the British electorate had done something that would have been unthinkable ten years earlier. It had voted for a female Prime Minister. Although people had little idea what Margaret Thatcher was likely to do once she was in power – for someone who would become notorious for her dogmatism, her manifesto had been peculiarly vague – that didn't seem to concern them. What she offered above all was a fierce, unreflective determination to halt Britain's slide into ruin and to restore its prominence in the world. This was such an unlikely prospect that she had to couch it in dream-like terms: 'Somewhere ahead lies greatness for our country again; this I know in my heart.'

Mrs Thatcher's election heralded the start of a new era – an era that would be harsher, more divisive, but ultimately more prosperous and less chaotic than the one that had gone before. It also served to emphasize just how far and how fast Jeremy Thorpe had fallen. Five years earlier, he had been within touching distance of power. Now, no longer an MP, shunned by the party he had once led, he was about to go on trial for conspiracy and incitement to murder. If found guilty, he could spend the next fifteen years in prison.

Peter Bessell was back in Manhattan when he heard the news of Thorpe's defeat. He took a late-night walk to try to shake off his sense of depression, but it wouldn't go away. Walking along, he thought back twenty years to Thorpe's first election victory, and to his own election as an MP five years later. 'Now it was all over and might never have been,' he reflected. 'All that was left were two discredited men in late middle age who had squandered the trust and hopes they had once inspired.'

Two days later Bessell boarded Pan Am Flight 100 to Heathrow. When he had flown to England in November for the committal hearing, he'd been convinced that he was doing the right thing. This time, facing the prospect of testifying against his old friend in open court, he felt sick with apprehension. 'What I was about to do I dreaded more than anything I could remember.'

PART FOUR

33

Ripped to Shreds

At 9.45, on the morning of 8 May 1979, a brown Rolls-Royce drew up outside the main entrance to the Old Bailey. It was driven by Sir David Napley, and inside were four passengers. The people waiting outside in the early-summer sunshine – some of whom had been there since dawn – might have imagined they were witnessing the arrival of a visiting dignitary. A stooped, hollow-eyed Jeremy Thorpe stepped out, accompanied by his wife and his mother, both dressed as if for a day at the races, and by his uncle, Sir Peter Norton-Griffiths. The party was met by the Keeper of the Central Criminal Court and then escorted to a room next to Court Number One normally reserved for consultations between barristers and their clients.

Arriving ten minutes later, Peter Bessell was received with rather less ceremony. First he went into the lobby, where he was immediately surrounded by journalists. If Bessell's haggard appearance had come as a shock at Minehead, he looked far worse now. Over the last five months he had lost almost a stone in weight. Inside his new pinstriped suit, he seemed to have shrunk away. According to the *Daily Mail*'s correspondent, he had 'the physique of a pipe-cleaner'. In California, Bessell had experimented with dyeing his hair a darker shade of brown, but as soon as he stepped under electric lights it turned the same sickly orange colour as before. To give him some privacy, he was shown into a waiting room by an Old Bailey policeman who insisted on frisking him for weapons before turning the three chairs and the table upside down to check for bugging devices.

Court Number One at the Old Bailey is the most famous

courtroom in the land. Past occupants of the dock include Dr Crippen, his fellow medical murderer Dr John Bodkin Adams and the Notting Hill necrophiliac John Christie, as well as the Nazi propagandist William – 'Lord Haw-Haw' – Joyce. The Thorpe trial, pundits confidently predicted, would outdo them all in terms of drama.

More applications for press seats had been received than ever before, and special arrangements made to ensure that people in the public gallery couldn't sell their seats to journalists. Whatever happened, it was going to be a notable trial in a number of ways. 'For the first time up-to-date electronic equipment is being used,' the *Daily Telegraph* told its readers excitedly. 'The jury and lawyers will be able to listen to tape recordings through earphones which have no wires attached to them.'

At half past ten Jeremy Thorpe, David Holmes, John Le Mesurier and George Deakin were led up the white-tiled staircase into the huge glass-sided dock. After the Usher had commanded the court to rise, Sir Joseph Cantley made his entrance, wrapped in his scarlet robes and wearing a horsehair wig – a wig which, as tradition dictated, had a hole in the middle. Although capital punishment had been abolished in 1965, Cantley, like all High Court judges, still carried the black cap, which used to be placed over the holes in their wigs whenever a death sentence was being passed. Behind the judge, dressed in a pale violet ensemble, came an Alderman of the City of London.

For the *Daily Express*'s Jean Rook, popularly known as 'The First Lady of Fleet Street', the whole spectacle was 'like a scene from Madame Tussauds. The carved wooden room, the lawyers in starched linen and stone-grey wigs, the dummy-silent figures in the dock.' She was particularly taken with Peter Taylor, QC, leading the prosecution as he did at Minehead – 'dark as a hawk with a fine Roman nose'. Cantley himself reminded Rook of a 'friendly North Country chemist I used to know with loose false teeth'.

After all the fanfare, the trial got off to a slow start. The first day was taken up by legal submissions. However tense Thorpe was feeling, his appetite seemed to be unaffected. He was reported to have lunched on steak pie followed by jam roly-poly and cream ordered from a nearby restaurant. Bessell, by contrast, could hardly eat a thing. Thorpe returned from lunch wearing a long black overcoat with a velvet collar. 'I hope you don't think it's discourteous,' Carman told the judge, 'but he tells me he is sitting in a draught.'

The next morning, Bessell had only just arrived at the Old Bailey when, to his surprise, he learned that the judge wanted to see him. Led into court, he saw Sir Joseph Cantley perched up on his dais with a face almost as red as his robe. Far from being friendly, the judge proceeded to give him a tremendous ticking-off.

'It appears you held something of a press conference here yesterday.'

At first Bessell had no idea what he was talking about. Slowly, he realized that Cantley was referring to an interview he had apparently given to a journalist the day before. In the few minutes that Bessell had been in the lobby, someone had asked him a question about his tea-drinking habits. Thinking this was unlikely to have any bearing on the case, he had given some flippant reply. According to Cantley, his behaviour had been completely unacceptable. 'You are not to discuss the case with anyone,' he told him. 'If a reporter approaches you, take his name and come and tell me about it. Otherwise you too will be in danger.'

Although insignificant in itself, this set the tone for what was to come. From the start, Cantley regarded Bessell with unconcealed suspicion, never wasting an opportunity to fire a rocket in his direction. It also gave Bessell his first glimpse of Thorpe since the committal hearing. Clearly the whole affair had taken a heavy toll on both of them. 'At Minehead Jeremy's eyes had been disdainful as he lolled nonchalantly on the front pew of the public gallery. Now, deathly pale, huddled in a dark overcoat, he was half-slumped on the upright wooden chair in that vast edifice; a defeated man staring into space. At Minehead I had known the worst my testimony could do to Jeremy was commit him for trial. I had always been aware that at the Old Bailey, if it was believed, it could send him to jail.'

But, as he saw Marion sitting a few rows back, a glimmer of the old Bessell resurfaced. She too had changed considerably since he had last seen her. In her case, however, the change had been for the better. 'No longer the homely overweight housewife with a garish artificial white streak in her black hair, she was slimmer, surprisingly relaxed and far more attractive.'

Even at this stage, he still had doubts about what he was about to do. 'As I walked through the swing doors into the lobby I wondered how I would find the courage to go back into that court and testify against him.'

Bessell would have a long wait to learn if his courage was going to fail him. On the afternoon of the second day, Peter Taylor stood up to give his opening speech for the prosecution. As he had shown at Minehead, once Taylor started talking he showed little sign of wanting to stop. 'Twenty years ago, in 1959, Mr Jeremy Thorpe was elected Member of Parliament for North Devon,' he began. 'During the early 1960s he had a homosexual relationship with Norman Scott. From then on, Mr Scott was a continuing danger to his reputation and career. It was a danger of which Mr Thorpe was constantly reminded by Scott pestering him for help and talking of the relationship with others.

'In 1967 Mr Thorpe was elected Leader of the Liberal Party. But the higher he climbed on the political ladder, the greater was the threat to his ambition from Scott. His anxiety became an obsession and his thoughts desperate.

'Early in 1969, at his room in the House of Commons, he incited his close friend, David Holmes, to kill Norman Scott. Peter Bessell, a fellow Liberal MP, was present. Holmes and Bessell tried, over a period of time, to dissuade Mr Thorpe from this plan, and to humour him. Other, less dramatic measures were suggested and tried – seeking to get Scott to America, trying to get him a job, paying him money, purchasing damaging letters from him. But Scott remained a constant and serious threat.

'Shortly before the first of the two General Elections in 1974, Scott went to live in Mr Thorpe's constituency. He had been talking openly about his relationship with Jeremy Thorpe, and he was seeking to publish a book about it. The accused, David Holmes, eventually became convinced that, as Mr Thorpe had repeatedly urged, the only way to stop this threat, both to Mr Thorpe and to the Liberal Parry, effectively was to kill Scott.

'Mr Holmes had connections in South Wales. He knew the accused John Le Mesurier, a carpet dealer. Through him he met the accused George Deakin, a dealer in fruit machines, and a plot was hatched to find someone who would kill Scott for reward. Mr Deakin recruited Andrew Newton, an airline pilot, as the hired assassin. Mr Deakin met him and briefed him. Mr Holmes also met him and briefed him further.

'The reward was to be £10,000. Attempts were made – but failed – to lure Mr Scott to his death. But eventually, in October 1975, Mr Newton met him in Devon, gained his confidence and drove him out on to the moors. There, Newton produced a gun. Scott had brought a dog with him. Newton shot the dog but failed to shoot Scott.

'Mr Newton was arrested, charged and convicted in March 1976. He had been charged with possessing a firearm with intent to endanger life, but at his trial the true history of the shooting did not emerge. He was sent to prison and on his release in 1977 he was paid £5,000, half the contract price. The cash was handed over to him by Le Mesurier at a remote spot in South Wales.

'The money to pay for this contract was procured by Jeremy Thorpe. He had persuaded Mr Jack Hayward, a wealthy benefactor, to make substantial contributions to Liberal election funds. Mr Thorpe then personally arranged for the money to be delivered by a devious route to Holmes, so that a payment could be made to Newton.

'In a nutshell, this is what the case is about.'

Taylor then proceeded to give a more detailed outline of the whole affair – far too detailed in the opinion of Bessell, who, once again, had to sit and wait until he was summoned. Finally, after another two and a half days, Bessell heard his name being called. As he walked slowly across the court, Auberon Waugh, watching from the press seats, thought he looked like 'a creature from outer space bravely going to its execution'. Standing in the witness box, Bessell held on to the sides to steady himself. Even the effort of lifting the reading glasses that dangled from his neck on a thin black cord seemed to take it out of him.

Cantley began, in the same stern voice, by reminding him that his immunity did not extend to perjury. As Bessell was well aware of the limitations of his immunity, he found this distinctly odd. 'The warning could only have caused the jury to regard me with suspicion from the outset.'

When Peter Taylor started his questioning, nervousness made Bessell speak so fast that the judge had to ask him to slow down. By the time the court rose at the end of Friday afternoon, Taylor was still only halfway through his questions. For Bessell, the real trial wouldn't begin until the following week. He spent the weekend at the Bloomsbury Hotel in Russell Square, feeling lonely and trying not to think about what lay in store.

George Carman meanwhile was thinking about nothing else except how to destroy Bessell. But, despite all his preparation, all the scrawled notes, all the rehearsals with his son, Dominic, he still hadn't finalized his cross-examination strategy. It was almost as if he had become so obsessed with the case that he couldn't think straight. Already several people suspected that David Napley had made a dreadful mistake.

On Monday, Taylor resumed his questioning. As Bessell recalled how he and Thorpe had discussed dumping Scott's body in a tin-mine, Thorpe gave an incredulous smile and gazed at the ceiling as if he had just discovered a keen interest in plaster moulding. At one stage Bessell revealed that he had recently been diagnosed with emphysema – an incurable disease of the lungs. This came as no surprise to Auberon Waugh, who had already reached his own conclusions about Bessell's state of health. 'It was as if we were listening to the ghost of a man giving a performance which had been carefully rehearsed when the body was animated.'

That evening, George Carman was invited to dinner with

Graham Boal from Kingsley Napley and his wife. They sat around the table in the Boals' kitchen, drinking wine and discussing their strategy. As usual, Carman did not stint himself on the alcohol. The longer they went on, the more concerned Boal became. 'By eleven o'clock I remember thinking, Christ, this man is a shambles. I have no idea where we are going. There were bits of paper all over the table with different suggestions on them – shall we do this, shall we do that? We sat up to about 3 a.m. working it out.'

When Boal eventually went to bed, he had a nasty feeling that disaster lay just around the corner. 'I was really seriously concerned.' The next morning, he arrived in court fearing the worst. But, once there, Boal witnessed an extraordinary transformation. Just a few hours earlier, George Carman had been so drunk he could hardly stand up. Yet the moment he put on his wig and gown, it was as if he changed into a different person. Physically small, Carman appeared to grow several inches. At the same time, his normally doughy features became much sharper and more defined. But it wasn't just his appearance that changed; so did his whole manner. All of Carman's intemperance, his lack of confidence, his chaotic rage, disappeared. In court – and only in court – did he succeed in becoming the man he wanted to be.

Meanwhile, Bessell was not only feeling extremely apprehensive; he was also in considerable discomfort. As he recalled later, the witness box at Court Number One 'could have been designed by a keen disciple of the Marquis de Sade – it is just too wide to enable the occupant to support himself by resting his hands on the side-rails, while the ledge in front is just too low for him to lean on.' All this ensured that he was already out of sorts before his cross-examination began.

At first, Carman could have been mistaken for a kindly doctor, gently teasing out embarrassing symptoms from a sickly patient. What had prompted him to come back to testify, he wondered? A sense of justice perhaps?

Knowing he was likely to sound pompous if he agreed, Bessell said simply that this had been a factor in his decision.

'Loyalty to the Liberal Party?'

'That was also a consideration.'

'Revenge?'

'No, sir,' Bessell said. 'I have no occasion for it.'

'Money?'

Seeing that Carman had a copy of his *Sunday Telegraph* contract in front of him, Bessell realized he had been backed into a corner. He denied that money had influenced him, knowing how unconvincing this must have sounded. For the time being, Carman moved on – to Bessell's religious faith. Bessell admitted he had been a lay preacher at the same time as he and Thorpe had, allegedly, discussed how Norman Scott could be murdered.

'Did that trouble your conscience?' Carman inquired, a few last shreds of his solicitous manner still hanging in the air.

'No, sir, it did not.'

'Did you not feel it was your duty to tell the party that its Leader was a man intent on murder?'

'My first loyalty was to Thorpe,' Bessell replied. 'I thought it could be prevented. I saw no purpose in seeking to damage his career in that way.'

'Didn't you think Mr Thorpe must have needed to see a psychiatrist?'

'Yes, I suppose that is true.'

All at once, Carman's sympathy fell away and out came the scalpel.

'A lot of things you have done are incredible and disgraceful, are they not?' he said. Before Bessell had a chance to reply, Carman continued. 'Let us pass on to something even more totally incredible. Before Mr Thorpe, on your account of the matter, had in mind sending Mr Scott to his death in 1971, in the United States, you have asserted he proposed the murder of another person to you, in 1970.'

'Yes, sir,' said Bessell.

'A man called Hetherington?'

'Yes, sir.'

Bessell described how he had picked up Hetherington – the would-be blackmailer – on the eve of the 1970 General Election, worked out that he was a fraud, then called Thorpe to tell him what had happened. Carman swatted this explanation contemptuously aside. 'If your evidence had a vestige of truth, the Leader of the Liberal Party had proposed the death not only of Norman Scott but of another person . . . this time it was not the unfortunate Mr Holmes but you who were to be the assassin?'

'That is correct,' Bessell admitted.

'What steps did you take to acquaint the Liberal Party, police, doctors, Mrs Thorpe, with the fact that the Leader of the Liberal Party was insane?'

'None, sir.'

'Yet when he got his vote of confidence in 1976 you were delighted?'

'Yes, sir.'

'Does this make you a thoroughly amoral person?'

By now the tension in the courtroom had risen sharply; the air itself seemed to have tightened. Bessell paused for reflection. This time he took longer to reply.

'I think it does,' he agreed.

'If you were preaching Christianity, add hypocrite?'

'Yes.'

'Amoral, hypocrite, liar – is that not a scoundrel?'

Bessell denied this, albeit without much conviction. By now, Carman's plan of attack had become horribly clear. Bessell had always known that he was likely to be portrayed as someone whose moral raft was listing badly under the weight of his past failings. Carman, though, plainly intended to go much further than that. He was going to try to show Bessell up as so untrustworthy that no one could believe a word he said. This was a high-risk strategy. However far his star may have fallen, Bessell was still a former MP – a public figure of some standing. What was more, he had never been convicted of any offence. But whether through luck or remarkable shrewdness, Carman had homed in on Bessell's weakest spot of all: his sense of shame, his desire to come clean. Somewhere deep inside Bessell the lay preacher still stirred.

Carman then asked if he had served in the war. No, said Bessell, he hadn't. First, he had registered as a conscientious objector. After that he had given lectures on classical music to members of the armed forces. As Carman was well aware, neither reply was likely to go down well with the jury.

Although Bessell didn't try to hide what Carman referred to witheringly as his 'credibility problem', he insisted he had turned over a new leaf since he and Diane settled in Oceanside.

'Have you told any whoppers since 1976?' Carman asked.

'Not to my knowledge.'

'You have told quite a few in this case, haven't you?'

'No.'

It was now 4.15 in the afternoon and Carman asked Sir Joseph Cantley if it would be a suitable time to adjourn. While Cantley reserved his sternest manner for Bessell, in other respects he showed every sign of enjoying himself. The *Washington Star*'s Judy Bachrach noted that the judge's 'tiny, girlish lips, set perpetually in a cupid's bow of dainty mirth, always seemed to be on the verge of a giggling spell'.

In his merriest voice, Cantley said, 'Oh, I think we have got time for one more whopper if you like.'

Bessell listened to this in disbelief. In effect, Cantley was telling the jury that he thought everything Bessell had said so far had been a lie. Ever since he had agreed to testify, Bessell had known he had such a bizarre story to tell that it would be a struggle to convince anyone it was true. He also thought it quite possible, likely even, that the British Establishment would close ranks to try to protect Jeremy Thorpe. But this was worse than he had feared. As the court rose for the day and Bessell made his way – silently – through the crowd of journalists in the lobby, he began to suspect that he wasn't facing just one adversary in court but two.

For the first few days of the trial, Thorpe had barely glanced up as he walked into the Old Bailey. One journalist described him as 'a walking cadaver' with the 'lumbering gait of an 80-year-old arthritic'. But, as he arrived in court at the start of Bessell's second day of cross-examination, Thorpe smiled and doffed his hat at the waiting crowds. He was looking rested and more relaxed than he had done in weeks. Possibly this had something to do with the fact that his mother was no longer by his side. Having accompanied him since the start, she now stayed away until the verdict.

Bessell, however, was not feeling at all rested. Ever since weaning himself off Mandrax, he had found it hard to sleep. For much of the night he had lain awake in his hotel room with a mounting sense of foreboding. Stepping into the witness box, he wondered when the first blow would fall.

He didn't have to wait long to find out.

'Mr Bessell,' George Carman began. 'Does it not prick your conscience to have entered into a contract by which you and your family achieve double the money on the conviction of a former true and loyal friend?'

'Yes,' said Bessell slowly. 'It does.'

'You are prepared to betray a friend for money, aren't you?'

There was another pause.

'I think that is an overstatement.'

The contract in question, of course, was Bessell's deal with the *Sunday Telegraph*. As far as Carman was concerned, this offered clear proof of Bessell's greed and untrustworthiness. Given that he would receive twice as much money if Thorpe was found guilty, surely he had a vested interest in Thorpe being convicted? Vainly Bessell argued that he was simply trying to make some money. He'd earned almost nothing over the last four years, he said, due in large part to his involvement with the Thorpe Affair. As he must have known, this was pushing it. The main reason Bessell hadn't earned any money was because he could no longer find anyone prepared to do business with him.

But this was only the start. Next, Carman homed in on the lies Bessell had told. Lies to Norman Scott, lies to Jeremy Thorpe, lies to Father Sweetman in Dublin, lies to his parliamentary colleagues. Lies to just about everyone. It wasn't simply that Carman was relentless – Bessell had braced himself for that. But what he hadn't anticipated was just how chilling he could be. How unnerving. Carman's voice was unusually classless for a barrister's, and he didn't have the fruity drawl of so many of his colleagues. Rather, it was as cold, as flat, as steel. Soon Bessell, the great Lothario, began to feel something he had never felt in his life before – emasculated.

'You lied, did you not, Mr Bessell, to Mr George Thomas, the present Speaker?'

'Yes, sir. On your client's behalf.'

'I did not ask you on whose behalf you'd lied,' said Carman. 'The fact is that you lied?'

'Yes, sir.'

'And all the time you were lying to Mr Thomas, who was, I believe, a lay preacher and fellow member of the Brotherhood Movement as well as a parliamentary colleague, you were going into the pulpits of the churches in Cornwall Sunday after Sunday as a lay preacher?'

'Yes, sir.'

'And you lied by your own admission while you were preaching the word of God?'

'Yes, sir.'

Whenever Bessell appeared to have regained some kind of equilibrium, Carman opened up another front. At one point Bessell was asked to read out a cutting from the *Western Morning News*, dated 16 June 1970. In a faltering voice, he did so. He was then asked to describe the photograph that accompanied the article. This showed him and Thorpe together at a political rally in Newquay – on the same day that Bessell claimed he had phoned Thorpe to tell him about the meeting with Hetherington.

Bessell pleaded that he must have got his dates mixed up, but Carman swatted this aside too.

'It takes a long time to nail down some of your lies. That is one we have nailed.'

'No,' said Bessell. 'I accept there is an error in days or dates. That is all, and given time I can provide the correct answers.'

'Yes, Mr Bessell, it takes time to explain lies. The error is in your distorted and tainted mind.'

Later, Bessell realized he had indeed got his dates muddled and dictated a note for his solicitor to pass on to Peter Taylor. But all this did was provoke a further rocket from the judge. 'I said you were to talk to no one,' Cantley told him, more sternly than ever. 'You have been extremely stupid.'

On and on it went, with Carman sometimes pecking, sometimes stabbing, but always drawing blood.

'Mr Bessell, have you ever been a drug addict?'

'No, sir!' he answered in astonishment.

'Mr Bessell, your immunity does not cover you against perjury, as my Lord has already pointed out. I ask you again, have you ever been a drug addict?'

'No!' he replied. Then, through a punch-drunk fog, a thought struck him. 'When you say drug addict, what kind of drugs do you mean?'

'Ah!' said George Carman triumphantly. 'So we have caught you in another lie, Mr Bessell!'

'You have not,' he insisted. 'I assumed you were referring to marijuana, cocaine, or something similar. Were you?'

'What about a drug called Mandrax?'

'That is a prescription drug, a sleeping tablet. Yes,' said Bessell wearily. 'I was addicted to it . . .'

'It affected your moral values, did it not?'

'That is possible,' he conceded.

Increasingly, as Bessell was only too aware, he was looking like a man with no moral values at all. In a masterstroke of humiliation, Carman took him, line by line, through two letters Bessell had written to Jack Hayward in 1974, asking him which parts were true and which false.

Within seconds, Bessell became hopelessly confused.

'Very well,' Carman told him. 'I am perfectly ready to accept the answer "partly true, partly false".'

After Bessell had finished with his litany of 'partly true, partly false' replies, Carman shook his head in artfully simulated sadness.

'Oh, Mr Bessell,' he said. 'It is a tangled web of lies that you tell.'

The more Carman pitched into Bessell, the more Thorpe's spirits rose. 'Although he looked grave in the dock, Thorpe was cheerful downstairs,' John Le Mesurier recalled. 'He was convinced that, provided we did not flap or panic, we could get off. He claimed we would totally discredit the prosecution case. The whole thing, he said, had come through the sewer and no British jury would convict on that sort of evidence.'

Meanwhile, Carman kept on stabbing away. By the middle of Bessell's third day of cross-examination, he was a broken man. A kind of dazed acquiescence had come over him; so much so that whenever Carman accused him of some new act of deception or skulduggery, he no longer made any attempt to deny it. Instead, he agreed, almost enthusiastically, with every charge that was put to him.

Carman: 'So you deserved to be put behind bars, did you, in January 1974?'

Bessell: 'Yes. What I had done in respect of Mr Hayward was in my view totally unforgivable, inexcusable, and therefore deserving punishment . . .'

At times, this got too much even for Carman.

'Mr Bessell, I do not wish you to use this box as a confessional box, I just want to find out the truth of what you say and the extent that your evidence can be relied upon.'

Bessell: 'I am sorry, sir. I was merely expressing the emotion of the moment.'

But it didn't take long for the self-laceration to resume.

Carman: 'Would it be a fair assessment to say that you had demonstrated you are a man capable of consummate deviousness in his business and personal activities?'

Bessell: 'I have to reply that you have shown undoubtedly that I have been guilty of deviousness, that I have been guilty of quite disgraceful behaviour.'

For those watching, this was a very peculiar sight – rather as if a gravedigger had begun to dig a grave, only to find that the person for whom it was intended had suddenly jumped up and started digging twice as fast.

Aptly enough, Carman finished off by asking Bessell about his two suicide attempts – in 1971 and 1973. Even here, he didn't let up, suggesting that on the verge of death Bessell had intended to perpetrate one last act of deceit: committing insurance fraud. Bessell had now spent more than ten hours in the witness box and was plainly exhausted.

When Carman asked his last question – 'I suggest, Mr Bessell, that you are right when you say you have a credibility problem. I suggest too that you are a person who is incapable of being believed?'– he didn't say anything at all.

The seconds ticked by. All Bessell's poise, all his vigour, all his love of the spotlight had gone. Now he sagged in the witness box with only the side-rail to hold him up. As the silence went on, everyone held their breath.

In the end, help came from an unexpected quarter. At this late stage, Sir Joseph Cantley took pity on him. 'You can't expect him to agree to that,' he told Carman. 'You're wasting our time. That is a question for you to put to the jury, not to him.'

At last, Bessell emerged from his torpor. 'If I believed I were no longer capable of being believed, I would not be here at the Old Bailey,' he said. 'I would be at Oceanside, California.'

Told that he could go, Bessell made his way slowly across the well of the court. In a taxi on the way back to his hotel, he gazed vacantly out of the window, barely noticing anything. Then, when the taxi stopped at a traffic light, his eye was caught by a newspaper hoarding. It said simply 'Bessell – Drug Addict'.

Three days after Peter Bessell had finished giving evidence, his daughter Paula drove him to Heathrow Airport to catch a flight back to America. During his time in London, Bessell had come to feel closer to his daughter than at any time since she was a child. Neither of them were physically demonstrative people, but they gave one another a long hug as they said goodbye. Then Bessell walked away towards the departure lounge. He would never return to England.

34

The Greatest Show on Earth

'Call Norman Scott!'

However dramatic Peter Bessell's cross-examination had been, this was the moment everyone had been waiting for. For months, Scott's name hadn't been out of the newspapers. He was the vindictive bloodsucker, the frothing maniac who had brought down the most popular politician in the country. That at least was how he had invariably been portrayed. Amid an expectant hush, people craned forward for their first sight of him. With longish black hair and smartly dressed in a dark three-piece suit, Scott didn't show any obvious signs of derangement. Now aged thirty-nine, he may no longer have been cherubic, but he still had the same sultry, bruised air that had captivated Thorpe.

After he had taken the oath, Scott looked around the court. To his horror, he saw his mother gazing back at him. 'I have no idea what she was doing there. It must have been ten years since I'd seen her. She certainly hadn't come to be supportive; I think she'd probably just come for a day out. It completely threw me. I was terribly embarrassed by the thought of having to explain what had happened in front of her.'

First, Peter Taylor went over the key points of his story: how Scott met Thorpe, the now-notorious night at Mrs Thorpe's house, the missing National Insurance card and so on. Whenever he was asked a question, Scott spoke so softly that the judge kept complaining that he couldn't hear. At lunchtime, he tried to talk to his mother in the corridor outside, to ask her what she was doing there. But before Scott could say anything, he heard Marion Thorpe's voice booming out, 'Stop that woman talking to the witness!'

It wasn't until the morning of 22 May – Day 11 of the trial – that Carman started his cross-examination. As he had done with Bessell, he began by adopting the manner of a kindly physician. Was Scott taking any medication at the moment, he asked in a voice that suggested anything told to him would be treated in the strictest confidence.

Scott wasn't fooled – 'I remember thinking he had eyes like a dead fish.' No, he said, he wasn't taking any medication. In the past he had suffered from a variety of emotional difficulties, but he hoped all that was behind him now.

Nodding understandingly, Carman then asked Scott about the incident in October 1961, when the police were called to a house in the village of Church Enstone, where Scott – then Josiffe – appeared to be having a nervous breakdown.

'I was very drugged at the time and some details may have gone out of my mind,' said Scott.

'You don't remember telling the police that you knew Jeremy Thorpe?'

'I still had a bundle of love-letters of Jeremy Thorpe that he had written to Van de Vater,' Scott replied.

The kindly doctor vanished as quickly as before.

'Never mind what you say are love-letters between Mr Thorpe and Van de Vater,' Carman snapped. 'Answer the question.'

Cantley was equally brusque. 'You are not giving a proper answer,' he told Scott. 'That was just a piece of dirt thrown in. Listen to the question and answer, and behave yourself!'

With Scott slapped down, Carman soon settled back into his stride. Referring to the fact that Scott had fantasized about having a relationship with Thorpe before he ever went to see him in London, he said, 'You met Mr Thorpe and talked to him for five minutes or less. He hadn't written you a single letter before you went to the House of Commons. Neither had you written a single letter to Mr Thorpe before that. Why did you say Mr Thorpe was a friend of yours when all you had done was speak to him for less than five minutes?'

'Because when I had had the therapy at the hospital I was going through a delusion and I had these letters,' Scott explained. These were the letters addressed to 'Dear Norman' that Thorpe had written to Norman Van de Vater. 'I was using these letters to say that I had a relationship with him already . . .'

'You were saying you had a sexual relationship with Mr Thorpe before you went to the House of Commons?'

'Yes.'

'Quite obviously, that was not true.'

'No, it wasn't.'

'In fairness to you, were you saying it because you were suffering from a delusion?'

'Yes.'

Carman then took Scott through some other stories he had told – including that his parents had been killed in a plane crash and that he was the son of an Earl.

'Was that another delusion?'

'No,' said Scott, apparently quite unabashed. 'It was a lie.'

'Do you think that was a wicked thing?'

'Yes, I do, but I have done so many wicked things in the past.'

Too late Scott realized his mistake. 'But I have not lied since that wretched man tried to kill me because I suddenly realized there was no point in all this lying,' he added hurriedly.

The damage was done, though. Carman had led Scott into a trap – exactly the same trap as he led Bessell into. He had exposed both men as liars. Liars who claimed to have seen the light and decided to tell the truth. But if they had lied before, who was to say they weren't lying now?

Carman then pointed out several discrepancies in Scott's various accounts of what had happened on the night he stayed at Thorpe's mother's house. In his statement to police in December 1962, Scott had said, 'I am almost certain his penis did not go into my anus. I am not sure whether he ejaculated, but he seemed satisfied.' But in later accounts he had insisted that penetration did take place – indeed, that he'd been in such agony he had bitten the pillow to stop himself from screaming. It seemed an odd sort of thing to be unsure about. How did he explain it?

Scott said that he didn't mention penetration in 1962 because homosexuality was still illegal and he didn't want to be prosecuted for buggery. He was also 'trying to make myself out a cleaner person than I was'.

So far the exchanges between Scott and Carman had been fairly placid. But all that changed when the court reconvened after lunch. Carman began by referring to another incident, when detectives had called at Thorpe's office to question Scott about the theft of Jane R's sheepskin coat. According to Scott, Thorpe had been trying to kiss him and stick his hand down his trousers at the time.

'Mr Thorpe had arranged for the police to come by appointment?' asked an openly incredulous Carman.

'Yes.'

And then, to everyone's surprise, except possibly Carman's, Scott cracked. 'Jeremy Thorpe lives on a knife-edge of danger!' he shouted.

This line may have had a suspiciously rehearsed air, but that didn't stop it from electrifying the court. Carman waited until Scott's voice had stopped bouncing around the walls before saying quietly, 'What about you?'

'I don't at all!' shouted Scott, even more loudly. 'I have certainly lived in danger of my life for many years because of your client.'

By now, Scott's face was flushed and shiny with sweat. From his high chair, Sir Joseph Cantley gazed down at him with appalled fascination. Although Carman's own face gave nothing away, his manner suggested that he had started to enjoy himself. The more he could rattle a witness, the more he knew he was winning the argument.

'You do appreciate that Mr Thorpe has consistently denied any homosexual relationship with you?' he said.

'Yes, sir.'

'Are you claiming the sexual activity on the first night at the home of Mrs Thorpe was without your consent?'

'There was nothing I could do because I was in their house, tired and very woozy!' If Scott had been shouting before, he was almost wailing now. 'I was broken and crying. I did not know what was happening until it was too late. I assure you it happened!'

'Don't get excited,' Carman said.

'I am not getting excited, but it is stupid. Do you think I enjoy saying these terrible things or talking about it? It is most horrendous.'

It was at this point that the judge made another intervention. 'If you only spoke like that when you began your evidence, we could have heard everything you said,' Cantley told him. 'It shows you can speak up.'

'Yes . . .' Scott said breathlessly. 'Yes, I can.'

Cantley: 'I will remember that.'

Possibly this was meant to be helpful, but it didn't strike Auberon Waugh that way. 'Unless I was very much mistaken, the judge, having seen that Scott was in a highly emotional state, was deliberately baiting him, rather as one might approach a lunatic waving a knife in the street and give him a prod with one's umbrella – uncertain of what will happen next, but sure that it will be interesting.'

If this was Cantley's intention, it had immediate results. Turning towards him, Scott said, 'Sir, I am in contempt of court. I will not answer any more questions.'

Cantley (grimly): 'You may find that an uncomfortable place to be.'

Scott: 'I have gone on enough over the years with this story. I will not say any more.'

Cantley: 'Do you want to go home now?'

Scott: 'I don't mind where I go. I won't have myself destroyed in this way when he knows very well his client is lying. I have had enough!'

The silence that followed was eventually broken by Carman. 'I am sorry, Mr Scott, but it is my professional duty to ask a considerable number of further questions. Are you going to answer them?'

Scott was implacable. 'I have nothing to say.'

Again, silence fell. No one seemed sure what to do.

'Are you going to answer further questions?' Cantley asked.

'No, sir,' said Scott. 'Not if I am going to be treated as a most dreadful criminal. I am not a liar.'

'Now listen here,' said Cantley, moderating his tone and sounding almost kindly himself, 'there are two sides to this case. You have made allegations against Mr Thorpe and it is his counsel's duty to put Mr Thorpe's version. It necessarily involves this sort of questioning. That is why you are being questioned and the jury in the end will decide what is the right answer . . .'

For a few moments it looked as if Scott were going to hold firm. Then all at once he crumbled. 'Yes, sir. I am sorry. I am sorry.'

When Carman resumed his questioning, he asked why Scott had been so upset about the fact that David Holmes had paid £2,500 for the letters he and Bessell had exchanged.

'I was afraid that I would be committed because of the whole story,' Scott said. 'Because of my lies in the past . . . I felt that people would regard my story as too fanciful for words and I would be committed to a lunatic asylum.'

What about the time when he went to the House of Commons with Gwen Parry-Jones? Was he not hell-bent on destroying Thorpe? Absolutely not, Scott insisted. He was merely trying to sort out the problems with his National Insurance card. Then, with great solemnity, he delivered perhaps his most memorable line of all, 'National Insurance is my lifeblood!'

As the court was digesting this, Carman asked Scott if he had ever boasted of having affairs with well-known actors.

'I have boasted of friendships with actors,' Scott admitted.

'Why did you do that?'

'Because I did – I just did . . .'

Half to himself, Scott added, 'I didn't think this court would ever sit, I can assure you. I thought the Establishment would cover it up.'

'Have you an obsession about this?'

'Of course I had. So would you if people were trying to kill you,' said Scott, not unreasonably.

'Let us once and for all clear up any mystery about this,' said

Carman. 'You knew, or had good reason to believe, that Mr Thorpe in 1961 had homosexual tendencies?'

'Yes, sir.'

'He was the most famous and distinguished person you had met at the time?'

'Yes, sir. I think so.'

'You were flattered that for a short time he introduced you into a different social world. I suggest you were upset and annoyed because he did not want to have sexual relations with you.'

'Of course that is ridiculous because he did.'

On the face of it there was nothing especially dramatic about this exchange. Behind it, though, lay months of planning. Carman knew that if he tried to pretend Thorpe had never been homosexual, Taylor would produce several witnesses who would swear that he had. Taylor had also told Carman that he was in possession of a sexually explicit postcard Thorpe had written to a man called Bruno in San Francisco. Admitting that Thorpe had once had 'homosexual tendencies' – leaving aside the question of whether he had ever acted on them – meant there was no need for Taylor to call any of his witnesses. Adroitly, almost without anyone noticing, Carman had skipped over a landmine.

The judge didn't even seem that interested in Thorpe's sexual tendencies. What interested him far more were Scott's financial arrangements.

'How are you supporting yourself now?' he asked.

'I am self-employed,' Scott told him. 'I give dressage lessons.'

He added that he owned three horses, and liked to hunt.

'Sounds very comfortably off,' said Cantley approvingly. 'How did you manage to get money to start the business?'

Scott said that he used money he'd been paid by television companies for interviews. There was nothing obviously noteworthy about this exchange either – but, again, it was more revealing than it appeared. Both the two main prosecution witnesses had been exposed as proven liars. Proven liars, moreover, who had made money from giving their side of the story.

That evening, the *Daily Express*'s Jean Rook sat down to write her account of the day's proceedings. Never one to err on the side of understatement, she did not stint herself now. 'It is as dramatic as *Hamlet*, as thrilling as the Derby, as gripping as Wimbledon,' she wrote. 'It is the greatest show on Earth.'

Norman Scott was washing his hands in the Old Bailey lavatories the next morning when he noticed a man standing at the next-door basin. Like Scott, this other man was in his late thirties, had dark hair and was wearing a suit. But there the resemblance ended. The last time Scott and Andrew Newton had seen one another was at Newton's trial, when Scott's evidence had sent him to prison. The time before that had been on Exmoor, when Newton had tried to kill him.

Now Newton was all smiles, behaving as if this had merely been an unfortunate blip in an otherwise warm friendship. Scott wasn't having any of it – 'I just ignored him.' He had only come to court because he had been asked to produce a copy of a newspaper contract that he had signed. Once Cantley had examined this, Scott was dismissed and it was Newton's turn to go into the witness box. At Minehead, Newton had arrived wearing a balaclava helmet. This time round he seemed less eager to play the jester – even though, like Bessell, he had been given immunity from prosecution.

Questioned by George Deakin's barrister, Gareth Williams, QC, Newton recalled speaking to Deakin amid the mayhem of the Showmen's Ball in Blackpool. 'I said, "I understand you want someone bumped off. If you have got nobody, I am your man" – or words to that effect.' Newton agreed that he had been extremely drunk at the time and this might have affected his judgement. 'You would probably agree it is a different world after sixteen pints,' he added ruefully.

To begin with, Newton had been told that Scott lived in Dunstable in Bedfordshire. He went there and spent two fruitless days trying to find him, only to learn that Scott actually lived in Barnstaple in Devon. It was not a very promising start, he admitted. At a subsequent meeting with David Holmes, Newton said he had been told that he could kill Scott and dispose of his body in any way he saw fit. As he had demonstrated before, Newton needed no second invitation to let his imagination run wild. After giving the matter considerable thought, he decided to kill Scott with a chisel – a chisel which he would conceal in a bouquet of flowers.

First, he planned to lure Scott to the Royal Garden Hotel in Kensington by promising him some modelling work for his fictitious agency, Pensiero Fashions. Then, once Scott was in his room, he would pull out the chisel and beat him to death – or 'bend it over his head', as he put it.

'Surely it would be easier to kill someone with a gun than with a chisel?' asked Williams.

'That is debatable,' replied Newton with a not entirely convincing air of expertise.

This puzzled Sir Joseph Cantley too – though not for the same reasons. 'But you were going to meet a man?' he said. 'Why was it necessary to have a bunch of flowers?'

Newton explained that this was a ruse to smuggle the chisel past any security guards, but still Cantley looked puzzled. The idea that one man might give another flowers was clearly one he'd never come across before. However, Newton had had to abort his plan when Scott didn't turn up. This came as a big relief, he insisted. Already he was having his doubts about the whole scheme. None the less, he went along with it – but only after making a crucial change to his plan. Instead of killing Scott, he would merely frighten him. That, anyway, was Newton's account of what had happened. He agreed that he was known to his friends as 'Chicken-brain', and that there was nothing malicious about this nickname. Rather, it was intended as a fair description of his mental capabilities.

Throughout his cross-examination, Newton stuck to his story that he was only ever trying to frighten Scott. This had been his intention when they had driven on to Exmoor on 24 October 1975, he said, but then the dog had gone and spoiled everything. If only

Rinka had been smaller, he wouldn't have minded so much. 'As it was, the dog was a monstrous size . . . so I shot it.'

Turning the gun on Scott, Newton then pretended it had jammed – all part of his amended plan, he claimed.

'Do you know what a buffoon is?' Gareth Williams asked at one point.

'Yes, I think so,' Newton replied.

'A buffoon would be someone who lacked moral sense.'

Possibly, he allowed.

'Why did you wear that absurd hat at Minehead?'

'I didn't want to make the press's job any easier.'

'Do you agree that it was the action of a buffoon?'

'No,' said Newton, before adding in a lordly if slightly injured voice, 'one is entitled to wear what one wants.' Then he nodded pointedly at Williams's horsehair wig. 'After all, I mean to say, you wear what is on your head.'

Once Newton had been dismissed, witnesses started coming and going with ever increasing frequency. Although neither they nor any of the onlookers knew it, the last act of the trial was already under way, the climax fast approaching.

On 4 June, Day 18, Jack Hayward gave evidence – 'a nice, respectable witness', as Lord Justice Cantley described him with obvious relief. Various letters were read out that Hayward and Thorpe had exchanged. In one of them, dated 20 April 1978, Hayward's frustration was all too plain: 'I am the last one to shirk a fight or desert my friends, but I do like to know who I am fighting, what it is all about and who my friends are. I am rapidly getting the impression that my friends have not told me the truth and it is also becoming apparent to me that I am being set up as a fall guy and a sucker of the first degree.

'All I have done (and God! how I regret it!) was to help the Liberal Party and various Liberals, despite the fact that I am not a member of the party and never was and disagree intensely with a lot of their policies. I feel a number of innocent people, including myself, have been or are being implicated in these Liberal machinations and I think it is time it stopped and the principals involved came clean.'

Cross-examined by George Carman, Hayward was assured that no one was claiming that he had been involved in anything underhand. 'So many names have been bandied about this court, I wanted to make it perfectly clear on behalf of Mr Thorpe that there is no suggestion you have been guilty of any kind of financial or commercial impropriety.'

'Thank you very much,' said Hayward. 'And thank Mr Thorpe,' he added.

Hayward was followed by Nadir Dinshaw. Not only was Mr Dinshaw a successful Karachi-born businessman, the court heard, he was also Rupert Thorpe's godfather. Dinshaw recalled going for a walk with Thorpe in St James's Park a year earlier. During the walk Dinshaw told Thorpe that he was going to tell the truth about the money he'd passed on to David Holmes – money which was subsequently used to pay Andrew Newton. Thorpe had implored him not to say any more than necessary. If he did, 'It will be curtains for me and you will be asked to move on.'

As far as Dinshaw was concerned, there was an obvious threat here – keep your mouth shut, or else you'll be deported. This conversation made him feel 'very, very sad, both for myself and for him', he said. 'Mr Thorpe has many virtues,' Dinshaw added in the same sorrowful tones, 'but an ability to control his feelings is not one of them.'

For some time, rumours had been flying about that George Carman was going to make an important announcement – an announcement that would affect the whole course of the trial. No one, though, seemed to have any idea what it might be. At 4.15, on the afternoon of 7 June, just as the court was about to adjourn for the day, Carman stood up. His manner gave no indication that he had anything significant to say, but, as he had already proved, he liked to take his audience unawares.

'My lord,' he said, 'on behalf of Jeremy Thorpe, I call no evidence.'

At first there was silence as everyone tried to take in the implications of this. It was followed by a frantic scramble of journalists rushing from the court to telephone their news desks. Carman, the man who had once lost so much money playing blackjack that he'd been forced to sell his house, had just taken the biggest gamble of his life.

35

The Judgement of Cantley

'Silent Thorpe' read the headline in the next morning's *Daily Telegraph*; 'No evidence surprise at the Old Bailey'. It wasn't just that Carman's announcement came as a surprise; there was also a widespread sense of disappointment, annoyance even. People felt cheated. For weeks they had been looking forward to seeing Thorpe fighting for his life. Now they were to be denied.

What did it mean? Some, inevitably, saw Thorpe's reluctance to give evidence as a tacit admission of guilt. After all, why would an innocent man pass up the opportunity to give his side of the story? Peter Bessell had his own theory. 'Throughout his life, he [Thorpe] had depended on others to extricate him from every personal crisis with which he was confronted. What could be more logical than that he should now depend on George Carman to do that which so many others had done before?'

Carman himself couldn't have cared less what anyone thought. His job was to get his client acquitted. He knew that if Thorpe went into the witness box, he risked being torn apart, just like Bessell. Thorpe was more arrogant than Bessell, and therefore more likely to get carried away by his own rhetoric. Carman also knew that neither John Le Mesurier nor David Holmes would be giving evidence. It was learning that Holmes had opted to stay silent that had finally made up Carman's mind. While Holmes was prepared to do a lot of things for Thorpe, he wasn't prepared to lie under oath. 'If I had given evidence on oath it would have been necessary to have told the truth about the occasions when Jeremy wanted Scott killed,' Holmes admitted later. 'In saving myself I would have convicted Jeremy on the incitement charge and that I was not prepared to do. I was not going to let him down at the last moment. I am not trying to sound noble. It was just unthinkable after ten years of trying to save him.'

As Holmes wasn't going to try to save himself, there was no need for Thorpe to deny any accusations he might have made. But that wasn't all; there was something else shaping Carman's thinking. He had calculated that he didn't actually need Thorpe to testify. The case against him rested, almost entirely, on the evidence of three men: Bessell, Scott and Newton. Already Carman had demonstrated that all three were liars. He had also shown that Scott had been fantasizing about having a relationship with Thorpe before he ever went to see him in London. If the jury couldn't believe what the three men had said, they would have to find Thorpe not guilty.

That, at any rate, was Carman's gamble. Of course, it was possible the jury might go the other way. They might feel that Bessell, Scott and Newton were unlikely to have made up the whole story, however much they had lied in the past. As Carman had always suspected, everything was going to depend on his final speech. He spent the weekend at his home in Altrincham in Cheshire, chain-smoking, scribbling notes on pieces of paper, and going over and over his lines.

On 11 June – Day 22 of the trial – Peter Taylor began his own closing address. The story of Jeremy Thorpe, he told the jury, 'is a tragedy of truly Greek or Shakespearian proportions – the slow but inevitable destruction of a man by the stamp of one defect'.

When Taylor sat down two full days later, one of the policemen sitting in the dock heard Thorpe mutter, 'The bastard!' Then came John Mathew, QC, for David Holmes, Gareth Williams for George Deakin, Denis Cowley, QC, for John Le Mesurier and, finally, on the afternoon of 14 June, George Carman.

In working out how to pitch his speech, Carman had to make certain assumptions. He knew that the jurors – if they were a representative cross-section of British society – were likely to be a fairly conventional bunch. While they might not agree with Thorpe politically, they would have been brought up to respect authority figures. As a result, they could hardly fail to be affected by how quickly, how catastrophically, he had fallen. In effect, Carman threw Thorpe on their mercy.

'Privately he is a man with a life that had had more than its fair share of grief and agony,' he told them. 'Nature has so fashioned him that at the time he had the misfortune to meet Norman Scott, he was a man with homosexual tendencies . . .' Just in case anyone doubted the extent of Thorpe's descent, Carman emphasized that he was now finished as a politician. 'You will recognize from the evidence that a political life and political future are now irrevocably and irreversibly denied to him.'

But Carman's approach was more subtle – and devious – than it appeared. Essentially, he was playing a double game. On the one hand he was appealing to the jurors' sympathy by pointing out Thorpe's human flaws. On the other, he kept reminding them how distinguished his client is – or was. 'Mr Jeremy Thorpe does not wish any advantage or disadvantage. He is now in your sole charge and he is content with that position. But inevitably because of the prominence he has achieved in the public life of this country, the case has centred to an extent on the life and times of Jeremy Thorpe – his frailties, his weaknesses have been exposed remorselessly to the public gaze.'

The next morning – presumably following protests from Thorpe himself – Carman engaged in some hasty back-pedalling on the subject of Thorpe's future. 'At his age, if your conscience and your oath permit you to say not guilty, there may still be a place somewhere in the public life and public service of this country for a man of his talents.'

He then advanced an entirely new theory about what had happened. Was it not possible that Holmes and Le Mesurier had cooked the whole thing up between them without telling Thorpe? This, of course, was the story that Thorpe had suggested Holmes should stick to a year earlier. Now, sitting in the dock just a few feet away from Thorpe, Holmes listened in astonishment to what Carman was saying. If he was going to take the blame for what had happened, surely Thorpe should have consulted him first? For Holmes, this was the moment when he finally saw his old friend in his true colours. 'I couldn't believe it. Then I realized that the whole nightmare had not been worthwhile.'

Having tossed out this red herring, Carman carried on much as before – carefully doling out alternate spoonfuls of sympathy and respect. Pleading with the jury to feel sorry for Thorpe, while suggesting in the next breath that his rightful place was on Mount Olympus. 'We learn, do we not, that idols sometimes have feet of clay?' As for Thorpe's homosexual tendencies, these should be treated in the same spirit of understanding. 'There are people who have propensities which we personally may not understand. To them, we have to extend tolerance, sympathy and compassion . . .'

The jury must not read anything into Thorpe's not appearing in the witness box, Carman said. 'It is a right invested by law that a defendant can stay silent. Everyone suspected or accused of a crime is entitled at the beginning and at every stage until the end of his trial to the right to say, "Ask me no questions, I shall answer none."'

Nor should they worry about finding Thorpe not guilty – even if they suspected that his hands might not be entirely clean. 'You must not suppose that a not-guilty verdict is some sort of certificate of innocence awarded by the jury. In law, it means that the prosecution had failed to make its case.' Again, the message may have been veiled, but it was clear enough. If the jurors were going to convict a man of Thorpe's stature, they must be absolutely convinced of his guilt.

The moment he moved on to the subject of Norman Scott, Carman's own supplies of compassion ran dry. Not only was Scott a liar, he was also an hysteric – though whether 'sad, mad or bad or a combination of all three, I care not'. And then, of course, there was the vilest, most contemptible creature of all: Peter Bessell.

'Mr Bessell may go down at the end of this case as the Judas Iscariot of British politics of the twentieth century, because he has three things in common: one, he seeks to betray a friend; two, he seeks to betray him for money; and three, he seeks to betray a man who, I submit, is innocent of the charges laid against him. If, by your verdict, you say not guilty, that may be the final epitaph of Mr Bessell.'

Carman had given more thought to how to end his speech than anything else. He knew he had to come up with something memorable, ideally with a lyrical flourish. Something that both stirred jurors' hearts and gave their insides a threatening squeeze.

'You have the right as citizens to vote in elections,' he told them. 'But you have a much more important right and a much greater responsibility to vote guilty or not guilty. Mr Thorpe has spent twenty years in British politics and obtained thousands and thousands of votes in his favour. Now,' he said, delivering a line his son Dominic had come up with two days before, 'the most precious twelve votes come from you.'

Then Carman slowly pointed at each member of the jury in turn. 'Your vote, and yours, and yours, and yours . . . In accordance with your conscience, I say to you, on behalf of Jeremy Thorpe, this prosecution has not been made out. Let this prosecution fold their tents and silently steal away.' With that, he sat down. A few moments later, Thorpe passed him a note from the dock. It read 'Well rowed, Balliol.'

'This is a very serious charge and a rather bizarre and surprising case,' declared Sir Joseph Cantley at the start of what would soon become the most notorious summing-up in British legal history. 'It is right for you to pause and consider whether it is likely that such persons would do the things these persons are said to have done . . . The four accused are men of hitherto unblemished reputation. Mr Thorpe is a Privy Councillor, a former Leader of the Liberal Party and a national figure with a very distinguished public record.'

In fact, Cantley was wrong on two counts. One of the defendants – George Deakin – had a criminal record for receiving stolen property. Another – Thorpe himself – had been criticized by a Department of Trade report for his role in the collapse of the London and County Securities Group. He then turned to Peter Bessell's evidence. Could the jurors trust it, given that he had sold his story to a newspaper? 'We can only play for safety,' Cantley said. 'We must look at his evidence with distrust if that is the conclusion we have come to about him and treat it as dangerous to act upon his evidence unless we find good reason elsewhere to believe it to be true.' In other words, no.

As for Bessell's character, jurors would have to make up their own minds about that. But in case they were having any difficulty, Cantley gave them a nudge in what he clearly felt was the right direction. 'You will have seen that Mr Bessell is plainly a very intelligent, very articulate man. He must have impressed the electors of Cornwall very much. He told us he was a lay preacher at the same time as being, as he put it, sexually promiscuous. And therefore a humbug,' he added.

As well as being a humbug, Bessell was a man who, as Cantley put it, had 'quite a record'. Lest anyone think he had gone too far, he reminded the jury that Bessell might – conceivably – be telling the truth. 'When I say you must look at Bessell's evidence with suspicion, it does not mean you cannot believe it if there is no corroboration.'

This bewildering triple-negative heralded the end of what Auberon Waugh considered to be 'as deliberate and prolonged a destruction of one witness as anyone was likely to hear. Whether it was justified, or whether it was an abuse of judicial power, is something which would have to be decided between Joseph Cantley and his Maker.'

But Cantley, it turned out, was only limbering up; there was plenty more where that came from. 'I now turn to the evidence of Mr Norman Scott,' he said. 'You will remember him well. A hysterical, warped personality, accomplished sponger and very skilful at exciting and exploiting sympathy . . . He is a crook. He is a fraud. He is a sponger. He is a whiner. He is a parasite.'

Once again Cantley gave the brake pedal the lightest of prods. 'But of course he could still be telling the truth . . . You must not think that because I am not concealing my opinion of Mr Scott I am suggesting you should not believe him. That is not for me. I am not expressing any opinion.'

Cantley didn't express any opinion of Andrew Newton either – beyond saying that he was a buffoon, a perjurer and, almost certainly, a fraud. 'What a chump the man is! To frighten or to murder – that is no way to go about it.' He went on to say that he doubted if Newton paid any income tax, as though this were the ultimate mark of moral depravity. As for George Deakin, 'He was probably the type of man whose taste ran to a cocktail bar in his living room.' What Deakin's taste in interior décor had to do with his guilt or innocence was anyone's guess.

After firing off a few more salvos at Norman Scott – 'a spineless neurotic character, addicted to self-advertisement' – Cantley came to what he considered to be the nub of the case. The evidence against Thorpe was 'almost entirely circumstantial'. Scott's claim to have had an affair with him 'was the kind of story people are so ready to believe these days, even if it wasn't true'. Any examination of his motives had to take into account the depths of his malice. 'You had the opportunity of seeing Scott in the witness box and you can see his vindictive attitude. Scott has said, "I pity him", but he doesn't – he hates him.'

Finally, Cantley told the jurors that they should start their deliberations by considering the charge of conspiracy to murder. 'You should ask yourselves if you are sure there was a conspiracy to murder Norman Scott . . . If the answer to that is "No, we are not sure", that is an end to it, because if there was no conspiracy, none of the accused can be guilty of it. If the answer if "Yes, we are sure", then you should proceed conscientiously to examine the evidence against each of the defendants in turn. If you find a doubt about any of the accused, he is entitled to be acquitted.'

Having done so, they should consider the charge of incitement to murder – against Thorpe alone. 'Again, you must ask yourself if you are sure that early in 1969 Thorpe seriously and genuinely tried to persuade Holmes to murder Mr Scott. If you are completely sure, you will convict, but if there is any reasonable doubt you will acquit.'

Cantley then smiled and gave a little wave. Wrapped in his red robe with its ermine trimmings, he looked more than ever like the elder of some woodland-dwelling clan. 'You may go now,' he said. 'Take as long as you like. There is no hurry. We shall wait for you.'

The first thing the jury did on being shown into the jury-room behind the court was to elect a Foreman, or Forewoman. Mrs Celia Kettle-Williams, a home economics teacher at a comprehensive school in South East London, was the unanimous choice – mainly, the other jurors told her, because she had been the only one who sounded confident when taking the oath. Mrs Kettle-Williams began by taking a straw poll to gain some idea of everyone's views. It resulted in an even split with six jurors for conviction and six against.

At the end of the day – with the jury still out – the four defendants were put in a police van and driven to Brixton Prison to spend the night. To stop anyone from photographing them through the windows of the van, the defendants lay on the floor, handcuffed together. When they arrived at Brixton, they were stripped, given a medical examination and told to shower. Holmes, Le Mesurier and Deakin had to share cells with other prisoners. Thorpe, however, complained that he had a stomach upset and – in keeping with the preferential treatment he had been accorded throughout – was taken to the more comfortable surroundings of the prison hospital. The jurors spent the night at the Westmoreland Hotel in St John's Wood, where they were given strict instructions not to watch the television news. As it was a hot night, they asked if they could go for a walk after they'd had their supper, and were taken, under escort, to Regent's Park.

The next morning the four defendants were once again handcuffed together and driven back to the Old Bailey, where they were locked in a private room. When he saw George Carman, Thorpe said cheerily, 'Hello, George, you look as if you've had a rough night.' As he had been when Thorpe was charged, David Napley was amazed by how relaxed he was. 'From all outward appearance, the calmest and most confident person of all those gathered there was Jeremy Thorpe himself. It really was remarkable.' At Le Mesurier's suggestion, the men passed the time by playing Liar Dice – a game which involved each of the players trying to deceive the others. While Thorpe enthusiastically joined in, Carman paced about the corridor outside, chain-smoking.

Meanwhile, Peter Bessell sat by the phone in a New York hotel and waited. A week earlier he had received a call from the editor of the *Sunday Telegraph*, John Thompson. Clearly embarrassed, Thompson told Bessell that the paper had decided to cancel its contract with him. After what they had heard at the trial, they no longer felt he was a fit person to appear in their pages.

Bessell did not try to argue. As the hours dragged by, he found himself hoping that the jury would be unable to reach a verdict. If there was a hung jury, the chances of a retrial were remote, he suspected. However unsatisfactory that might be in legal terms, at least his conscience would be clear. 'How could I welcome a jury decision that sent Jeremy to the misery and degradation of a prison cell? But I certainly could not rejoice over an acquittal.'

At the end of the second day there was still no decision. Once again the defendants were taken back to Brixton Prison – where, once again, Thorpe complained of a stomach upset and was taken to the prison hospital. Midway through the next day his stomach had recovered sufficiently for him, and the other defendants, to enjoy a lunch of smoked salmon, rare roast beef and Chablis sent in by Thorpe's friend and fellow Liberal MP, the food writer Clement Freud. They too discussed the possibility of a hung jury. Thorpe said he thought that it was unlikely that Bessell would attend any retrial. He had also heard that the *Sunday Telegraph* had cancelled Bessell's contract.

And then, at 2.34, on the afternoon of Friday, 22 June, fifty-one hours and forty-nine minutes after they had started their deliberations, word came through that the jury had finally returned. Led into the packed courtroom, the four defendants stood shoulder to shoulder in the dock. None of them looked at one another. Rather they stared straight ahead as the door in the back of the court opened.

In silence, Sir Joseph Cantley took his seat. Then the clerk of the court asked the Forewoman, Mrs Kettle-Williams, to confirm that they had reached a verdict.

Yes, they had, she said.

First she was asked for the verdicts on the charge of conspiracy to murder. Each name was read out in turn.

'David Holmes.'

'Not guilty,' said Mrs Kettle-Williams in her clear, confident voice.

As the verdict was announced, Holmes swayed and seemed about to faint. One of the wardens held out his hand to catch him if he fell.

'George Deakin.'

'Not guilty,' said Mrs Kettle-Williams again.

Slumping forward, Deakin burst into tears.

'John Le Mesurier.'

'Not guilty.'

Le Mesurier pursed his lips and nodded to himself.

And finally Jeremy Thorpe.

'Not guilty.'

There was a sudden intake of breath from all around the court, a collective gasp. Then came the separate charge of incitement to murder. How did the jury find the defendant?

'Not guilty.'

To begin with Thorpe didn't react, not even when Le Mesurier grabbed his arm to congratulate him. For several moments he stayed staring straight ahead with his hands still clasped behind his back. All at once his face broke into a grin. Turning around, he said to Marion, 'Darling, we did it!' Then came a glimpse of the old Thorpe, the inveterate grand-stander. Taking the three cushions that had been supporting his back throughout the trial, he hurled them over the glass partition of the witness box. Amid all the excitement, Carman showed no emotion, busying himself with tidying his papers. Later, he would describe the moment as being beyond words.

Clearly annoyed by this disturbance, Cantley told everyone to stay where they were – 'Keep still, stand still, or regret it!' But no one took any notice, least of all the reporters.

For Gareth Williams, David Holmes's barrister, 'It was the most incredible scene I have ever seen. When the verdict came in, Holmes was swaying on his feet like a drunken boxer. He was totally gone, out on his feet, supported by the wardens. But Thorpe had a look of total equanimity, a sort of told-you-so expression. In five seconds he was unfazed and was thanking the coppers in the dock and kissing the lady usher. He was saying to the press, "I will see you outside." Poor old Holmes. I went down to the cells and took him to my car. I ran him down the road and put him in a taxi.'

Outside the court, the crowds were standing ten deep, held back by a row of police with their arms linked together. When Thorpe appeared in the doorway with both his hands held above his head, people surged forward. Fights broke out and a policeman's helmet was knocked off. Thorpe and Marion were bundled into Napley's Rolls-Royce. They were driven back to Orme Square, where Thorpe gave a televised statement: 'I have always maintained that I was innocent of the charges brought against me. The verdict of the jury, after a prolonged and careful investigation by them, I regard as totally fair, just and a complete vindication.'

When Ursula Thorpe was asked what she thought of the verdict, her reply was more revealing than she might have intended. 'He is so lucky with his women,' she said. That evening, after drinking several bottles of champagne, Thorpe, Marion and Ursula emerged on to the balcony, where the three of them stood like marionettes waving stiffly at the crowd below.

Norman Scott was not in court to hear the verdict; he had gone back home to Devon to be with his animals. He was not greatly surprised that Thorpe had been acquitted, he told waiting reporters. He had always suspected that Thorpe might get off, despite the weight of evidence against him. 'I hoped and prayed that he would go to prison because he had done such appalling damage. But somehow I knew it would happen; I felt the Establishment would look after their own.' Asked what he was going to do next, Scott said that he might go on holiday – to Tibet.

Writing in the following day's *Evening Standard*, Max Hastings said, 'Inevitably, rumour, speculation and controversy will surround "The Scott Affair" for generations to come.' In an editorial the paper expressed confidence that Thorpe would be able to bounce back to some sort of prominence. 'Considering the unswerving loyalty and support of his immediate family, there is every reason to hope that Mr Thorpe can achieve the same sort of redemption as Mr Profumo.'

Others, though, were not so sure. 'Mr Thorpe exercised the right of every citizen,' declared the *Daily Telegraph*, 'but his public image might have been better served had he explained the whole course of his behaviour publicly and on oath.' The *Daily Mirror* was blunter still: 'He has been cleared of the criminal charges against him but the uncontested evidence puts an end to his public life.'

However ambivalent people's reactions were, one man at least had no doubt that justice had triumphed. On Sunday, 1 July 1979, the Reverend John Hornby, the vicar of the parish of Bratton Fleming in Thorpe's old constituency, held a thanksgiving service for Jeremy and Marion Thorpe. Expecting far more people to come than the little Victorian church could hold, Hornby had arranged for speakers to relay the service to people in the nearby village hall. But the village hall was empty and, apart from Thorpe, Marion and Thorpe's son, Rupert, the congregation consisted almost entirely of journalists.

Undeterred, Hornby told them, 'We have the opportunity to give thanks to God for the ministry of his servant Jeremy in North Devon. In the long, dark days of Minehead and the Old Bailey, God granted Marion and Jeremy that fantastic resilience which has aroused the admiration of the whole world! The darkness is now past and the true light shines! This is the day the Lord hath made!

Now is the day of our salvation! Thanks be to God, for with God nothing is impossible!'

Peter Bessell was still in New York when a journalist telephoned to tell him that Thorpe had been acquitted. By coincidence, he was staying in the same hotel where he had heard the news that Thorpe had been arrested. But now there was no electrical storm, no lightning dancing symbolically on the horizon. Now, as Bessell put down the phone, there was only silence, solitude and sadness.

36

Awkward Bows

Peter Bessell died, of emphysema, on 27 November 1985, aged sixty-four. He and Diane had carried on living in Oceanside – they married in 1978 – where he took a keen interest in local politics. To the end, Bessell remained convinced that Jeremy Thorpe had been protected by an Establishment cover-up: 'Indisputably, there was a deliberate cover-up, or series of cover-ups, for almost eighteen years of Jeremy's relationship with Scott. Certain ministers of the Crown, branches of the security services and more than one police force knew about the cover-up and took no action to prevent it.'

He felt sure that the police investigation, the committal hearing and indeed the trial itself had been affected as a result. He was baffled by the way in which the Director of Public Prosecutions' office had approved his deal with the *Sunday Telegraph* – only for it to be cited, repeatedly, in court as a key reason why he couldn't be trusted. Then there was the way in which Joseph Cantley – 'that sozzled old eunuch', as Bessell called him in a letter to Auberon Waugh – had made it clear to the jury that he considered Bessell to be a compulsive liar.

But Bessell wasn't the only one who suspected there had been something amiss about the trial. Detective Chief Superintendent Michael Challes, who had persuaded him to testify, told Diane that Sir Joseph Cantley's summing-up was the worst he had ever heard. Challes also wrote to Bessell saying bluntly, 'The judge failed in his public duty.' Three weeks after the trial ended, Lord Hartwell told the House of Lords that 'The extraordinary, or bizarre, aspect of the trial was the relish with which the judge made himself the ally of the defence in this connection. Between them the judge and defence counsel savaged the prosecution witnesses, including Bessell.'

Gareth Williams, later Baron Williams of Mostyn, who died in 2003, was equally convinced there had been a bias in Thorpe's favour. 'I don't think the witnesses were objectively treated. I don't think the prosecution case was fairly assessed by the judge. I think there was too much kow-towing to Mr Thorpe's social and political position.'

There were those too, including Auberon Waugh, who believed that Peter Taylor, QC – later the Lord Chief Justice – had not prosecuted the case as vigorously as he might have done. Even George Carman was puzzled by Taylor's restraint in court – something he put down to his being too much of a gentleman to go for the jugular. Others thought that Taylor had one eye on his own ambitions and didn't want to ruffle too many feathers.

The idea that there might have been a concerted attempt to protect Thorpe was lent weight by what apparently happened to Dennis Meighan – the man first approached to kill Scott. Meighan later confessed to his role in the affair and gave a statement to police about his meeting with the 'representative of Jeremy Thorpe'. A few days afterwards he was asked to call in at a police station in west London to sign his statement. But the statement he was shown – Meighan claimed – bore little resemblance to the one he had given. In particular, there was no mention of either Thorpe or the Liberal Party.

Before the committal hearing in Minehead, Bessell had written an aide-memoire, as he called it – an account of his involvement in the case, from the moment he had first met Jeremy Thorpe back in 1955. After the trial, he expanded this into a book, entitled *Cover-Up*, in which he outlined his reasons for believing that Thorpe had been protected by his influential friends. As he had so often done before, Bessell tried to get to the bottom of Thorpe's behaviour, but in the end he rather gave up and fell back on Mark Twain's quote: 'Everyone is a moon and has a dark side which he never shows to anyone.'

No commercial publisher would touch the book – not surprisingly in view of some of the allegations made – and Bessell paid for 2,000 copies to be privately printed. Convinced, as always, that a change in his fortunes lay just around the corner, he made sure that the words 'Limited First Edition' were prominently displayed on the title page. But there was never a second edition and, when he died, the garage at Oceanside was still full of unsold copies. Nor did Bessell ever manage to find a publisher for his children's book about the little alien and the kindly man who tries to educate him in the ways of the world.

His obituary in the *Los Angeles Times* paid tribute to his involvement in local politics and, in particular, to the campaign he had mounted to replace eroded sand on Oceanside's beaches. 'Bessell, a dapper, silver-haired man, who settled in a beachfront home with his wife here in the mid 1970s, was perhaps best known internationally for his involvement in the Jeremy Thorpe Affair, a lurid political scandal that rocked England in the late 1970s . . . In Oceanside, his activities were somewhat more pedestrian. But his impact on the North San Diego community was significant, friends and political colleagues said . . .'

'Peter was the most fascinating man I've ever met,' said former Oceanside councilwoman Melba Bishop, a close friend. 'He had been at the very top of the political spiral. He had talked with kings, queens and presidents, and negotiated war and peace issues. And lo and behold he winds up involved in local politics in Oceanside. Frankly, he brought a lot of class to this town.'

In January 1981, David Holmes was arrested for 'importuning for an immoral purpose' on the Old Brompton Road in South Kensington. Two Police Constables told West London Magistrates' Court how they had seen him approach several men before walking off with a man wearing tight jeans. When they arrested him, Holmes begged them to let him off. 'Look, I promise to go straight home, only not this,' he was reported as saying. 'I'll never come back here again, please.' The policemen remained unmoved. Holmes was fined £25.

The story was picked up by the tabloid press – 'The Sex Shame of Thorpe's Friend'. By then it wasn't just Holmes's reputation that had suffered. Shunned by Thorpe – they never spoke again after the trial – his former business colleagues also gave him the cold-shoulder. Holmes had moved from merchant banking into consultancy, but, unable to find work in the financial sector, he became the Manager of a roller-disco in Camden Town, North London.

Five months after his arrest, Holmes's account of what had happened in the Thorpe Affair appeared in the Sunday scandal-sheet the *News of the World* – a deal negotiated by the paper's then-Deputy Editor, Stuart Kuttner. 'It was plain that David had come down in the world, but he didn't seem bitter and I didn't have any sense that he was motivated by revenge. I think he just wanted to set the record straight.' Nor was Holmes motivated by money. Despite his reduced circumstances, he refused to take a fee from the paper, telling them to give it to charity instead.

Although he had no reason to corroborate Bessell's version of events in *Cover-Up*, in all key respects the two accounts tallied. Holmes recalled how, in the winter of 1968/9, he had first heard the name Norman Scott. 'During the following two or three weeks, Jeremy, Peter Bessell and I had several talks about the problem of this lunatic boy. At the third meeting Jeremy was frantic. He told us he wanted Scott out of the way – a job in Mongolia, anything, anywhere. "And," he said, "if all else fails, kill him." '

David Holmes died, of cancer, in 1990, aged fifty-nine. After his death, his solicitor, David Freeman, said, 'He was a very nice chap. One of the nicest I have ever defended. Thorpe was the *deus ex machina,* no doubt about that . . . He [Holmes] was taken in by Thorpe's tremendous superficial charm. Who will rid me of this pestilent Scott? So Holmes rode forth – and buggered it all up.'

As David Napley had predicted, the Thorpe trial was the making of George Carman. Overnight, he became the most famous barrister in the country. Everyone wanted to ingratiate themselves with him – or almost everyone. When the trial was over, Carman assumed that Thorpe would write him a letter of thanks. Under the circumstances it was the least he could do. But a month went by without any letter arriving. Puzzled as well as hurt, Carman told Napley that he hadn't heard anything.

Another six weeks passed. By now Carman was feeling more angry than hurt. Again he told Napley that he hadn't heard from Thorpe. But still no letter was forthcoming. Eventually, almost four months after the trial had finished, a letter did arrive. Although it was full of gushing praise, Carman felt that something about it didn't ring true. The letter struck him as the sort of thing that had been dashed off in a couple of minutes. Like so much else Thorpe did, it was all froth and bluster. Before the trial, Thorpe had also promised Carman that if he got him off, he would present him with an antique sword that the last Tsar of Russia, Nicholas II, had given to Thorpe's grandfather. But afterwards this promise was conveniently forgotten; the sword stayed put in Orme Square.

Carman's success in the Thorpe trial made him the first choice for what proved to be a long line of celebrity clients. He successfully represented the comedian Ken Dodd – accused of tax evasion – and won high-profile libel cases for Robert Maxwell, Richard Branson, Elton John and Tom Cruise. But fame and prosperity did nothing to drive away his demons. When he wasn't in court he remained as volatile, as self-destructive as ever. All three of Carman's marriages fell apart, with each of his ex-wives claiming he had physically and emotionally abused them. One of them, Celia Sparrow, recalled how Carman had once taken two large knives out of their kitchen cutlery drawer and said, 'Which one do you want in you first?'

Winning was the one thing that boosted Carman's self-esteem, that blanked out, however briefly, the sense of emptiness within. But in the end even this lost its lustre. In 1999, he was diagnosed with inoperable prostate cancer – he died two years later. As he lay dying, Carman asked his son, Dominic, to bring him an envelope that was on the top shelf of his bedroom cupboard. Inside he kept his most precious possessions. There weren't many of them: his father's war medals, the programme for an Oxford Union debate he had taken part in, a few other bits and pieces – and the letter Jeremy Thorpe had finally got round to writing him more than twenty years earlier.

Although he had been acquitted, Thorpe soon discovered that almost everyone thought he was guilty – and treated him accordingly. In the summer of 1981, a memorial service was held in Knightsbridge for the musical accompanist Ivor Newton. At the end of the service, Thorpe and Marion were making their way down the aisle when several members of the congregation very deliberately turned their backs on him. The writer Hugo Vickers recalls being at a reception with the Queen Mother and the Thorpes. When Thorpe was presented to the Queen Mother, she gave him the chilliest of nods and moved swiftly on. 'I remember thinking he had the look of someone who almost expected to be slighted.'

Thorpe's hopes of being given a public role were soon dashed too. In 1982, he was chosen to be the Director of Amnesty International's British section – the same organization that he and the former Lord Chancellor, Lord Elwyn-Jones, had once been Trustees of. But, after a public outcry, the job offer was withdrawn.

Possibly it would have been better for Thorpe if he'd been found guilty. Then at least he could have served his time and tried to start afresh. As it was, he was forced to lead a kind of half-life, shut away in the decaying grandeur of Marion's house in Orme Square, ignored by his former colleagues and seldom appearing in public. As far as Bernard – now Lord – Donoughue was concerned, the way in which Thorpe was treated was entirely in keeping with the British Establishment's desire to protect itself. 'It suited the Establishment for him to be found not guilty. On the one hand they were protecting him because they were protecting so many other things as well – things they didn't want to come out. But then he was effectively locked up in a cupboard so that he couldn't say anything.'

In the mid 1980s, Thorpe was diagnosed with Parkinson's Disease, something he bore with great fortitude but which took an increasingly heavy toll on his health. One of the symptoms of Parkinson's is hypomimia, a form of facial paralysis giving the sufferer a peculiarly blank expression. For Thorpe, it meant that the Mandarin Mask was fixed for ever. But, however ill he was, he still had one last ambition – to be given a peerage. This, he felt, would signal to the world that he was no longer an outcast, that he still had a role to play. Much to his annoyance, though, he was turned down by one Liberal Leader after another.

What Thorpe didn't know – and never found out – was that David Steel had done a deal with the Party Chairman and the President, who had wanted to pursue him for the return of the money that had been used to pay Andrew Newton. 'I told them, look, we've had endless bad publicity already. Just forget it. There was no way we are ever going to get the money back. But the condition for not trying to get it was that he would play no part in the public life of the party – by which we meant he wouldn't be given a peerage.'

In desperation, Thorpe turned to Peter Mandelson, Minister without Portfolio during Tony Blair's first term as Prime Minister. 'In 1998 Jeremy asked me to go to Orme Square,' Mandelson recalls. 'He explained that nobody in the Liberal Party would give him any support and said, "I'm a former Leader of a political party and I would like the Prime Minister to nominate me as one of his peers." He reminded me more than once that he had not been convicted and felt that people should be more magnanimous. I went back to Tony, who said he really didn't think he could do anything unless the Liberals wanted it.'

With all avenues to the Lords blocked off, Thorpe tried to find another path back into the light. In 1999, he wrote a book, *In My Own Time*, a highly selective account of his life in and out of politics. The book was published by Politico's Publishing, a company that had recently been set up by the broadcaster Iain Dale. 'I got this phone call towards the end of 1998 from this man called Jeremy something. He couldn't speak very well and at first I thought it was a lunatic. Eventually he said it was Jeremy Thorpe. Even then I didn't entirely believe him.'

Like Mandelson, Dale was asked to go to Orme Square. 'The house was very grand, but rather rundown and grubby. I remember peeking into one room and there were dust-sheets over all the furniture. It was also very old-fashioned, with servants to bring in the food.' By now the effects of the Parkinson's Disease were unmistakable. 'When Jeremy spoke he could be hard to understand and he spent an increasing amount of time in a wheelchair, but he was always immaculately turned out and it was obvious that his brain was unimpaired.'

Dale tried to persuade Thorpe to write about his trial, but he wasn't having it. 'He just said, "I'm not going to go there."' When the book was published, there was a launch party at the National Liberal Club. To Thorpe's delight, several senior Liberals came, and he clearly hoped this might signal the start of his rehabilitation. But it proved to be one of his last public appearances. In time, Parkinson's robbed Thorpe of his movement, his speech, his ability to feed himself and finally his sight.

Among the friends who continued to visit him was Steve Atack, a former member of the Young Liberals who had known him since the 1960s. 'Towards the end he used to communicate with his thumb. Thumb up was yes, thumb down, no, and thumb in the middle meant don't know. In a way I think he found the isolation from the Liberal Democrats more painful than the isolation from his decreasing well-being, but he never complained. Despite everything, Jeremy didn't want to die. He fought death to the last gasp.'

Throughout his illness, Thorpe was nursed by Marion – although latterly she too was confined to a wheelchair after suffering a stroke. A special lift was installed in Orme Square to enable the two of them to move from floor to floor. When Marion died in March 2014, aged eighty-seven, the house was put on the market and Thorpe moved to a serviced apartment around the corner in Porchester Gardens.

At four o'clock in the morning, on 4 December 2014, Steve Atack was woken by the phone ringing. 'The carer called me to say come over as fast as you can.' Atack rushed round, but, a few minutes before he arrived, Jeremy Thorpe died. He was eighty-five.

Death brought Thorpe the respect that had eluded him in the last thirty years of his life. His funeral service took place on 17 December 2014 in St Margaret's Church, Westminster, opposite the Houses of Parliament – the same church where Caroline's funeral had been held in 1970. All five of Thorpe's successors as Liberal – or Liberal Democrat – Leader attended, along with most of the party grandees. The coffin was draped in a Union Jack and topped with Thorpe's familiar brown trilby.

During the service the choir sang an anthem that had been written by the composer John Ireland. The anthem took as its text a number of phrases from both the New and the Old Testaments. Among them was one from the Gospel of St John – 'Greater love hath no man than this: that a man lay down his life for his friends.'

Fifty-two years earlier, following a brutal purge of his Cabinet by the then-Prime Minister, Harold Macmillan, the young Thorpe had made what was considered to be a brilliantly witty remark – 'Greater love hath no man than this: that he lay down his friends for his life.' As the mourners filed out of the church into an overcast December afternoon, they were left to ponder which of these two quotes best applied to Jeremy Thorpe himself.

At the time of writing, Norman Scott is seventy-five. He lives in a village on Dartmoor in Devon with seventy hens, three horses, a cat, a parrot, a canary – and five dogs.

Postscript

Letter to Norman Scott from Peter Bessell, 13 July 1976

PO Box 2145
Oceanside,
Cal. 92054.

Dear Norman,
I was very glad to get your letter. I tried to telephone you about ten days ago but was told your number was out of order. I wanted to thank you for telephoning me. It was good to hear your voice again – you sounded the same as ever.

We have all been through a searing experience and I can imagine how much worse it has been for you in the midst of it . . . From the moment when Newton – cum Kean [*sic*] – took you on to the Moor nothing could prevent the full facts from emerging. Although the whole truth has still to be revealed, in the fullness of time it will come out. It is one of the tragedies of the whole saga that none of us are totally without blame. From 1965 onwards, it was my first concern to protect Jeremy, as he asked me to do, from any form of public scandal. At the same time, as you have recognized, I was genuinely concerned about you and wanted to find ways of helping you. I was very moved by some of the kind things you said about me to the papers . . .

Weeks after the Newton Trial, I read your comment in the witness box when you were asked if you had blackmailed me. You said, 'Mr Bessell in the end will tell the truth.' I admit, Norman, that your faith in me as expressed by that reply brought tears to my eyes.

Congratulations on becoming a father again. Try to get all the joy you can out of that experience. Children and animals are so dependent upon human kindness and by giving of your love to your daughter you will get much love in return. My children have stood by me in my troubles with fierce loyalty and it has been a great strength to me. One day, Norman, you will grow old too!

I am sure you have read about Diane in the papers so you will know I have been greatly blessed by the love and care of a beautiful, gentle and wonderful girl. The papers made it sound rather sordid in some instances but of course it is nothing of the sort . . . She asks me to send you her warmest regards and kindest good wishes.

I cannot understand what happened to Jeremy's mind at the end. The greatest shock to me was his statement to the *Sunday Times* of 14th March. His categorical denial of any knowledge of things which he not only knew about but in many instances instigated was bad enough, but his attack upon you must have shaken many, many people. Strong, secure and powerful men do not attack their fellow humans in that way. It was an act of fear and weakness which did more than anything else to persuade me that, in your words, 'in the end' I would have to tell the truth . . .

The important thing is that we must all be willing to face the absolute truth, even if the consequences are not entirely pleasant for any of us. If we are prepared to do that, we shall, in the end, be judged fairly and what more can we ask?

There is a wonderful side to Jeremy's character which I shall always admire and hold in affection. That does not excuse his actions in respect of you – or, for that matter, in respect of me – but he needs understanding and sympathy just as much as the rest of us. The higher one climbs the ladder, the greater the fall. It is important to guard against bitterness. I have found it difficult to do this sometimes and I know you must have had the same struggle, but it only hurts or destroys ourselves if we allow it to overcome us.

Write to me again soon. I shall look forward to your letters.

God bless you.

My warmest regards,

Peter

Acknowledgements

I could never have written this book without the help of three people in particular. Norman Scott was enormously generous with his time and kindly let me see a private memoir he had written about the Thorpe Affair. Paul Bessell talked to me at length about his father, Peter, and greatly deepened my understanding of this most contradictory – and fascinating – man. And, by no means least, I'm indebted to Dominic Carman, who allowed me not only to pore over but also to take away an extremely large crate containing the case notes made by his father, George Carman, for the Thorpe trial.

I am also very grateful to the following people for their help: Roy Ackerman, Steve Atack, Lord Avebury, Paula Bessell, Graham Boal, Leslie Bonham-Carter, John Campbell, Stephen Claxton, Michael Crick, Paul Dacre, Iain Dale, Lord Donoughue, Keith Dovkants, Sir Harold Evans, Cathy Fehler, Michael Gove, Miriam Gross, Stephanie Hook, James Hugher-Onslow, Marigold Johnson, Paul Johnson, Diane Kelly, Joyce Kennedy, Stuart Kuttner, Goggi Lund, Tatiana Lund, John Macdonald, Kevin Macdonald, Yasmin McDonald, Lord Mandelson, Tom Mangold, David May, Dennis Meighan, Jan Moir, Charles Moore, Richard Moore, Christopher Murray, Matthew Norman, Geoffrey Owen, Stewart Purvis, Dominic Sandbrook, Lord Steel, Marie Taylor, George Thwaites, Hugo Vickers, Sarah Vine and Alexander Waugh.

My agent Natasha Fairweather at United Agents has been staunchly behind this book from its first stirrings and has lent much-appreciated support and friendship.

I want to thank my editor Venetia Butterfield at Penguin, along with everyone else who worked on the book.

I would also like to thank Donna Poppy for her exemplary copy-editing.

*

I have read a lot of books about Jeremy Thorpe and the period – principally *Private Member* by Leo Abse; *Cover-Up: The Jeremy Thorpe Affair* by Peter Bessell; *Jeremy Thorpe* by Michael Bloch; *No Ordinary Man: A Life of George Carman, QC* by Dominic Carman; *Jeremy Thorpe: A Secret Life* by Lewis Chester, Magnus Linklater and David May; *The Thorpe Committal: The Full Story of the Minehead Proceedings* by Peter Chippindale and David Leigh; *Downing Street Diary* (2 vols.) and *The Heat of the Kitchen: An Autobiography* by Bernard Donoughue; *Rinkagate: The Rise and Fall of Jeremy Thorpe* by Simon Freeman and Barrie Penrose; *Quest for Justice: Towards Homosexual Emancipation* by Antony Grey; *Not Without Prejudice: The Memoirs of Sir David Napley*; *The Pencourt File* by Barrie Penrose and Roger Courtiour; *State of Emergency: The Way We Were: Britain 1970–1974* and *Seasons in the Sun: The Battle for Britain 1974–1979* by Dominic Sandbrook; *Big Cyril: The Autobiography* by Cyril Smith; *Against Goliath* by David Steel; *In My Own Time: Reminiscences of a Liberal Leader* by Jeremy Thorpe; and *The Last Word: An Eye-witness Account of The Thorpe Trial* by Auberon Waugh. All the exchanges between Jeremy Thorpe and Peter Bessell come from Bessell's book, *Cover-Up*, or from his 'aide-mémoire'.

It is customary for writers to rise to a grand climax at the end of an acknowledgements section by thanking their wife/husband/partner for putting up with their volcanic temper tantrums and agonies of self-pity during the long decades it took them to write their book. While I have no wish to break with tradition, I rather suspect that I was in a much better mood when I was working on *A Very English Scandal* than I normally am. Those peculiar noises emanating from my study were more likely to be chortles of amusement or – just as often – gasps of disbelief than groans of despair. That said, my wife, Susanna, has been both an invaluable sounding-board and a diamond-edged critic throughout, and this book would have been an infinitely poorer thing without her.

Index